Uplifting Defeat: My Journey

An explosive display of Hopes, Destiny, Mental Illness of my loved one, Shattered Dreams and the Rebirth.

Sue Joshi

Copyright ©2023 *Sue Joshi*

All Rights Reserved.

Dedication

Should I dedicate this book to my ex? Yes, I did hear him say to the whistle blower after 43 years of marriage that I was not his type anyway! But then is it not the truth that he is the one who gave me the heavenly experience of the Motherhood and the most beautiful Family of Ten?

Or should I dedicate this book to Ken? Again, I agree that after merely 17 days of encounter, he had declared that sorry, our wavelengths are different! But is it not the fact that he is the only one who actually gave me the wonderful 3 in 1 experience? This was the most beautiful somewhat romantic but much more emotional as well as divine attraction (Or? Love,) I had felt for the first time at the age of almost 74 & half years?

Or, should I dedicate this book to that divine figure tucked safely in a cute little memory box, somewhere deep in my mind, it's presence unknown to me for almost 55 years? This savior of mine, the Lord Krishna and his most beautiful wife appeared at my doorsteps exactly when I needed them the most?

Or, how about I will just dedicate this book, my Biography to my late parents? After all, they are the ones who are responsible for this one of a kind, most wonderful existence of mine on this strange planet named Earth?

Acknowledgments

Interestingly as far as being thankful to someone for the origin of this book is concerned, I can think of only one person, and that is Amelia! She, out of the blue, called me sometime in June of 2022. She works for Amazon publishing company. "Sue, when do you plan to write your story!?" It goes without saying that I am thankful now to all those in her group.

When Amelia called me, I absolutely had no clue whom I was talking to. It so happened, in August or September of 2021, almost 9 months before she had called me, a wonderful volunteer named Jody had contacted Amazon on behalf of me. Jody wanted information as to how to get a small book printed that was written by me.

By the time Amelia called me last year, all the events, both beautiful as well as some sort of devastating were already in place. They were the precursors for this biography. I was in the process of completing self-analysis.

Being a strong believer in Destiny, as well as being obsessive, I guess I will have to thank my own character called OCD! I will like to thank Jody as well for getting the ball rolling.

Not sure if it is my inborn habit, but as long as I remember, I always believe in thanking anyone needed to, ASAP. Maybe because I will forget, my OCD or whatever. Before every meal or after getting up every morning, my hands automatically join in prayer 🙏 to thank God(the Superior Power) and at night for the forgiveness of the whole day's sins!

First, I will like to thank my now ex who said "Yes" to marrying me in 1972. He is the only causative factor for making this story possible. My two most wonderful sons, their own beautiful families, including their in-laws, our 4 precious grandchildren and their very thoughtful babysitter Farah, are the next ones to thank. They All were there helping me tirelessly one way or the other for months especially after I became homeless on Christmas Eve 2015.

Next, thanks to Shaila, my friend from NJ, who without thinking twice, gave me immediate shelter on the evening of that dreadful Christmas Eve and continued supporting me physically as well as emotionally for months that followed. Tomy, along with many of my friends from the hospital, including nurses and my friend Olivia from Old Tappan, I can never forget your heartfelt support. I want to thank Chris cook, Teresa, Diane and all others from my Woman's Club of Old Tappan, especially including Pamela, our President of WCOT, who has always been there to cheer me up by sending wonderful and thoughtful greeting cards wherever I was sheltering. Another friend whom I had met around 2013, in a restaurant called Rolling Pin in Westwood, her encouragement through letters, emails and calls can never be forgotten.

My sisters, my brother and his wife, my cousins, my nieces and nephews, especially my two nephews Salil and Samir, their daughters and close relatives, my nephew-in-law from Dallas, Texas and many more relatives, you all have helped me one way or the other.

Ken, you are one of the most important causative factor for the year 2022, being declared as the best year so far out of my 75 years of existence on this earth! Equally important are my classmate and his wife who appeared as my savior, as if as God and Goddess. It is because of 3 of them my ongoing quest regarding myself as to why I am the way I am, was successful. The answer came to a full circle and self-analysis was completed.

Actually, the list is endless! Everyone from the knitting group, many from my vast adopted family at Brookdale Battery Park, countless other friends and acquaintances, the lawyers, the bankers, Mr. and Mrs. Bhide, our old friends, there are so many of those I can think of! Equally important is to thank some of those whose negative feedback helped me to be where and how I have come to understand myself today.

Including those whom I may have forgotten, also My Angel, my mother, Padmakala, my Living God, I will like to thank all of you from the bottom of my heart.

Table of Contents

Dedication i

Acknowledgments iii

Introduction xii

Chapter 1: Early Childhood Through Primary School 1

Chapter 2: Middle and High School 9

Chapter 3: Life as a Premed 17

Chapter 4: Medical School Days 24

Chapter 5: A Stress-Free Year of Internship 36

Chapter 6: My Choice For Postgraduate Study 41

Chapter 7: Marriage Story 45

Chapter 8: Can I Call This Beginning Of Act I? 59

Chapter 9: Days and Months that Followed 66

Chapter 10: Departure and Arrival 77

Chapter 11: The Goal Oriented Life 83

Chapter 12: Aim To Succeed Continued 91

Chapter 13: Life In Boston, Mass. 97

Chapter 14: Springs Summers and Winters That Followed 101

Chapter 15: Story through Different Seasons Continues 110

Chapter 16: Completion of Residency and More 114

Chapter 17: The Best of the Dream Come True 123

Chapter 18: Destiny Never Stops Surprising 129

Chapter 19: Three Most Wanted Months in My Life 139

Chapter 20: Back to Routine 144

Chapter 21: New State and Environment, New Agenda 151

Chapter 22: Next Few Years of My Career 157

Chapter 23: It Seemed Never Ending 164

Chapter 24: Can It Be the Final Chapter of My Career? 177

Chapter 25: Farewell Cake Wish 188

Chapter 26: Retirement with Specific Goal In Mind 198

Chapter 27: Retirement Years Continue With Some? 206

Chapter 28: Finally The Truth Was Revealed 218

Chapter 29: What Followed The Life Train Derailment 229

Chapter 30: Scene II Act 2 238

Chapter 31: Trip to the Police Station 250

Chapter 32: First Visit to the Court 257

Chapter 33: Detour To 5 Star Prison Instead 263

Chapter 34: Scene III Act 2 268

Chapter 35: There Is No Proof But… 279

Chapter 36: Beggars Can't Be Choosers 286

Chapter 37: Nothing Seemed Like Working Though— 293

Chapter 38: Scene IV, Act II 300

Chapter 39: There Is a Myth About All Lawmakers Being Lawful!... 304

Chapter 40: Hoping To Finish Act II and Move On To… 316

Closing Chapter 325

Arrest on the morning of Christmas Eve, 2015.

The date, December 24, 2020, will go in the History of America as ***Anthony Fauci Day*** in celebration of his 80th birthday.

5 years ago, the person responsible for making me homeless declared his victory over me. Those in his support can go to hell; this is what one person said, and the same person, my personal lawyer, **HAILED VICTORY** in my support, assuring as I have also rid myself of him.

Off with the shackles!

I may have lost my **ONLY DREAM OF INTACT FAMILY**, but the amazing and huge bundle of the treasure of life experiences will surpass anyone's Estate.

Learned among everything is the meaning of true friendship. Thanks to those who opted to walk away and those who decided to welcome me. Today will, of course, go in my book as *History Making Day*; in my own maybe inconspicuous life.

Introduction

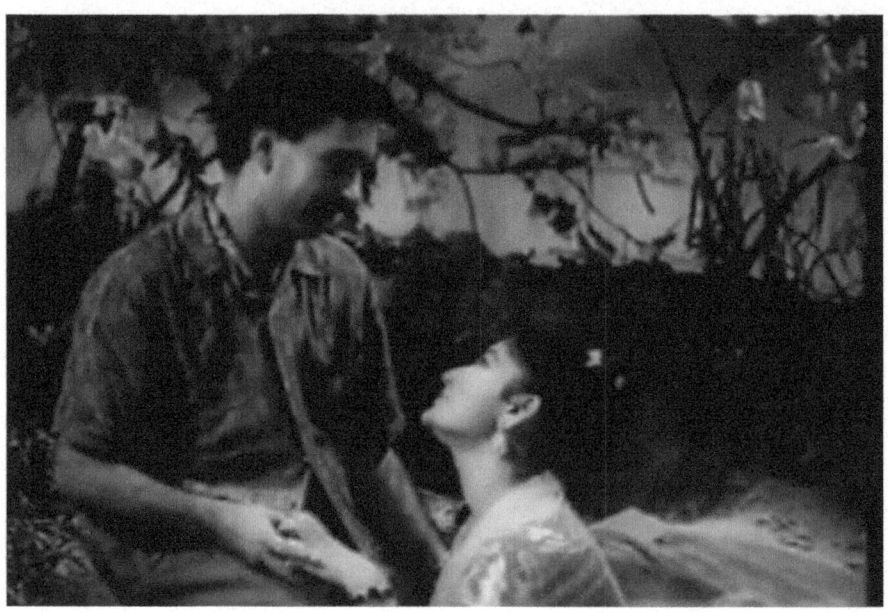

This is a story of a dreamer, a big-time one. But it seemed like her dreams were playing a cruel game of keep-away with her destiny and aspirations. Perhaps it was like playing Waltz, moving towards and then away from each other. Just never seemed to dance close to each other.

Well, that's how I, Sue Joshi, at least, perceive my life. I had only wished for a beautiful, happy, and intact family, but little did I know that it would be destroyed so easily. My dream of an intact family of ten, after 38 years of marriage, took many twists and turns through multiple dark tunnels, finally did find the light at the end of the length of a seemingly unending road in that tunnel.

This book is a glimpse into my life through many layers. I had never imagined that it would come to this stage, but as Marilyn Monroe quotes, *"Everything happens for a reason."* You just have to prepare yourself for what comes next. You can't have success without suffering at least a bit of pain, defeat, and regret. Eventually, you learn to grow and mature from tragedy and hardships. The reason I say this is, because now I'm back to being mentally and emotionally strong, maybe stronger. I have found the real purpose for my existence on this earth.

Just recently I had completed self analysis and had come to realize something that was very simple. Once the routine had set in and my work place had turned out to be my No.1 priority, the only thing I wanted was to be with someone who was willing to listen to me. Just this closeness behind the closed doors of our master bedroom was more than enough to quench my stressed mind while practicing Pedantic Anesthesia for 30 years. It was Shrikant, my then husband who seemed to be very attentive to my story telling about the whole day's events, the frustrations, lack of cooperation from my colleagues along with some satisfying, gratifying daily occurrences at the hospital. Even though this communication turned out to be just one sided, it was more than enough for me to get up next morning and restart the routine with the same zest, same vigor. This was all till the day I retired at the end of 2002.

Now it is middle of 2022. A lot has happened in those 20 years. There were plenty of times when may be the worst unthinkable mishaps had already taken place. I had come out intact, walking through an inferno after my arrest over six years ago. And again something has happened that has drastically made me loose peace of mind, may be even worse than ever. Once more I am in dire need of someone so that I can spill out my misery for the hundredth time. I have been too desperate, unable to function.

I am missing Ken. Even before we actually met in person, we had spent hours on the phone. He was the first man other than my ex I was about to meet. He spoke my language, wanted to know everything about me and my story. It is too long, I was telling him again and again. He wanted to listen to it all. And then we met in person, again and then again. In between we again spent hours on the phone. And just after 17 days after we first met, we have spent time in each other's company, he has gone on a cruise that was planned way before we were destined to meet. I have this premonition that again a huge tidal wave is waiting to engulf me, my simple dream to be just close to someone is about to shatter in millions of pieces right this moment.

Finally it so happened, my intense, unmatched prayers were heard. My dreams and my destiny got engaged in a beautiful dance which involved just being close to each other in the tune of some soft music. It seemed like they finally decided to abandon the waltz.

Once again my Angel, my Mother had used her broad wings to protect her daughter named Pratibha. She had once more acknowledged the severe despair, the silent but unimaginable cry of her devotee.

To anyone's disbelief, I actually met this Lord Krishna and his beloved wife in person. They appeared at my doorsteps as Vitthal and Rakhumai, the God and the Goddess. As if a miracle had taken place. They were my classmate and his wife! I met them after 55 years!

Together we walked, rested along the Hudson River. I had something to say and they both were eager to listen.

I was able to spill out my story again for 100th time.

Lord Krishna

Chapter 1: Early Childhood Through Primary School

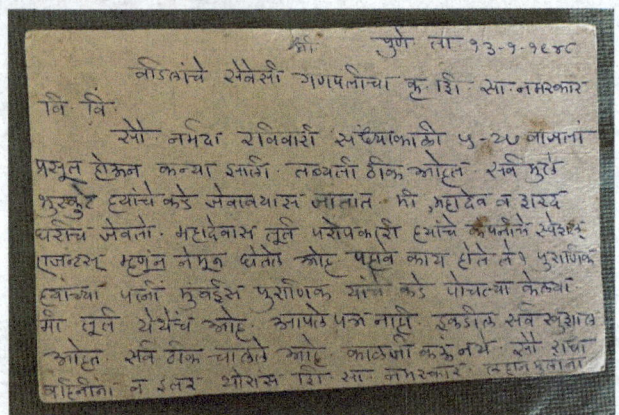

Amidst twinkly lights, festive cookies, gingerbread houses, and trees decorated with lights and ornaments, where everyone had just begun celebrating Christmas Eve in 2015, I was being shackled by the police of Old Tappan, New Jersey.

The whole life that I had built was collapsing in front of me. After spending at least 8 weeks in the psychiatric hospital, getting 11 shocks to my brain, and failed attempts at suicide, I'm still alive.

I didn't get the justice I was hoping for when it came to the emotional torture I endured. Instead, I got a restraining order that shut me up and forced me to leave my home with only 20 minutes to pack up my belongings. I was left to figure out who to beg for shelter.

But before I begin talking about what happened next and how all of this actually took place, let's rewind into my life and go back from where everything originated.

Simple, naïve, and innocent – that's who I am, and that's how everyone I have known so far in my life has observed and judged me. My maiden name is Pratibha, which means creativity. Then, I was going by Suhasini (the one who smiles), given by my ex-husband, Shrikant, during our wedding ceremony in India. I guess he liked my smile and the meaning of my given name, which I thought was a bit difficult to pronounce for my American friends. So, mainly for the convenience of others, I go by Sue now. Sue Joshi.

Just recently, I jotted down my reflections on self-analysis, wherein I asserted that my personality is a product of my observations, interactions, and my parents' general behavior. Consequently, determining what to discard and what to embrace has been the most straightforward way to explain the shaping of my personality. Luckily, it never got influenced by any external forces at any given time.

Believe it or not, I've got a letter from my dad to his older brother from the day I was born back on January 11, 1948. He wrote it on January 13th, saying, "Nami, my mother, gave birth to a baby girl on Sunday. Both mom and baby are doing fine!" Back then, and probably still now, babies weren't named when they left the hospital. They wait for a special naming ceremony on the 11th or 12th day after birth. I was officially given the name "PRATIBHA" on the twelfth day of my life, after I came into this world with a loud cry to prove my existence. The name means Imagination and Creativity, which will be important in future chapters.

My father and his siblings lost their parents when they were young, and my father looked up to his older brother as a father figure. As a matter of fact, I have nearly all the letters, mostly written by my father but a couple from my mother, addressed to his elder brother. It was only a few years ago when I asked my 90-year-old paternal cousin, Sharad dada, if I could have a couple of those letters. His response was, "Why only a couple? You can have them all! Besides, no one from your siblings is interested in them anyway!" At that moment, I felt like I had just discovered a huge treasure!

My cousin and I have a somewhat peculiar relationship, dating back to my early childhood. I have always regarded him as my real brother, rather than just a cousin, despite having one male sibling. Eventually, I realized why this was the case. My cousin came from a village and was brought by my father to Pune for his high school education. He stayed with us from 1947 to 1951, making him 15 years older than me. I believe that due to this shared experience, I began to think of him as my brother. My actual brother is only 3-4 years older than me. Additionally, I find it easier to talk with my cousin, and he is one of the few people who have witnessed my life in the USA firsthand, in a meaningful way.

As someone who is naturally curious, I have always been interested in learning more about my family history and my own personal background. This curiosity intensified after my retirement in December 2002, and I began asking my mother, older sisters, and anyone else who had known me since childhood about my personality and behavior growing up. I was eager to learn about everything from my appearance to my social interactions and even any conflicts I may have had. Even now, at the age of over 74 years old, when I run into old friends from school, pre-med, and medical college, I find myself uncovering new and intriguing details about my past that I never knew before. There is always more to learn, and I've always been excited to explore and discover more about myself and my family's history.

When I was just 19 days old, I stumbled upon an interesting discovery while going through one of my mother's letters. You see, my mother was a Freedom Fighter, having left school at the age of 16 to join Mahatma Gandhi and other crusaders in the fight for India's independence from British rule. She even spent a few months in jail during this time. However, tragedy struck on January 30, 1948, when Mahatma Gandhi was assassinated by a Brahmin man. In retaliation, an angry mob began to burn down the residential buildings of Brahmins in the area. Despite the chaos, my mother took me in her arms and bravely walked down the two steep staircases of our building, imploring the mob to stop their destructive actions. She reasoned with them, saying, "What are you going to achieve by burning our buildings? Please calm down and return home!" Eventually, others from our building came out as well, but it was my mother's courageous actions that stayed with me and inspired me throughout my life.

My second oldest sister (Sulabha) finally told me, after repeated inquiries, that the only significant thing she remembered about my childhood was that I used to fight for some space to study. Apparently, I would frequently demand some time alone for studying, and the elders had to finally intervene and tell me to stop studying and go play with my friends from the building. I also discovered that I was a chubby little girl who, on one occasion, disappeared after being dressed up in a beautiful frock. I couldn't be found anywhere. As it turned out, I had walked all by myself to a nearby playground with a big water well for swimming. After an extensive search, they found me sitting at the edge of that well. What was wrong with me?! I wonder.

At the time of my birth, my father's factory business of producing beautiful crookery, including cups and saucers with gold trims, was apparently in a boom. Deccan Pottery Ltd. was one of the first signs of industrialization in Pune. My mother told me that they had celebrated this fortune with all the workers to show their thankfulness in appreciation.

When I was around 2 years old, I recall going on a train to Chinchwad, where my father's factory was located. I also have a memory of my father driving us in his car to pick up my newborn sister from the hospital on May 21, 1951, when I was about 3 and a half years old. Despite growing up without any photos of myself, I do remember my father once jokingly telling me that I was not born to them and that they had sold "Hay" to purchase me. While this statement could have been interpreted in different ways, I never questioned my father's meaning while he was alive. Looking back, I wonder if I was perhaps the odd one out among my six siblings, or was it due to something else? However, I never felt envious of them or attached much significance to my father's jest.

Although I have trouble recollecting many aspects of my childhood, there is one particular incident from my first grade that has stayed with me. During our school's annual gathering, my teacher, Ms. Devbai, selected me to perform in a play. Attending an all-girls school, I was given the lead role of a young boy named Dhruva, which I later discovered is the Marathi translation of North Star.

The story of the Play goes like this — My father was a King with two wives, two Queens. I was the son of his less favorite wife named, Suniti. Once, both, my stepbrother and myself, we were sitting on the lap of my King father. His favorite queen, named Suruchi, saw me and immediately pulled me off my father's lap, saying that I have no right to be sitting there. Only her son has the right. I was devastated and determined to find a place from where no one could remove me by force! I ran for a jungle. Standing on one foot, day and night, with a definite goal in my mind, I prayed to God. I ignored the rain, the heat, the cold, and the storm. Lord Vishnu was pleased, appeared in front of me, and asked me for any boon. He gave me a permanent place in the northern skies. Other stars appear to change their location. But one can always see this North Star in the same position in the northern part of the world.

My memory of this seemingly insignificant incident is so vivid that I don't recall many other things of much more importance. I can still visualize myself standing in the corner of a large stage, facing a huge audience. My father had instructed me to speak loudly, and in my determination to fulfill his wishes, coupled with the amplification of the loudspeakers, my speech came out roaring!

The significance of this simple act and its impact on my personality modulation is too obvious in my future life. The North Star served as a sky marker for navigators, astronomers and escaping slaves. Unlike all other stars in the sky, Polaris always points to the North. And is helpful in determining the direction. Over time, this has helped it to gain symbolic meanings such as guidance, hope, luck, freedom, constancy, and even life's purpose. Whether you are a dreamer or an adventurer, your own North Star will guide your journey ahead.

In my future life, some significant events occurred. The fact that I had worked with children for over thirty years as Chief of Pediatric Anesthesia and the vivid memories of my own early childhood has brought me to a clear understanding. Children can remember a lot of things from a very early age. So it is up to us as parents to how to help our children create their own personality.

According to my children, the grandchildren will easily overcome the memories of the unfortunate events that occurred in their Aaji and Aba's lives. I tend to disagree with that.

In the first grade in a play, me acting as a boy named North Star. The prayer is for the Lord Vishnu for a request to secure a permanent place in the Northern Skies.

Chapter 2: Middle and High School

The only purpose of writing this book is to shed some light on the fact that mental health is one of the most important reasons why many wonderful relationships come to an end. During the period while I was firsthand witnessing the destruction of my simple dream of an Intact Family, I became aware of so many similar situations in multiple families either known to me or through the stories being told during the conversations. Every coin has two sides. At least in my case, I did try to make my loved ones aware of the complex personality disorder my now ex has been suffering from.

Personally, I wanted to be there for him during his tortured emotional moments. I had volunteered, no one had forced me, and I had decided to tie the matrimonial knot with him 43 years ago. I had walked the seven steps hand in hand, promising him the wedding vows on December 30, 1972. The Holy Fire, the Priest, the relatives, and the closest friends were the witnesses to that ritual called SAPTAPADI. I had understood him. I had started caring for him unknowingly through those 43 years. I had analyzed both sides of the coin. The one side everyone has experienced, just like me, his simple nature, no smoking, no drinking, talent, great conversational abilities, good looks, and many more acceptable ones.

To experience his other side of the coin, unfortunately, I was the only witness. I was the only one who had shared his life for 43 years. Also, I was the only one who had first-hand witnessed the genetic nature of this disorder. His brilliant mother, with a master's degree in Sanskrit and English, had revealed very similar behavior. I stayed with my in-laws for 8 months after marriage and during several more visits to India or during their two or three visits to the USA. As a concerned wife, a physician, and the mother of his two wonderful sons, their wives, and the four grandchildren, I was ready to do anything. I had discussed this issue with my psychiatrist friends. They told me that, yes, there is a treatment available for these complex mental issues. I tried my best to share this information with my loved ones. Unfortunately, Destiny took the upper hand. So be it!

Middle and High School Days

Somehow I don't have much recollection of my middle school days except that sometime after my first grade, we moved to a new school under the same title, "Bhave School". The original one became an all-boys school, and ours became "Bhave School for the Girls". This all-girls school is literally located in the back yard of my residential building. We could easily leave our apartment after the school bell rang for the first time.

Being lefty, it was not that easy for me to be accepted in some mass physical activities which needed handling certain equipment. Well, I did play some games similar to Volleyball, Badminton, Rubber Ring throw and catch across the net, etc. I do remember hurting the knuckle of my right ring finger during one of those sports. I actually had my own gold ring on my ring finger at that time. The tissue around that metacarpal joint swole so fast that the ring could not be removed with all the normal tricks like applying soap and all that. The ring actually needed to be cut by the goldsmith in order to remove the pressure on that ring finger.

I was really obsessed with the specific design for my ring!

This particular ring has its own little story. This ring, with the specific design with two clear stones on each side with a small Ruby stone in the middle with a tiny gold ring to encompass all three stones, was the MUST, I should have! This is where one can have a bit of a glimpse into my OCD. Obsessive Compulsive Disorder!

I think in seventh grade, I joined some classes outside the school for additional knowledge in Sanskrit and English. There I had befriended a girl of similar age from another school. The same girl named Prema, who attended a different school and premed college, became one of my best friends in the future, actually till this date. This was when we both ranked within the first ten in first-year medical school! Her beautiful handwriting, and especially the ring she wore from an early age on her left ring finger, was something I thought that I must have. So it was in my tenth grade when I won some special monetary prize. I had that ring and a tiny matching necklace made for me. The ring was eventually repaired and went back into the same right ring finger of mine.

Another obsession I remember even from those childhood days was I would constantly wash my hands from the tap right next to where my mother used to cook. I remember she was getting a bit annoyed, but I just could not help it.

Friendship is something that has always been number one for me as long as I remember. I did play a part in various stage activities like dance, plays, etc. One time I had accompanied one of my best friends Kirti who was participating in a play for our annual gathering. Our drama teacher needed someone to play the role of another male actor. Here I was actually asked if I wanted to try. WHY NOT? This is what I said to myself. I was accepted right on the spot by the drama teacher. This is how I knew that I was very good at ACTING! (according to others who watched!) This is how in all my four high school years, I played important male roles in the annual gathering. I think it was in 9th grade when I got to play the most important role in a famous play at that time. They had someone from outside to guide us. He took us all those acting in the play to watch the same play running at that time in a theatre wherein the actors and actresses were all professional ones. Just this one observation improved my acting tremendously. Yes, I did feel proud of myself. It was the perfect acting for a girl in 9th grade.

Anyway, this is only part of the reason why I was on the stage at every Annual Gathering throughout my 11 years of school. It so happened, I was always the number one student throughout all four classes of the same grade. We had a total of about 200 girl students in every grade. I was called upon the stage so many times each year to accept various prizes for my achievements. Actually, there was a girl who was much superior in scholastic knowledge, but I think because apparently, I had better overall scores because of extracurricular activities like drawing, sewing, physical education, etc.

Every year upon arriving home after receiving the annual report, I remember my father waiting for me on the 3rd-floor gallery outside our apartment. I still remember his finger gesture asking about my ranking. And without failure, it was always No.1. Who knows, maybe this was the reason why he may have said jokingly that I was not born to them, but they had bought me by selling the hay!? Again who knows the truth!? I know for sure all my five siblings were equally or may be even more talented than I was. But don't you agree that I should find at least one positive explanation for his statement regarding me?

My dad was always happy to know that I stood first in every grade for 11 years of my scholastic education.

A few of my very close friends used to get together at my school on weekends. This was always with partial truth-telling to our parents that we were going to study together. Along with the studies, we used to make fun of our teachers. It was always more talking and less studying. We had plenty to talk about. So, to some extent, we were very mischievous! I do remember being punished by a couple of our teachers a few times. The entire class of 50-plus girls was made to stand outside, far away from the school building. Actually, in times like this is when we seek out the opportunity to find some raw Tamarind fruits hanging from two huge trees or those freshly fallen on the ground. They tasted yummy, sweet, and sour. Those were the days!

One of my friends Alaka and myself, we used to share one desk during daily classes. I still remember the dance wherein I was the playful Lord Krishna, and she was Radha, Krishna's very close friend, but he was not supposed to be in her destiny to marry him or whatever, something like that! Just like anything else, I took our friendship very seriously. I think it was in 8th grade. I kind of noticed that her behavior had changed. As per my observation, I thought she became very serious. I can't explain why (definitely not any homosexual crush), but I was so sad that I actually developed something called Alopecia Aerate, in which patches of baldness develop on the scalp. It is believed to be related to emotional stress. Later I found out that she was going through some age-related hormonal changes. Soon after that, I myself went through similar changes. Similar baldness occurred one more time due to another emotional blow in 1978, 16 years later. That time I had sent my three-and-a-half-year-old son to India. In later years, this is how I eventually came to analyze myself.

I take things too seriously! Looks like I just can't help it!

A few of the other random memories I have, two ladies from a college for teacher training had visited my parents. They wanted to analyze my IQ as part of their training. Don't remember the exact numbers, but the score was definitely above average.

Another interesting memory is my class teacher, Ms. Kelkar, used to invite me to her home to help her out while evaluating and scoring the terminal examination papers. I was to add the score from all the pages and write it on the front page of the examination papers.

One vivid memory of mine is that my parents went through real bad financial ups and downs in my late childhood as well as early adulthood. For my final certification examination at the end of 11th grade, we had to pay 60 rupees for the application fees. It wasn't that easy to have that much cash for that kind of purpose. My mother had hidden that money in the wheat grains container, and it came in handy at the right time.

Another thing, in my final high school year, most of those students who could afford attended private classes, especially for math. For whatever reason, I lost my confidence in mathematics for the first time. It was my father who taught me the basics of the unfamiliar portion of mathematics. In the final examination, I scored 96/100. As I recall, I liked and did much better in the English language than in Marathi, my mother tongue, as well as Hindi, our national language. Can't answer why so. Sanskrit was a great subject for higher scores.

During holidays, we were allowed and were actually encouraged to play different card games, carom, a board game, etc. Most of the girls in our building would start one project like curtain embroidery or something, and everyone would follow them. But according to my father, we must finish anything extracurricular before the Summer Vacation was over. Throughout the year, there were various festival celebrations. We all found happiness in small things. Those were the good old days. No one was poorer or richer than the other. There was innocence all over in every family.

Chapter 3: Life as a Premed

As I said before, I don't remember much about my life in general while growing up. Both our parents were very well educated for their time period, especially my mother. As a woman being a college graduate, it was almost unheard of. Even for my father, being without parents from childhood, being dependent on someone from the relatives for shelter and education, and being one of five brothers as siblings, it must have been very difficult. I wish I had the inclination to learn about my father's life either while he was still alive or through his close relatives, or at least from the elders of the next generation. I have tried to learn as much as I could from my cousin/my imaginary real brother, Sharad dada, and will continue to do so in the near future. Because of his age and that of a couple of my other paternal first cousins as well, maybe I am already running out of time.

We had very serious financial issues, especially because my father couldn't keep a steady job. During the recession following 1951-52 or something, my father had lost everything. The one-of-a-kind factory needed to be closed, and loans to be paid off. I can totally imagine how he must have been devastated. I actually have in my possession the letters he had sent to his older brother asking for 5-10 rupees at that time, and this is the only way I can understand the way he behaved later on, I got to witness it that time, but after almost 70 years, I got the proof for the answers I have always been searching for. This is the way my father turned out to be later on. He was always very hard-working and had big ambitions, goals, and dreams. Therefore was never satisfied with what he was able to accept and undertake in order to take care of his six children and wife. But every time he got lucky and was able to make some money, he was not just thinking about himself and his close family of 8. He will always share that money with his own siblings and their children. I definitely owe it to my keen observation of my father's behavior that I always have this strong desire to succeed along with others and not at the expense of them. Not having sufficient funds to take care of a growing family with growing needs was one of the most important reasons why my mother used to get upset now and then. The end result was the physical abuse she had to tolerate, and we siblings had to witness helplessly much more than what could go unnoticed.

Even now, especially in America, where there are ways to report, just the sheer memories of my father's beast-like behavior during those moments make me clench my fists. Though, now I have a better understanding of his behavior at that time. This is because now I have witnessed firsthand what it is all about. It is because of their own shortcomings, they make the life miserable of those of the weaker sex! My mother was the victim, and I was my ex-husband's. I didn't experience any physical abuse at all, which at least could have been visible. Mine was all emotional abuse, and in addition, no witnesses. It was always about what he said, I said. For my mother, it was physical and had the witnesses who dared not utter a word!

Occasionally I still experience those episodes occurring in my dreams, and I wake up sweating with anger. To add to this was the constant feeling of humiliation while thinking of the neighbors paying close attention to what was going on next door.

Trust me, these types of situations were not uncommon at all around the neighboring families in the building. This is in spite of all families belonging to the middle class, at least somewhat educated, and Brahmins. When I say that I created my personality only through my observations of my parents' behavior, without knowing the concept of me having my own children, I had taken a silent oath that I would never raise my hand towards them or anyone in anger. I have letters from my mother. There are vivid memories of her own, constantly juggling while taking care of her own children, working 24/7 to earn the most needed money, along with the inconsistent income from my father. But in her memoir, she never mentioned any of this physical and emotional abuse or any real sad memories. Also, I never knew the details, but there was always someone there, unknown to me, at least, to offer financial help. One major factor was my mother's contact with prominent people while she was in prison as a freedom fighter at the age of 16 years. Also, it was because of my father's friends from the past, who were willing to pay back for his good deeds.

Anyway, all the siblings being very good at studies, were very well educated. For both of our parents, education was the number one priority. All of us did very well financially later on. My eldest sister got married on May 19, 1963. She passed away on April 6, 2011. She was so beautiful, petite, and very simple in her behavior. She eventually completed her Ph.D. She worked for Bhabha Institute in its atomic energy division.

For my first year of premed studies, I joined M.E.S. College. It was at quite a bit of walking distance. I had requested and was granted permission to be exempted from the first period of physical education! Many times my older sisters used to walk me to the college for safety reasons. I remember myself being very casual, was never fussy about clothes or the way my hair was combed and breaded, etc. I think I didn't mind being pampered, and my older sisters didn't mind taking care of me, even at the age of 17.

During this first year, my physics professor was so good and methodical in teaching that I fell in love with that subject. I took English as an additional subject. I had befriended one African American girl. Somehow I can picture her but just cannot remember her name. We sat next to each other, and we conversed together all the time, only in English. This helped me tremendously in the future regarding my communication ability. As such, from the time we started learning English from the seventh grade, English was my most favorite subject in languages. My friends don't believe me that as long as I remember, my thoughts have always been carried on in English and not in Marathi, my mother tongue. Mathematics was another of my favorite subject. Even in my first year of college, I passed the finals scoring 100/100 in Mathematics!

During the break after my first year of college, my next elder sister (Chimi) and myself had gone to stay with my brother in Bombay. I don't remember having any goal in my mind regarding my future. It was my father who decided that I would be joining the "B" group for the second year of premed! It means that he wanted me to be a doctor. This had nothing to do with the idea of making money in the future. We had a very big extended sane family. There was no doctor so far. Hence it was my duty to be a doctor to serve them in the future. Therefore I was ordered by my father to attend premed classes in Botany and Zoology by joining the "B" group. Looks like I was not meant to be a Mathematician! He is the one who filled my application at my home town and it was submitted to the office of another college called S. P. College. This college was much closer to our residence, and there was no need for a chaperone. I was a big girl now. I remember very little about my second year. Even as let as now, in September of 2022, I am learning something more about myself being in that year, in that college. I do have a very slight recollection of doing some earthworm and cockroach dissection, but that's about it! But one thing I do remember is the final exam results. I did stand first in the "B" group from S.P. College, one of the prestigious colleges in Pune. I did receive some monetary prize. This money was used to buy Grey's Anatomy Book, second hand, from my older sister's friend, Ms. Chandorkar.

Not sure if this is the right occasion to tell my future story, but I will spill it out anyway. In 2014, I went to visit one of my best friends, Vidula's father, in Pune, my hometown. As per my obsessed mind, it was a must that I pay my respects to him and his wife and offer them a copy of my book written in the Marathi language at the end of 2002. It was about my tribute to my mother before she passed away. It was during this visit in 2014 he revealed something so precious to me, helpful for my future analysis of myself. "Pratibha, you were so selfless. The college officials gave away one of the monetary prizes to Vidula, my eldest daughter. It actually was supposed to be for you, but you never showed any anger or disappointment!" The words coming from a 94+ years old father of my future best friend from 1966 onwards till now was a total surprise for me, and I did feel good about myself, maybe for the hundredth time. I have just finished my self-analysis. My elder sister and nephew, who had accompanied me, were the witnesses in 2014. Not only did I not know this, but a more surprising fact was that I did not even remember that Vidula was with me at S. P. College in 1965. I was under the impression that I met her in medical school. Also, just a month ago, in August of 2022, I visited a friend of mine in Yardley, Pennsylvania. She seemed to remember me much more than me having the slightest clue. She told me that she was my classmate in the same college during that same year. She is the one who told me that I was very studious, seemed very much focused on my goal, and will go to the library before and after classes punctually. I really don't know what to do about my selective memories!

In pre-med year 1966, leaving the library after studying in the evening.

Chapter 4: Medical School Days

Our Group in Medical School for Clinical Rotations in the Hospital for 2nd and 3rd Years

Thus my future was planned for me by someone other than myself, and it was by my father. Trust me, I have absolutely no regrets at all that I became a doctor, not even in my famous dream world. Don't remember if someone did it for me or if I filled out my own application to enter medical school. May be my information is not correct, but there were only two of those government medical schools, one Military and the other that I applied for. Yes, I was accepted at B. J. Medical College, Pune. I was the seventh in ranking out of 200 students that joined the school as a First Year Medical Student in July of 1966.

I will like to tell you a bit about the financial prerequisite for medical education. I was to get MBBS Degree at the end of a minimum of four and half years of medical education, followed by one year of internship. I was scholar enough to get 7th-ranking admission to the school but was not in the top 150 students all over Maharashtra in my final high school examination two years prior. Therefore I was not granted any scholarship. Yes, my father had the dream of his daughter, Pratibha, becoming a doctor for the family. But the only person to fulfill his dreams was my mother.

As I mentioned in the previous chapter, she was a freedom fighter. She had worked with Mahatma Gandhi. In fact, she had some letters from him during that period. At the age of 16, in 1930, she was jailed by the British for about 6 months. This is because she had participated in the Freedom Movement for India from the British. This very fact came in handy 36 years later, just when it was badly needed. One of her friends, who was also jailed at that time, mentioned to my mother that she could apply for a Government pension.

To this day, I feel so privileged, so lucky, to be able to get all this MUST NEEDED information to fulfill my ongoing quest, to know about my family, to know about myself. About 15 years ago, I met a gentleman named Mr. Bapat in NJ who was actually on the committee to grant those pensions. In 2006 after my mother passed away on September 15, 2006, I was trying to get the original book translated into English so that our children and my friends in the USA will be able to know about my mother and her life.

A prominent businessman, Mr. Vaidya from Swastic Rubbers, had visited us in NJ at that time and had promised to get the book translated into English as soon as he went back to India. Even being so senior, Mr. Vaidya had actually expressed his thankfulness that may be he did not win any money but did win my friendship in a Casino in Las Vegas! This was the place my husband and myself had first met him just by chance while vacationing. The book was first written in the Marathi language as a tribute to my mother. One English professor in India had agreed to translate it. Mr. Bapat had seen the book on that professor's desk in Pune, India. He took one copy of the original with him to the USA during his visit to his daughter. He got hold of me from the address on the back of the book and got in touch with me. I absolutely have no words to describe how I felt when I met Mr. Bapat in person.

So, not only my mother started getting the monthly check, but both my younger sister and myself started getting money every month for education, books, etc., along with the tuition fee. This, I believe, was the ultimate gift my mother got for her own indescribable hard work through out her life till 54 years of her age. I can totally relate to her feeling proud of herself for leading a financially independent life till she passed away at the age of 92, just two weeks shy of her 93rd birthday. Obviously, why it was my very strong, almost obsessed desire to thank her while she was alive. The original Marathi book was my tribute to her before she left this world.

During our first year, the main subjects were Anatomy and Physiology. Especially about Anatomy, I was not thrilled at all. It was too much of remembering by heart. There was no imagination, no creativity involved. One of the most memorable things was the dissection of the human body. Prema, Sunanda, Mana and myself, from different high schools, we four decided to be partners in crime to dissect the dead body in order to educate ourselves. I do not remember how we chose ourselves to be together, but we were all among the first 10 from the merit ranking.

Each one knew at least one other of the four but not all of the other three! Later on, we all became very good friends and were part of "The Mission Impossible" of the 9 girls as friends. Mostly the first two would do the job very sincerely, one of them will read the book and guide, and the other will do the nice and clean separation of the skin, muscles, nerves, blood vessels, etc., which is called the "Dissection." Mana and myself were mostly engaged in talking, not gossiping, but who knows what we were actually talking about. I met Sunanda after a long time in 2020 while I was visiting my hometown Pune in India. She actually remembered how I used to hate my feet dangling without support while sitting on the small stools provided. Even now, I always look for something to rest my feet on, something like a pedestal or footstool. What a memory! Hats off to Sunanda. No wonder she was No.1 in Pune and No.3 in ranking in the entire Maharashtra. This was during my final year of high school.

I still remember our first Part 1 oral examination after 3 months of the completion of a portion of the dissection. I do remember that I failed the first attempt. I don't remember about two other partners, but I definitely remember about the third one and passing it on the first attempt, even when she was absent from medical school for more than a month due to hepatitis. A thought did come to my mind occasionally if it had anything to do with her connection to the higher authorities in our school. The same thoughts came under similar situations regarding possibly privileged connections of other students in my batch. But truthfully, none of this really mattered in any significant way over the years in developing the friendships. At least in my mind, they were and still are one of the many best friends I had for myself.

One of the muscles that I had correctly identified in one of the part examinations that I remember even now is called "Sterno- Cledo- Occipito- Mastoid!" This muscle on each side of our neck has attachments to four and not three or two bones - sternum, clavicle, occipital bone, and mastoid! Our demonstrator's name was Dr. Duddy. I think I used to like him, but nothing like a crush, the term I came to know way too late in my life!

I actually have nothing much to write about Physiology, Pathology, Biochemistry, and not even sure if there were any other subjects we were taught in the first and second years of medical school. The only thing I remember is I think Dr. Mrs. Lata Gokhale used to like me or at least my hair.

The 9 totally benign members of our "Mission Impossible Group" were Prema, Sunanda, Mana, Meera, Perin, Radha, Uma, Pravina, and of course, myself, Pratibha. There was a sense of hierarchy among some other groups, either due to jealousy or some superiority. We did notice, but like any other good girl, we didn't care and said nothing. We just kept engaged ourselves in talking and eating. We all used to eat together in the ladies locker room, a huge one, and would exchange whatever eatable things were packed lovingly by our mothers and dutifully delivered on time by the Tiffin Carrier guy five days a week. In this group of nine, there were two of my friends, Meera and Perin, both of their families owned bakeries. The life long fascination of mine for only the right type of cakes has its origin right in that locker room! Now, this reminds me of another incident. Mana's parents had once invited us to their huge bungalow at Lonavala, a hill station. The vegetable Pulav had big Masala cardamoms specifically for added flavor. Unknown to their existence in the list of spices I was familiar with, I thought they were big dead bugs. Especially because we were served delicious food on the balcony, surrounded by beautiful green trees. I did take my first bite and another one, unafraid, without anyone noticing the confusion in my mind.

More than the subjects taught in the second year, I remember the total fun I had, in general, that year. Don't even remember much specifics, but I think it was the 75th Aniversary year of our medical school. The only activity that I remember very well is the fact that I had participated in one drama. I played the role of a pregnant woman! Yes, a Woman! Because all the previous major roles I had played in the school were male roles. After all, it was an all-girls school anyway. One of the other actors in that play was Vilas Pathak. Not sure what role, but may be as my husband? Who knows!? I don't even remember the story of that play. The only thing that I heard many more years later was that, apparently, Vilas Pathak had a crush on me while in medical school. Now that I have decided to get to the bottom of everything as per my OCD, I won't have the opportunity to ask the question directly to him through WA. Unfortunately, he passed away some time ago in a car accident. So any possibility of the truth to this rumor will go unanswered forever! Unless any of my classmates know about it and are willing to share it with me at the age of 75 years or later. Nothing is likely to change anyway.

A picnic was planned by our group of friends during the 2nd year of medical school in 1968.

I had so much fun participating in various activities during the 75th-anniversary celebration that year, which involved lots of talking. I actually lost my voice for a while. I think this is the year I may have started liking some good-looking guys, from various levels, from being a surgeon, registrar, houseman senior student, and maybe someone from my own class. The funny thing is I never thought it to be necessary and therefore had not kept anything of this as a secret. Few of my close friends knew all about it. But even today, the fact still remains the fact. I absolutely had no clue as to what it was all supposed to mean. Nor did I ever dwell on any of those feelings. I always remained just a happy-go-lucky girl with zero sense of reality. Didn't care, didn't bother, and didn't see the need to explore, even out of curiosity. My OCD was not in service!

One unfortunate event did occur in August of this second year of medical school. In August of 1968, one late morning, I got a message from a guard. My father was admitted to Sassoon Hospital, which is located on the same premises as the college. I had a premonition that morning while leaving the house to attend classes. Seems like I had already predicted that he was coming to the hospital. He had developed dumping syndrome following peptic ulcer surgery a few years ago and was unable to absorb proteins. The end result was a very low protein value and swelling of the dependent organs like legs. Not sure if it was due to aggressive treatment to reduce the swelling using diuretics which ended up in significantly low potassium levels and cardiac arrest. As far as I knew, his heart and blood pressure were always perfectly fine. One week after the admission, it was all over. Not that I had wished this to happen, but even then, one thought did come to my mind. I am truly sorry to say, but I thought that my mother finally got her true freedom.

In the third year of medical school, we had lectures and rotations through different branches of surgery, like general surgery, ENT, obstetrics, and gynecology. There were groups of 13 students or two groups of 13, which means 26 in attendance at a time. The housemen or registrars used to conduct bedside case discussions. Usually, my position was at the back of the class, trying to avoid anyone's attention. My practice of simultaneously achieving a minimum of two or maybe more things all at one time had its origin when I was a medical student. I used to crochet or do tatting, which required minimum materials, just thread and special needles. Along with this, I used to pay attention to what was being taught at the bedside. And maybe, if possible, simultaneously used to chat with any friend standing next to me. I think this is why my ENT professor, Dr. Bhutala, used to call me an absent-minded professor. The medical term in the USA for the same is called Attention Deficit Disorder. Perin, a friend of mine from the Mission Impossible of Nine, reminded me just recently. In the library, everyone used to concentrate on studying. But her observation about me was, many times, I used to be engaged more in playing with my long curly hair. I used to pull part of a hair and then try to separate the split end of that same hair further. Can anyone imagine studying and engaging himself or herself in such dual activities? I know I did it, but I absolutely have no explanation. That is the way I was. I still pull my hair, especially if thinking seriously about something. Except that my hair is very short, and I don't go exploring further about my split hair. I concentrate on the texture of each and every hair that is pulled out of me. I think it is part of my OCD, obsessive-compulsive disorder. It becomes more apparent when I am engaged in deep thinking.

Hopefully, the reader will be able to picture me dealing with my hair now and then.

I distinctly remember our OB Gyn rotation. We were required to assist in 10 normal deliveries and get the signature as proof. I was determined to get proof without assisting with a single delivery. I really don't have the answer to why I was bent on doing so. But yes, I did succeed. During that time, one Hindi movie, named ARADHANA, was just released in the movie theater. It was supposed to be one of a kind, romantic movie. I never got to see that movie during that period, but I did hear from several of my classmates how they had all fallen in love with that movie and especially with the main actor Rajesh Khanna. I did get to see the movie in later years and, of course, did understand what it was all about.

Anyway, finally, the final examination took place. I think it consisted of written as well as oral tests. I especially remember about the Anatomy written test. They were not multiple choice but were essay-type six questions. Out of that, I think we were supposed to answer five. To this day, I get nervous thinking about potential consequences. It so happened that out of 5, I had written absolutely, totally wrong answers to 2 of them. Basically, I did not flunk for whatever reason, but the answers to the remaining three must have been the ideal answers, and the examiner must have been happy to credit full or at least the passing marks.

I had passed the final M.B.B.S. examination just by sheer luck on the first attempt and was supposed to get the certification. I think we had to wait till we completed one year of internship before getting the actual degree in our hands. But this did not stop me from celebrating. One of my favorite teachers in the high school was Mr. Ingle. I went to visit him with my close school friend Kirti. As per customary practices, I handed his wife and him some sweets and in return, he declared, "Pratibha, congratulations. Now you got the license to kill the patients!" I knew that he was truly happy for me.

Thus I did pass my final examination and was all ready with the sleeves rolled up to face anything as well as to serve. From January first, 1970 I started my internship year.

Not too long ago, I finally decided to inquire regarding what I had in mind for a very long time. I called my paternal cousin/ imaginary real brother Sharad Dada. Yes, it was always the truth. I was the first doctor in all of our extended Sane family. And he was the first engineer in the same extended family. My father who was no.1 proponent of education, did bring him to our house for his high school and college education.

Chapter 5: A Stress-Free Year of Internship

Finally, on January first 1971, we all kind of began to disperse. The days of being together for rotations, clinics or lectures etc., came to an end. Even our private (!) group of 9 from Mission Impossible didn't get a chance to get together during the lunch hour. But the most important and desirable change at least for me was no more studies for the sake of passing examinations. This continued to be a frequent occurrence in my dreams earlier and even now, after so many years, I would dream about appearing for examinations unprepared. These are some of the times I have absolutely no desire to keep dreaming. Being awake was and still is the only way I would find some solace!

Again as usual, I am not 100% sure but I think we had to do six months of internship at Sassoon General Hospital. Both Prema and myself went to a small town called Shirur for only 15 days as part of the rotation. I remember this as one of the best parts of that worry-free life. We both girls and boys, would talk on the verandas outside our apartment rooms. One friend was good at analysing the personalities according to the way we wrote our signatures! The horizontal line under the signature and the two dots under that line meant I am very firm in whatever I do or mean and may be very sure about what actions I plan to undertake. Later after the marriage, obviously my signature changed from Pratibha G. Sane to Suhasini S. Joshi in a normal scribbling way. Drawing a line and two dots under it remained the same!

A classmate analyzing the personality by studying the signature.

One other thing I distinctly remember is way past normal sleeping time, and I always used to hear roaring laughters and joyful conversations coming from outside of our rooms. Later I learned, the Bridge card game lovers were responsible for that activity. It made me very curious and kind of obsessed in later years and I decided to learn to play Bridge. In 1975, when our first son was born, my husband and I played as partners with another young couple with a small child as well! This is whenever I was not on duty, and we would eagerly wait for the babies to finally fall asleep! I do remember that I played with my own convictions, my own rules of the game of Bridge. Basically, I had nothing to do with competition.

Any way, after 15 days, rest of the 6 months both Prema and myself did internship at a very small village called Wagholi, very close to Pune by public transportation. There we had two more roommates. By this time Prema was already in touch with her prospective husband residing in USA. It is too long a story but she had already started studying for ECFMG, an entrance examination needed to be cleared before starting any residency in USA. She tried to encourage me to study with her. My answer to her was absolute NO! I had opted to embroider her green sari instead! During our third year, we both had studied together several nights prior to the final examination. But since I had never entertained the idea of going to America, studying for that prerequisite exam was absolute No!

It turned out to be that both the other two classmates and Prema had already started thinking about their future with specific partner in their mind. Obviously I had nothing to do with it. The thought of marriage had never entered my mind at all, forget about anyone specific occupying my mind. Actually it is in just recent years, while I am trying to finalize my self analysis, I did discover something very interesting about my own self! I think during the years following the second year of medical school, for whatever reason, I always used to be in my La La Land World of Dreams. Nothing specific, no one in particular, nothing to do with the reality. Can't even say for sure if I was even dreaming about any of the good looking guys that I kind of used to like! Who knows, I gave up even thinking about the puzzling mind of mine! I distinctly remember about one supervisor from the clinic at Wagholi bringing me to her house to show me the picture of her son in Military uniform. Her family name was Joshi. I vaguely believe that she wanted to find if I was interested in marrying her son in that picture!

In my La La Land World of Dreams

Any way the whole year of internship was over. When we had finished the final year, we had to sign a bond to serve the government for 2 years. If not, the penalty was going to be 5,000.00 rupees. Since Prema and myself like few other classmates had done six months of rural service during internship, we had to serve only one year instead of the two. If we don't serve that one year means the penalty should be only 2,500.00 rupees. This logic needed to be applied because

Prema did get married to her Pen Pal, her future husband and moved to America right after the internship. And for me now the time had come to choose which specialization I should choose for post-graduation studies?

Chapter 6: My Choice For Postgraduate Study

Now that I have decided to write my biography, it seems like the dots are getting connected very easily. What I realized was how my future was already being molded and created because of the choice I had made to specialize in.

I love children. That means Paediatrics would have been the right choice. In our E.R., during internship rotation, many times, we used to get severely dehydrated babies. To start an intravenous in order to hydrate them meant torturing the children further. Their desperate, weak cries would make my heart ache. Therefore Paediatrics was out of the question. I also used to love surgery. But it meant compulsory rotation in OBGyn for one full term of six months out of four years total. As I have mentioned earlier, for whatever reason I hated OB-Gyn. So basically, in order to at least watch the surgery being performed, I chose Anesthesia for post-graduation!

Not sure about other hospitals but in Sassoon General Hospital, I don't remember residents being trained by actual professors in Anesthesia on a regular basis. We were trained by senior residents called registrars or housemen. We did not have any monitoring devices. The practice of Anesthesia was based 99.99% of clinical observations. Intubation, meaning inserting a breathing tube through the trachea or windpipe, is one of the most common parts of Anesthesia Induction. In order to achieve an ideal condition, the patient first needs to be put under reversible sleep. This is routinely achieved in an adult by first securing an intravenous followed by administering Sodium Pentothal or anything else equivalent. A short-acting muscle relaxant called Succinylcholine is used to facilitate intubation. This basically needs practice! I am trying to describe this in detail because of the potential risk associated with repeated doses of this muscle relaxant was not taught as something of importance. Dr. Halabe, our registrar, repeated its administration as many times as needed till we succeeded in the process of intubation! This muscle relaxant, if repeated can cause the heart rate to slow down significantly maybe sometimes even leading to cardiac arrest! In reality everything went fine. I did soon learn to feel comfortable intubating a patient within the first attempt!

We used to get many babies for procedures like cleft lip, and cleft palate among others. These procedures are very risky from an anesthesia management point of view. On top of that, the location of the operating rooms was remote from the main hospital building. Now after fifty years, even if I think there was a blessing in ignorance, it is very difficult to convince my colleagues from the Anesthesia field here in the USA. We were equally comfortable in these kinds of primitive settings!

This is the same remote area where we were trained to provide anesthesia for ECTs — Electro Convulsive Treatment for patients with severe mental depression. The brain is actually zapped with electric shocks while the patient is under anesthesia-induced sleep of very short duration. This is one of the very old fashioned treatments still used and must be all over including in the USA. The reader will come to know in later chapters that there was a time when I, myself underwent anesthesia for exactly the same reason!

I especially remember one incident during my first year of training in Anesthesia. In six months, I kind of became senior enough to have some juniors under my wings! There was a call for an emergency cesarean section. Before my senior and myself reached the operating room, our junior resident in training had already put the patient to sleep and didn't follow the correct procedure. She proceeded to assist breathing for the patient before securing the trachea with intubation. This precaution is a must and one has less than a couple of minutes to prevent oxygen deprivation. It so happened that this patient had a full meal which was not digested, which rose in the mouth, blocking the trachea or windpipe. The patient expired due to lack of oxygen. The surgeons were super fast. One healthy baby came into this world without her mother to take care of her.

This turned out to be one of the few incidents which I would never forget! I must admit that when I say that I actually hated Obstetric Anesthesia, this was one of the significant reasons why. We brought the patient back to a big room where many live patients were admitted for various reasons. The patient was declared dead upon arrival to her bed in that room.

I never got a chance to complete more than one year of training in Anesthesia. The requirement for Diploma in Anesthesia was two years and for M.D. in Anesthesia, it was three years.

It was during this year of 1972 my future predetermined destiny was also beginning to shape up.

Chapter 7: Marriage Story

"Sue, was your marriage an arranged one?"

I had retired at the age of 55, which was by the end of 2002. Thereafter, due to various reasons, my life has been associated with mostly non-Indians. Out of curiosity, the question asked repeatedly has been regarding my marriage! My reply always has been, "My marriage was neither a love marriage, nor was it arranged for me in a way you all may have heard about any Hindu Marriage. It was never predetermined by elders, neither was it forced on me or on my now ex-husband." We both had willingly decided to tie the matrimonial knot.

It all started sometime during the year of 1972. Somehow the concept of marriage or the feelings supposed to be associated with it in a girl of my age had not yet entered my La La Land of Dreams! The younger reader from this generation or even some from my own generation, may think of this being not normal. Unfortunately, I am not in a position even to comment on it. This is because I myself have no answer for the same! But then, just like for any other girls or boys of my age, the elders had started taking action. As if it is their duty, responsibility towards their younger ones, sons or daughters, brothers or sisters or as a matter of fact any close relative or a neighbour, to get them married.

In my case, my two elder sisters and their husbands had taken charge! It was decided that somehow I would be introduced to any boy of my age, of good family background and of equivalent education. I doubt very much if my name was registered somewhere similar to "Shadi.com" or any matrimonial registry. I don't even remember how many but definitely not more than five of the doctors of my age, that I was introduced to.

For me, it was just like casually chatting with my batch mates! At the same time, when I don't remember so many important events in my life, then why is it that I remember one conversation very distinctly? My mother had said something to me during those days. That time I had thought of it to be one of her casual statements. "Pratibha, if you don't want to marry, it is okay with me!" But her other sentence that followed at the same time was, "I will like you to take me to America later on in your life!" I had come to know later on through her letters to me that my mother had always loved travelling. But believe me, at that time in 1972, no such idea of my future in America was even entertained or was in the picture.

Eventually, I thought about it. My older sister, Chimi was married at that time and had joined her husband in America in 1968. My mother was forward thinking. She must have thought that my sister would be able to sponsor me to come to the USA in the near future.

Anyway, I do remember 3 of the incidents. One of them was a trip to a small town called "Shrirampur." I think it is famous for Sugarcane production and factory. My second eldest sister Sulabha had accompanied me. The boy was of the family name called Agashe, and I think he was a doctor (who really remembers?). I believe their message in return must have been that they or the boy himself was not interested in tying the matrimonial knot with me! The second one was from Bombay, a doctor with a family name "Joshi." I think he was the brother of one of my professors in Anesthesia at Sassoon Hospital. The fact that he lived and was practicing in Bombay, therefore my eldest sister Mangal from Bombay and her husband Ramesh had accompanied me to their house. Actually, during the same time, for the first time, a good-looking guy named "Shrikant Joshi," the first non-doctor, that also a potential match from America, paid a visit with his parents to our house. I distinctly remember him sitting very obediently between two of his parents. I don't even remember if I had prepared the snacks by myself and served them with tea or maybe coffee in order to impress the other party!

In general, this actual process during those days was followed by the 'Wait and Watch' game! The strangest fact is the answer "YES" to the proposal, first came from this Shrikant Joshi's family and I think just within 2-3 days, the same positive answer came from Joshi # 2 from the Bombay family. To this day after what happened to me by the end of 2015, 43 years after my marriage, my elder sister Sulabha continues making the remarks that we should have accepted the "other" proposal from Bombay!, Joshi for Joshi, a doctor for an engineer! At least three out of 4-5 were "Joshi" anyway, including the one in that military uniform picture! Initially, I tried debating, then arguing with my sister. Now I just ignore her ignorance.

Trust me, after the first eight months or so after the marriage, I was totally content in my married life just like any other couples of my age and time. In fact, even after I was made homeless on Christmas

Eve 2015 till the day I ended up filing for divorce by the end of November 2017, I always remained hopeful to go back to this Shrikant whom I had willingly married on December 30, 1972. After all for many years, especially after my retirement at the end of December 2002, I was always just daydreaming of him as a possible friend or at least a vehicle through which I was hoping to keep my beautiful Family of Ten intact.

Whether anyone wants to believe it or not, from the day we got married on December 30, 1972, Shrikant, my then husband, was the only man in any physical form who had access to my mind, my thoughts, and my dreams. This was till I bumped into this stranger named Ken. On March 25th of the year 2022, this Ken had come to pick me up as planned through the previous conversations on the phone or texts. Even till May 5th of 2022, the presence of that tiny cute box with the content of a divine figure somewhere deep in my mind was totally unknown to me! Also the validity of its presence remains unconvincing to anyone except me and my conscience!

Shrikant and myself soon got engaged. It was a very small and simple ceremony. I received a gold engagement ring (the word, a diamond engagement ring was unheard of, at least by me!) and a pink polyester-cotton sari from Shrikant's family. We did go out a couple of times just by ourselves, once in a garden and another time to see a movie (English). At least once, I visited him in his house and we were left alone to talk to each other about our future. "How many children will you like to have?" To this my answer was "whatever!"

Please don't laugh at me. Even being a doctor, I truly had no concept, no inclination to know anything about marriage. The way I was, I am not even sure if I would have been ready anytime to step out of my dream world! And the worse thing was I didn't even know the significance of those dreams. I myself find it kind of pathetic but I refuse to blame myself!

Shrikant's parents and all the extended family were very good natured. He has only one younger brother and many cousin sisters and brothers. There was actually nothing to complain about though I didn't even know what was I supposed to complain about! There were restrictions on larger gatherings for lunches or dinners, including during the weddings. I am not sure but I think it was related to some kind of National Emergency, War. My best friend Vidula's father had played the key role as a senior person in charge.

Our marriage took place in the early evening at an auspicious moment called " Muhurta", according to Hindu Calendar. It was followed by simple and short post-marriage rituals. This definitely included one MUST FOLLOW Ritual called "Saptapadi." We both walked seven steps, hand in hand, promising each other at every step to be there for each other at every stage of life as lovers, partners and companions till death parted us apart! The Holy Fire, the Priest, the loved ones from both sides, the friends and relatives from both sides, they all were the witnesses!

Even though it was an arranged marriage, we both had a choice to marry each other or not. I admit that we didn't have much time to get to know each other very well, but I doubt it would have made much of a difference. My mother had always been supportive of my life choices, and she had told me that I didn't have to get married if I didn't want to. However, I feel like my destiny has been to go through all of the experiences that this human life has to offer. There are a few things I regret, but for the most part, I love everything that my destiny has given me so far.

Our marriage ceremony was held in India, in my hometown, a traditional Hindu marriage that is not complete without Saptapadi vows. Saptapadi, which consists of seven Feras (rounds) around the Agni (holy fire), is the most important rasam(tradition) in a Hindu marriage., and it's a 5,000-year-old Vedic ceremony. The seven rounds of the Indian wedding ceremony are a representation of the couple's love and commitment to each other. Promising each other at every step in front of the holy sacrificial fire is the heart of every Indian wedding. I have made an effort to put forth the essence, the soul of this timeless wedding ceremony.

Saptapadi is a 5000 year old vedic tradition.

Saptapadi, is an integral part of any Hindu Wedding Ceremony, however small or elaborate the ceremony may be.

During the first four rounds or circumambulations, the groom leads, and the bride follows, holding each other's right hand.

- **Step 1**- The groom promises, "I will nourish you physically, mentally, as well as spiritually."
- **Step 2**- The groom says, "I promise you, we will grow and evolve together."
- **Step 3**- The groom says, "I promise to bring you abundance and care for your needs."

- **Step 4**- The groom says, "I promise to serve you with the happiness in my being and bring you happiness as well."
- **Step 5**- The bride says, "I promise to care for our children with love."
- **Step 6**- The bride says, "I promise to love you in all seasons of your life, in your youth and old age as well."
- **Step 7**- The bride says, "I promise you true friendship all my life."

Different cultures in India have different traditions when it comes to weddings. In some, the bride and groom take turns leading certain aspects of the ceremony. For example, the groom may lead the first six steps, and then the bride will take the last step. In other cultures, the bride may lead the last three laps around the fire. Other traditions involve the bride touching seven beetle nuts in turn with her toe while her groom helps her keep her balance.

Among other cultures, instead of seven steps, they do *Mangal Pheras*, which is also a sacred Hindu ceremony in which the bride and groom walk around the *Agni* four times, symbolizing their union and commitment to one another. This cultural tradition is commonly found among the Gujaratis and Sindhis, though there are slight discrepancies between each religious interpretation. With the Saptapadi, the couple ties themselves together for seven lifetimes before their friends, family, and the gods as a representation of their eternal love and bond.

Society often perpetuates the idea that marriage is the key to happiness, but the adjustment period after marriage can be tough for many couples. It's not uncommon for couples to feel like they are "not totally themselves" even when they share a bed or shower, and their "real selves" are more likely to emerge after marriage.

Society expects that the woman needs to be ready to make the marriage work. It is seen as her responsibility to follow her husband's lead to be receptive to resolving issues. A good wife also understands that her husband cannot be perfect, so she doesn't try to change him. Instead, she adjusts to his personality and corrects his shortcomings when necessary. A good wife displays qualities that not only help build a home and family but also help her project herself as a good human being. Apparently, my husband is the one whom I have to respect and love in order to get my life sorted. However, in reality, as they say, it takes two to tango. Unknowingly, I put in my all and expected the same in return. But little did I know that my life would make a sharp turn very soon.

After the ceremony, it was time for my Vidaai (farewell). The Vidaai, or Bidaai depending on the region, is a very emotional moment during a Hindu marriage ceremony where the bride's family bids farewell to their daughter as she leaves with her new husband. This is one of the most memorable moments of the wedding day for both the bride and her parents.

The bride's family and relatives accompany her to the exit of the wedding venue, with her parents leading the way. Before she crosses the threshold, she is given a handful of rice or coins, which she is supposed to throw over her head behind her as she leaves. This is supposed to symbolize a repayment to her parents for all that they have given her throughout the years. By doing this, she conveys good wishes to her parents and shows them gratitude for loving and caring for her all her life. In this way, she ensures that the house of her childhood remains happy.

Our traditional marriage ceremonies are elegant, intimate, and culture-rich festivities which also means never-ending traditional rituals. After the Vidaai, once we reached Shrikant's home we had our Griha Pravesh; it's when the bride pushes a jar full of rice with her right toe to enter her husband's house. This signifies that the bride has been now accepted as a member of the family.

Seriously, if anyone thinks that I understood the significance of any of the rituals including this "SAPTAPADI", sorry, that was not the case at all! By now, I had attended so many weddings over my 24 years of existence on this earth. I had never paid any attention to the various components of this Holy Marriage Ceremony. Only one incident that I remember was one of my beautiful maternal cousins was made to marry a very old-looking guy who actually was an Indian Prist or something! I was so upset without knowing any details and never tried to explore later on. Basically, I remained clueless for many more years! My beautiful cousin is still alive, and I believe she had a wonderful marriage like others. I have visited her a couple of times during my visits to India. I even talked to her on the phone a few times till a few months ago.

So by the night of that date of December 30,1972, I, whose birth certificate said " Pratibha Ganesh Sane", ended up applying later on for a marriage certificate with the name of "Suhasini Shrikant Joshi! Each and every component of my maiden name was changed! Did I take any objection? Absolutely I did not! After we got married that evening, I believe, before even the reception program started, a small ceremony had taken place in the wedding hall itself. My then husband, Shrikant, wrote his preferred first name for me with the gold ring he had gotten from my family just a few hours ago as a wedding gift.

He wrote it on a silver dish filled with rice grains, flattened to make it easier to scribble the name! Without any previous discussion, conversation or my permission, he wrote the name "Suhasini!" It means the one who smiles! I guess he had liked my smile! Needless to say, he never confessed or said so in the next 43 years of being together! Nor did he call me using that name Suhasini, which he himself named me as, he always talked to me or referred me to others as "Pratibha!" Yes, it does sound strange but it still remains the fact, the truth!

Nevertheless, I have my own proof from hundreds of my friends, mostly non-Indians and also only a couple of my Indian friends. Not only do they love my smile but they have told me more than just a few times, " Sue, never give up the smile!" This short form, "Sue," is my idea. I believe we have talked about this in the previous chapter.

I guess on my first wedding night lying next to my husband Shrikant, we must have at least kissed good night to each other for the first time. Later that night, in the dark, I must have been thinking for the longest time but I don't remember what about. It had never occurred to me during my first wedding night that when my mother named me "Pratibha" during the naming ceremony on the 12th day of my birth, she had already predicted my future. Her new born baby was going to be the one with lots of Imagination, lots of creativity!

Hence the name Pratibha was decided. Neither was I aware of the fact that in the very near future, I would be compelled to act as per my given name Suhasini, the one who smiles, as façade! It so happened that I had no choice but to be successful in my art of Acting mainly for the others watching me from every corner of my husband's house! My past hobby of 'Acting' during high school and medical college in annual gathering plays has definitely come in handy at various stages of my post-marriage life.

I was hoping to share some of the pictures from our Wedding Album. Over the years, one of the most important tasks I had undertaken especially after my retirement, was to arrange all the pictures chronologically in multiple albums. Is it not true that nothing remains the same forever? The pictures serve as memories to forward and share them with our loved ones, grandchildren and on and on. This has been the practice since ancient days except because they didn't have anything to write or draw on, the walls of the caves, the papyrus papers or something similar was used. The computerised labels and descriptions for our albums were the volunteer help from both of our sons. Finally, after more than four years, actually 4 years, 2 months and 13 days to be exact of being forced to leave my home on Christmas Eve 2015, I was allowed to enter my own house. This is the only home I had known as my own for 31 years. This was the only one I considered mine among the total of 14 houses we happened to have been owning over thirty years!

According to the court orders, the presence of a police to accompany me and also to be paid by me was a must. Presumably, it was for the sake of my ex's safety. On March 6th, 2020 for the first time and then March 13th, 2020 for the last time, I entered my home with a few of my friends and the police named Drew Craft. The friends were there to help me move out my belongings, as allowed by court orders.

I witnessed with my own awake and open eyes, my "Home Sweet Home" Dream had shattered real bad. The " Love, Laugh, Dream and Inspire!" board, created by me, once hanging right near the entrance was nowhere to be found. All the albums except one or two along with more than 80 percent of the belongings from the six-bedroom home had disappeared!

Wedding Cake offered by Shrikant Aunt.

Chapter 8: Can I Call This Beginning Of Act I?

Now that I am compelled to write my story, as part of my OCD, I am not sure whether to refer to this chapter as Part 1 of my Life Drama!

When I left my mother and the rest of my close family last night following my own wedding ceremony, I became Shrikant's wife first, then my in laws' daughter-in-law, and Shrikant's brother's sister-in-law! On my Vidaai, I am not sure if I had shed any tears while leaving my family or noticed any one of my own family including my mother doing the same. It has become a bit difficult to remember much that took place almost fifty years ago. I am not sure if it is just because of the age finally catching up with my brain activity or because I don't want to remember it or is this the memory loss that is caused by the eleven brain shocks called ECTs I received in the psychiatric hospital sometime in April of 2016? It is hard to tell. The twelfth ECT I had refused.

It must be as per the customs, both Shrikant and myself visited my mother the day after our wedding. Here again a tiny, post-wedding Hindu ritual took place. Some solid form of Turmeric or something similar was tied to one of the wrists of both of us. We untied each other's wrist wraps and that was the end of the ritual! We ate some sweets prepared by my mother. Both of us together bowed down touching my mother's feet, asking for her blessings. "You both may live hundred years of healthy life and raise a wonderful family of your own!"

This type of boon or blessing is not uncommon at all. Every time any married couple bowed in those days would remember hearing something similar to this. This act of touching the feet of elders is also an age- old Indian tradition that is considered to be a mark of respect. This gesture can be seen in almost all Hindu families, both in India and abroad. In fact, some Bollywood movies and daily soaps have also depicted this common practice. Indians believe that when a person bows down and touches the feet of their elders, their ego gets suppressed, as this gesture indicates respecting the age, experience, achievements and wisdom of the person whose feet are being touched. The elder person then, in turn, blesses the person touching their feet. This act is called Padasparshan.

Walking towards our 5 Star Honeymoon Hotel.

Soon after our marriage, my husband and I were both sent off for the Honeymoon. I believe the arrangements were done by my father-in-law in a five-star resort at a hill station called Ooty. Being a well to do family, it must not have been difficult to honour my husband's desire especially because he was a visitor from America.

Located in the Nilgiri Hills, Ooty is a beautiful hill station popularly known as the Queen of Hill Stations. With beautiful and breathtaking views of the mountains and surrounding lakes, this place was the perfect retreat for Shrikant and myself.

Nilgiri Hills, Tamil Nadu, India
[Watermark Image Source: Getty Images]

This was the first time we were both literally alone, just the two of us. No one that we both knew was anywhere in any nearby rooms. Somehow now at the age of seventy-four and $3/4^{th}$ years, I am really not that uncomfortable writing a bit in detail about what happened next. Yes, Shrikant, my husband took care of my virginity. It wasn't that hurtful at all. No screaming, no shouting, in fact some strange feeling occupied my whole body and mind for the first time.

It was an experience that I would never forget because at that time I felt it was special and was meant for me. We did manage to sleep comfortably very close to each other. It was during the next morning after the longing for each other had subsided at least for the time being, I noticed something different in the person whom I had given everything I could last night. He literally became mute! Shrikant kept his mouth shut! Because it was for the first time I was too close to a man and it was impossible for me to figure it out. I tried finding out what was wrong. Was there anything I did wrong? Was there anything I could do? His answer to multiple of such questions of mine, repeated again and again was his lips being zipped! Eventually we had breakfast, lunch, dinner, little stroll in the garden for fresh air, repetition of everything again and again, the next day and the day after may be for almost 7-8 days.

We returned to his home. In a few more days it was time for Shrikant to go back to USA. During day time we visited a few of his relatives, and then he started packing his bags. I did not have much to do except just to observe. On several occasions I had noticed that his mother was trying to have some conversations with her older son, Shrikant, but his response was always non-courteous as if he didn't want his mother bothering him! We spent the last two days with one of his close relatives in Bombay.

I remember something about them being very close to the Movie industry. Again the repetition of the same routine as in Ooty. Intimacy, silence, question mark, intimacy silence……..As I remember, the last day of Shrikant's stay in India for me was one of the worst days in my life for that time period. I was going to miss his closeness at the same time his mood swings were totally destructive to my tiny, inexperienced, innocent mind. Yes, these were his mood swings, this was his behaviour, it was literally torturing me every single moment of my awake time, which was actually twenty-four hours of the last day of us being together prior to his departure to the United States.

Mood swings are the correct terminology used in medical terms for the description I had to provide later on to a big group of psychiatric personnel. I learned about it when I was interviewed by a number of doctors and other healthcare professionals 3 days after I was forcefully admitted on my birthday in Heaven Facility, a five-star prison(I call that psychiatric hospital a prison for a specific reason).

This is where and when I was officially diagnosed as a "Bipolar patient." It was on my birthday on January 11, 2016. From that day everything had officially started going wrong. It was the wrongful diagnosis labelled to the victim of mistaken identity. I was not the Bipolar patient as they thought, it was someone else. Actually there was absolutely nothing wrong with me except that I was actually frustrated. From June 2010 till the day of Christmas Eve, 2015, I was trying to get the attention of my loved ones. I was trying to tell my children that their father needed help. In fact, there was something wrong with Shrikant right during those days of marriage or may be even from before. Unfortunately till this day no one has shown any interest in seeking the truth, nothing but the truth!

Anyway, I will get back to this part of the story later on.

Getting back to Shrikant's departure to USA, Air-India or any flights leaving Bombay Airport fly abroad invariably at odd hours of very early morning. There were so many of us at the airport, his as well as my closest relatives were all gathered to bid farewell to Shrikant, my husband, whom I hardly knew at that time. There are pictures in one of the albums, both of us standing next to each other, he wearing the fresh flowers garland given by one of his cousins and was holding one flower bouquet in his hand as well. Even after so many years, it is just impossible for me to describe the total devastation caused by the storm, the cyclone swirling in my mind non-stop. This was the aftermath of the fact that we willingly had said "YES" to each other and had actually walked those seven steps during that SAPTAPADI promising each other something. Without me knowing, I had been snatched out of my La La Land of Dreams by my DESTINY. I was totally numb. I was unable to figure out what else was going to be offered by this Destiny, this "Karma" as a result of my some doings from the previous life!

I feel so good about myself that this concept of Destiny or Karma has not really affected my consciousness or my self-awareness in any negative way. The concept has not caused any permanent, irreversible damage to my tiny mind. I still remain hopeful even when so many times I have felt the damage created by hoping for hopeless dreams. I have accepted all the colors whole heartedly that my Destiny has provided so far, whole heartedly with open arms, as it is. What is led ahead by part of my predetermined Destiny for the future is obviously unknown to me. I have decided not to think about it and just to continue concentrating on moulding part of that same Destiny that is in my hand.

Chapter 9: Days and Months that Followed

One of the most auspicious days in the Hindu Calendar is Makar Sankranthi. It's a festival celebrated in January, dedicated to the religious Sun God, Surya. According to an old calendar, it's I think, January 10, but the general consensus is that it's celebrated on January 14. This celebration marks the end of winter and the beginning of longer days as the Sun takes a northward journey.

In fact, on this day, we were able to plan our younger son's birth – the auspicious day of January 14. It was a planned cesarean section. My obstetrician was going to be on vacation on his due date of birth roughly two weeks later.

This day is celebrated throughout India, and in our customs, it can be celebrated at any time over the course of almost one month. The newlywed bride or girl is adorned with a variety of costume jewelry, including a black sari and a special get-together takes place. On that occasion, Shrikant's paternal aunt gifted me a beautiful set of sapphire earrings and an expensive silver decorative band/belt. Many ladies from relatives and neighbors were invited, and I allowed myself to be celebrated by my mother-in-law and others in a special way.

Today, I'm describing this in detail for a *very* specific reason. Later in my life, I was told by some trusted friends that the "Makar Sankranthi" celebration as the first one for any newlywed girl is considered a bad omen for the woman. If it follows any other auspicious Hindu celebrations, then it's okay! It so happened because it was the first Holy celebration, the one following our wedding on December 30, 1972, and thinking that I may soon join my husband in America, hence was the haste.

Years later, after our younger son was born, around the day of the same Makar Sankranthi, January 14, every year, I used to celebrate it. Up to 40 friends, including husbands, wives, and children, used to enjoy dinner and get-togethers. They all used to look forward to this occasion. It was arranged for Saturdays, and Sundays were occasionally used as Snow Days! Because I was working, the preparations would start at least one week before. Every lady and girl would get some special personally handmade gift as a token.

In all, for at least 30 years, this was a yearly fun-filled event for everyone, especially during the winter season. Unfortunately, later on, unpredictable weather turned out to be one of the most stress-causing factors for me. I had to make the painful decision not to celebrate the occasion anymore. Needless to say, after that fateful event of homelessness on Christmas Eve 2015, this same Makar Sankranthi celebration has become kind of just a legendary story of the past!

There are so many beautiful pictures in chronological years arranged in so many memory albums. I guess none of my loved ones have any interest in salvaging them. Maybe they think it is better to wipe out those memories. But I don't want to forget. I want to remember the good times we had together through those photos.

My routine started in that hardly familiar home of my in-laws after Shrikant's departure to America. Shrikant's maternal grandparents had decided to stay back after our wedding. I think they both adored their new granddaughter-in-law. I knew very little about cooking because there was hardly any chance to learn. Besides, my in-laws had a full-time cook. Occasionally, if I tried something like a snack or two, the grandparents were the first ones to appreciate it.

For the first month or so, there was hardly any time for me to think privately by myself. Both in-laws had many relatives all over the place. A trip was planned (Procession) with two cars that my father-in-law owned (through his company). We visited several of those relatives with at least one overnight stay everywhere. In fact, we traveled far distances over three to four weeks. We had even reached Bangalore! None of those relations got registered on any of my brain cells. We all came back with many more gifts for the newlywed. They were all tucked away somewhere by my mother-in-law, never to be found again on time!

Soon the reality set in. My alone life at night in our bedroom became a place where I could let out my tears uninhibited. From day two of our honeymoon, I remained horribly crushed between the two sets of totally opposite feelings. The wanted feeling of being touched, and then the tortured feeling from those repulsive mood swings of my husband – both feelings became my constant inward witnesses. For the outside world, I always remained "Suhasini", the one that smiles! I have a very good friend, Vidula, whom I have mentioned before. She got married just a few days or months before I did. I remember going for a walk with her after Shrikant had left for States. It was behind the famous Hill called Parvati. We sat on a rock, and I asked her a puzzling question as to how one is supposed to react during the process of lovemaking. I then realized that I had done nothing wrong on our first Honeymoon night and those that followed. Here I will like to point out to the reader that in those days (1972), many of the girls, even well-educated, had absolutely no idea about what is involved in the actual process of lovemaking! Who knows, they may have started getting the so-called hormone-related feelings at the right age but had zero education regarding it.

Before he left, Shrikant had written down some assignments for me, a kind of homework. I should learn to drive and type. These two were the important ones. As far as driving was concerned, our car driver taught me to drive. I think eventually, I learned enough that the driver and my father-in-law felt confident that I could drive with the driver next to me. I never learned parallel parking, and even now, I have never done it. It was never needed. In India, I gave the driving test, and after adequate payment, I got the International Driver's License. During my unexpected extended stay in India, eventually, I started working again as a "Locum" in our Sassoon Hospital in the same Anesthesia field. Occasionally I drove the car with the driver, and in the locations where one is not allowed to honk, invariably, I made that honking sound!! Just couldn't help it!

As far as the typing assignment was concerned, I actually hated it beyond anyone can imagine! Even now, one of the main reasons why I never wanted to learn computer technology is because of what I was forced to do by my husband at that time.

Parallel to this daily routine, my married life was in total shambles right from the beginning. The only reason I kept attending the typing class was that it was very close to my mother's house. Every day I would visit her after the typing class. Trust me, I never told her anything about what was going on in my personal life. Over the years, she had witnessed so many unpleasant circumstances in her own personal life that I had absolutely no desire to make her feel miserable again. Till she passed away on September 15, 2006, she had heard nothing negative from my earlier years of married life. The same thing goes for everyone else. Till the year 2010, there was absolutely no one who knew about one of the two sides of my marriage story except one person, and that is Shrikant's father, my father-in-law.

Soon after Shrikant left for America, I started receiving aerogram letters from him. They were more rare than occasional. The tone in those letters was too disappointing, too discouraging, too disheartening. One of the sentences, which I will never forget, was, "You are better off dying!" There is no way anyone can imagine what state of mind this Suhasini may have been in, how she may have faced everyone in the house on a daily basis. My father-in-law was a businessman and was not home that often. One evening, I got a chance to talk to him privately. His driver drove us to a distant temple-like place called Ramakrishna Mission. It was a beautiful shrine. He read the letter but I don't remember exactly what he had to say. He did support me emotionally but gave absolutely zero clue about his older son's nature or some unwanted behavior of him while growing up.

Please, no one question me, please don't ask me what was wrong with me, and why I did not file for the divorce right away. Did I keep the letters as proof? Are they kidding? The word divorce was not even in my dictionary! It didn't occur to me at all that I should let my mother know. I have thought over the various scenarios millions of times. I'm unable to come up with any alternative thoughts about what may have clouded my mind during that time period. I'm not sure if it is because I have always been a strong girl like the Warrior Queen of Jhansi! My eldest brother-in-law used to refer to me as being like her. Or was there the presence of that cute tiny box with its beautiful content of a divine figure may be of Lord Krishna? Though unknown to me for almost 55 years, was he always residing somewhere deep in my mind, well secured? Was this unknown entity always had been the driving force? It is very difficult for me to figure it out after hours and hours of thinking.

Warrior Queen of Jhansi

It was my father-in-law who offered me his time to expedite the passport requirements. Because I was not going to serve the one-year bond, it was necessary to pay 2,500 rupees. I really felt uncomfortable that he had to pay that for me. Also, I didn't know but soon found out that some of our professors from medical school were his friends. I did accompany him during his visits to those professors! It reminds me of one wonderful occasion that took place only because of my father-in-law. He arranged a big party in a well-known restaurant for all my friends and professors from the Anesthesia department at Sassoon Hospital. I had noticed that he had a kind of soft corner, especially towards his nieces. One of his brother's daughters, named Anju, is a bit younger than me, she became my younger friend. My father-in-law always allowed us to enjoy the evenings together. We both actually traveled by ourselves and visited some of the closest relatives of Shrikant. One incident I remember very distinctly. We both had planned to see a movie. Apparently, my mother-in-law had planned to take me with her for some family function. She insisted vehemently that I accompanied her. I was new to her tantrums, but Anju knew her very well. She defended on behalf of both of us with her uncle, my father-in-law. We won! We saw the movie, and then only my mother-in-law's wishes came true!

This was only one of the minor incidents related to my mother-in-law, Shrikant's mother. She was actually very talented and had a Master's degree in English and Sanskrit. But on a daily basis, her behavior didn't reflect her level of education at all! She would constantly kind of harass the servants in the house. They always had to obey her ever-changing commands, her demands. She was actually a control freak! Each and everyone that was in her daily vicinity had experienced it without any doubt. If things went her way, then usually there was no problem. Almost on a daily basis, the furniture arrangements were demanded to be changed. Just recently, I came to know one of the facts, the truth. Her husband, my father-in-law, had long given up going against her. Just to avoid her, for many years after he retired, he was seen in his younger brother's house most of the time. In fact, I came to know the truth from a totally unexpected source!

Later on, my in-laws visited us in the USA twice. Both times their minimum stay was for six months. There were plenty of similar encounters that I personally had to sort out almost on a daily basis. It was left up to me to choose whose presence was most vital, and I must choose between my mother-in-law or my housekeeper.

Again, the fact that I'm going into details about this part of my life with my mother-in-law is for a reason. Over the years, while leading my life with Shrikant, I was constantly puzzled but was not able to draw any conclusions with 100 percent surety till 2010. That was the year it was the must that I needed to get my loved ones involved. I was hoping all six of us, our two sons, their wives, and both Shrikant and myself, would try to figure out a solution for the future of a Happy Family of Ten, including our four beautiful grandchildren. Over the years, we as a family had visited India several times. Sometimes it was only the three of us without Shrikant. Again, on several occasions, I witnessed my mother-in-law's behavior. Not only was she a stubborn but pathological liar, hoarder, and control freak, her behavior was almost repulsive many times. She would get whatever she demanded as long as my father-in-law was alive. One thing is she didn't have control over her husband's money.

Just 10 days ago, in October of 2022, I received a message on WhatsApp from one of my batch mates. It was shocking but not surprising. When Shrikant decided to visit my family and me in 1972, his family did some detective work. To me, it sounded like a conspiracy theory! They collectively decided and asked one of their relatives, Dr. Bhide, to find out about my character and if I had any love affair or affairs! It so happens, this Dr. Bhide was our ENT professor. He had inquired with my batchmate, who was his postgraduate student at that time! As per my batchmate friend, her answer to him was, "Pratibha is a lovely girl, sincere, and has no affair at all!" I actually have nothing against Dr. Bhide. He was a thorough gentleman who just did his job. He had passed away, but the most astonishing part is he and his whole family, including his in-laws, have visited us in the USA in the past. I know all his four daughters and actually just recently met his widowed wife in the USA again.

Strange are the ways how the TRUTH finds its way to the surface! Because I had decided to write my biography, I have been in touch with many of my classmates, including the ones from my childhood. I have requested them to let me know about both my good and not-so-good characteristics. In my language, there is a proverb meaning, *"Only a thief has to worry about the starry night!"*

I guarantee none of my family members, including, of course, myself, had ever thought of digging into Shrikant's family history or, as a matter of fact, about him. It was back in 2010 that I finally decided to seek some information regarding his childhood. I wanted to know about his childhood and was any emotional trauma or anything that may be reflective of his behavior. The attempts did not succeed, they reached a dead end.

It took much longer than normal to first get the passport. Later on, somehow, the visa papers arrive from Shrikant from the USA. Now the preparation begins to pack my bag. Again, I had noticed that my mother- in- law wanted to stay closer to me.

I think I arrived in New York somewhere around October 23, 1973.

Chapter 10: Departure and Arrival

Again, a large number of relatives, this time more mine than Shrikant's, gathered at the Bombay Airport to see me off. It was past midnight. Again, I wish I get hold of those well-arranged photo albums dumped in one of those hundreds of boxes by my ex-husband. Those truly are the memories that I really wanted to hold on to, especially because it is not that easy for the younger generation to be able to spare sometime for the oldie, there priorities are obviously different.

Anyway, this was my first travel by plane and that was also far away, beyond the seven oceans, to America! I happened to get the window seat and tried to peep out of the window, the right side of my head resting against that same window. Soon I fell into deep thinking. I had left all my friends, including those from my childhood. I knew that most of them were married but then we still used to meet once in a while because they were settled in Pune, anyway. From my medical school, one friend was visibly sad when she learned that I was getting married and was eventually moving to America. It was Mana Pandit.

Friends hugging each other after the send-off party arranged after my engagement.

From the first year of medical school, we had become very good friends. During our first year of houseman-ship, we all, many from our Mission Impossible group, had rejoined and had enjoyed each other's company again. When the batchmates learned about my engagement, there was a send-off party arranged. Shrikant had accompanied me to our headquarters for that occasion. In fact, that was the first time I had tasted Chicken Curry. It was the first time I had eaten something non-veg and had realized then that I would not mind eating something that is not vegetarian. At the same time, also I can easily do without eating non-veg.

Along with my friends, I had also left behind wonderful families, both mine and my in-laws'. I had voluntarily left them in search of only one person, hoping to be with him forever. I was not even sure if I would recognise my husband. I had barely known Shrikant for a month or so. I didn't even remember if I had ever looked deep into his eyes and had the chance to preserve his picture in my brain, my memory box. My main concern was whether he would come to the airport to receive me or not. And even if he showed up, would I spot him out of that big crowd at JFK? Neither was I sure if he would recognise me or not! Once again my brain was a total chaos. Also, it was my first experience in a plane which got repeated several times in the future. It is almost impossible for me to fall asleep on the plane. However, I have learned the trick now. The best thing is I keep on watching a movie or documentary, something or the other, continuously. If I end up falling into my dream land, it's okay, if not, then also no problem! I know eventually I will catch up with my sleep.

There was no option for a nonstop flight those days. Don't remember which country we took the break in between. But eventually, the plane did land safely on the afternoon of October 23, 1973, almost 10 months after we got married. Later over the years, I did get accustomed to the routine that usually follows the international arrival to my country of acquired citizenship. Eventually, I knew to stand in the line for U.S. citizens.

I got my Green Card right at the airport. I think it was handed to me by the customs officer. Did follow others to the carousel to pick up my checked-in bags, paid for the cart to carry them and yes, I came out and did spot my husband named Shrikant.

I don't want to pretend but I really doubt if I was excited to see him or not. In fact my mind was full of total apprehension. There was absolutely no feeling of "True Mutual Love" to start with. This, I can't say, was the fault of either of us. After all we had not really "fallen in for each other." At least I was sure about myself, and I had not even entertained the idea of falling in love, had no concept about it either. We had chosen each other from among the few of those prospective husbands or wives we had visited once or may be more than once prior to making up our minds. But the way our life together had begun, I never even got the chance to feel what that love is supposed to be!

Now, I don't really mind confessing about this first-time experience of falling into so-called LOVE. Because this experience is one of the reasons why I was compelled to write my biography. Just recently at the age of 74 &1/2 years, by March end, 2022, I actually felt something for the first time that others may define as me having fallen in love!

Shrikant hailed for the taxi and we did arrive at our one-bedroom apartment in Brooklyn, located somewhere around Avenue J and Coney Island Avenue.

Less than 24 hours ago, I had departed India, my Country of Origin and now I had arrived in America, my new Country of the future.

And this is the way our real married life started. It must have been just the way with many other professional girls of my age. The late sixties and early seventies was the period when a vast number of male students with B.S. or equivalent degrees from India had gotten a chance to pursue their post graduate studies in America, the Land of Opportunity. After achieving their goal and securing a job, many of them had decided to visit India, their country of origin. They all had exactly the same goal in mind. Their plan was to look for a partner, a prospective wife, and get married. Some of them were somehow able to bring their wives with them. But most of them had returned back to the USA, obtained the visa papers for their wedded wives and after a few months, the wives had followed their husbands and stepped in the USA.

In fact, this is exactly what Ken had mentioned to me during one of our conversations. He also had come to the USA as a student, had obtained an additional postgraduate degree and then had gone back to India. He had liked the girl that was suggested by one of his relatives from another town. According to Ken, if he had stayed back in India after his M.Tech. Degree from IIT Bombay, he would have definitely fallen in love with someone like me! I had to stop him right there. I didn't want him to wipe off all his wonderful memories with his late wife, whom he had cared for all those years including through her debilitating illness. I was almost sure that he had actually followed all the seven steps of that SAPTAPADI, the promises he had given to his wife during that Holy ceremony of the Hindu Wedding.

He had loved the daughter they had both brought into this world as the symbol of their love (?) for each other. I had to explain to him the role of Destiny. This happened to be one of the conversations on his 75th birthday on April 11, 2022.

My life with Shrikant started in Brooklyn on October 23, 1973. It had always remained as less talking and more doing including love making. That was the case till I had finally decided to retire at the end of December 2002. I was two weeks shy of being 55 years old.

Chapter 11: The Goal Oriented Life

Being living by himself, not so keen on cooking or may be not much fussy about the choice of food, Shrikant was more dependent on prepared food from grocery shops. Rye Bread, Coleslaw salad, Potato Salad, yellow American Cheese, lettuce, these were among the frequent items on the grocery list. Later on, somehow I never wanted to eat some of those items, especially the Rye Bread. I can never forget one very funny story regarding my culinary expertise. One item from the grocery list, Lettuce, I thought it was cabbage and one day decided to surprise Shrikant by making so called Cabbage Bhaji.

This is one of the Indian recipes frequently prepared by any wife who is generally in charge of the kitchen. I followed the instructions from one of the Indian cookbooks called "Ruchira". This book was the must for every Indian household coming to America! Including the taste and appearance, everything came out okay except the total amount of that Bhaji if one compared it to the size of that lettuce head! The total amount was barely 5-6 tablespoons! This was in spite of the fact that I had added some frozen peas for some color along with that chopped so called cabbage! Truly for years we all had laughed while telling this story again and again!

The following weekend, we took the subway to buy Indian grocery from Kalustyan's on Lexington Ave around 29th street. The plan was to buy some authentic ingredients for my future cooking endeavors.

Without any discussion initiated by either of us about the last almost 10 months, including the Honeymoon period, our happy life together as husband and wife had truly begun. There were a couple of Indian families that Shrikant knew living in Brooklyn. One of them was a couple, Mr. and Mrs. Shobha Bhide. They are still one of my much older and more respectable friends. I owe a lot to both of them, especially because they were there for me through one of the most difficult periods. Mrs. Bhide invited one more family, and we three ladies prepared the sweets for the upcoming Indian Festival of Lights. That was total fun. We soon had 2-3 parties in the name of "Diwali," the Festival of Lights.

Festival of Lights Celebration, for the first time as Married Couple.

One of those parties took place in Amrit and Sanju Bakare's house in Somers, Westchester. Sanju is Shrikant's maternal cousin and was his next kin for many years from the time he came to America, and the same thing for her till they both married later on. Shrikant told me to meet him at Grand Central Station on Friday evening. Within less than two weeks, I had my first experience traveling by Subway by myself. I should congratulate myself again and again, even now! Suhasini being comfortable traveling by subway even at the present age of 74 & 3/4 can easily be the reason for jealousy for those suburbans who are prone to be jealous!

Sanju welcomed me with open arms and heart. We celebrated our first Diwali as one family at Sanju and Amrit's house. Amrit's two brothers and their wives were also there. We remained much more than 'Just Family' for many more years. For me, they both became actually number one as far as being closest relatives and friends. Arun and Surekha Adya for me became the second closest friends. Surekha's parents were very close friends of my in-laws. They both knew almost everything about Shrikant and me. The funny thing is they always referred to me as 'Pratibha' and not as 'Suhasini!'

I think just 2 weeks later, one of my best friends, Prema, from medical school, arrived in New York with her mother-in-law whom we always called Tai in later years. Prema's sister-in-law, Lilatai, was doing residency in Pathology at Coney Island Hospital. Shrikant and I visited them at Lilatai's apartment, which is very close to the hospital. I think we bonded right away. For many more years, Shrikant, Lilatai, and we three had spent numerous evenings and weekends together. Lilatai introduced me to a married girl of my age named Shiva.

She was originally from Ceylon. Both Shiva and I studied in the Coney Island hospital library for an exam called ECFMG (Educational Commission for Foreign Medical Graduates). Passing this exam was a must in order to pursue future studies in medicine. Later on, for many years, Shiva, her husband, and we remained close friends.

I think this examination was in early January. It consisted of two parts, medical knowledge and another regarding understanding the English language, giving 3 hours for each. This was the first time I had to choose one from the five multiple choices for each questions. Not sure if I regretted studying for it with Prema when I was offered the chance during our internship! I was mostly worried about the English language part. Someone from the examiners read some English story or something on the loudspeaker. Then we were supposed to answer the questions on the paper, and I don't remember if it was also in the form of multiple choice.

Somehow that year, the results for ECFMG were declared late. It was almost the end of March. Yes, I passed this first examination with flying colors! Shrikant, my husband, was visibly happy! I did not realize at that time that I had cleared one major hurdle for him. More for him than for me, the goal was, I must succeed in my career. He had planned his future, his dream right when he had come to India, he was to marry a doctor!

My father wanted me to become a doctor because there was no doctor in my extended Sane family at that time. Definitely, money was not at all the reason for my father, and for me, as I have said before, growing up, I didn't have any goals. Shrikant was well aware of the fact that doctors make money! He knew it very well that Sanju, his cousin who then became a general surgeon, had worked extremely hard during her residency and had started earning a good amount of money.

I started realizing my husband's motives later on in my career. But the 100% proof I got was in the year 2019! For the first time after I came out of my depression, I attended one very big Indian gathering in Dallas. I met Prema's sister-in-law. She is the one who told me regarding this fact. She herself was looking for a match for her sister at that time in 1972. Shrikant had declined to consider her sister for a possible wedded partner. Her sister did not have M.D. degree.

For me, I am happy that I did not know about Shrikant's future plans at that time when I passed that exam and succeeded many more times during the next 38 years of my married life. Whatever anyone wants to think about how my life turned out to be later, it doesn't matter to me at all! Because yes, I really had a wonderful life for almost 38 years with the partner whom I had agreed to marry. I had willingly said "YES" to Shrikant's proposal in December of 1972.

Again, I am talking about only what I personally felt about my marriage with him. What I still keep hearing from a whistle-blower from his family even now after almost 7 years out of his life, Shrikant still continues to repeat the same. His complaint through this whistle-blower is that I was not the right choice for him! I know he is totally out of his mind by now. I am afraid that once a possibly treatable personality disorder of his has become irreversible. I still feel sorry for him but absolutely have no repentance. I had tried my best that his personality disorder finally gets identified and that he gets treated.

Under Shrikant's guidance, I started requesting applications for Internships from various hospitals in New York. I think I got invited for only one interview from Beth Israel Hospital. A vacancy had opened because someone, I believe a prospective first year Indian resident from that hospital, had committed suicide. The hospital finally decided to freeze that position and therefore I was declined that position. During our visits to Coney Island Hospital, both Shrikant and myself used to say hello, especially to any Indian-looking resident in a doctors' white coat that we met. Would talk to them about getting applications from various hospitals where they may go for rotations during residency training.

It so happened one afternoon, I was all ready to get out of the apartment. I had worn the same pink sari I had gotten from Shrikant at our engagement. That day I was to join him for his final visit with his psychiatrist! As I was about to leave the apartment, there was a knock on the door. It was not very common. But as I opened it, to my surprise, one of those Indian residents we had met actually came with the internship application! He did enter the apartment. To this day, I still get horrible Chills thinking about the possibility of being raped.

This word, "rape", was unknown to me at that time. Definitely, someone was watching over me. Now I believe it was always my Mother, my Angel. He started leading me backwards as he moved forward towards our bedroom. Some unknown entity alerted me. I quickly moved forward to the entrance door, compelling him to get out before me, and locked the door, telling him that my husband was waiting downstairs for me. Luckily, I have never felt unsafe the same way again so far.

How much I have tried to recollect that occasion, the psychiatrist, and the purpose of Shrikant's prior visits to him, I never could remember anything that had gotten me worried. I do remember asking Sanju about it in 2010. She had told me that after Shrikant came back from India in January of 1973, he was extremely depressed. She is the one who had suggested him to see her friend, who was a psychiatrist.

It took me actually 38 years of marriage to get a clear picture of Shrikant's behavior. It was in 2010, I think I witnessed the FINAL BLOW! The events that took place after June 1st, 2010, must be considered as the beginning of the last act of my marriage story. This was the first time I had no choice but to alert my children, requesting them that their father needed help.

Chapter 12: Aim To Succeed Continued

Sometime in March of 1974, my older sister Chimi, just two years older, from Columbia, S.C., came to visit me with her husband and beautiful toddler daughter. Since there was no pressure to study for any examinations, at least for the time being, we enjoyed roaming around in Manhattan. Don't remember the exact details, and don't even remember who's idea from two of the men it was. We went to see one X-rated movie!

Needless to say, with the general consensus, we walked out of the theatre much sooner than later. While in our apartment, I still remember the presence of one picture, possibly lost forever in one of those albums. In our living room, my brother-in-law was fanning himself, his toddler next to him. I was going through the postal mail, which included one application for residency. The picture was actually proof of how I still continued being engaged in pulling my hair!

Perin, one of my friends from our Mission Impossible, residing now in Temple, Texas, had just recently reminded me of that from the year 1967-68! My habit has never left me! It is actually one of my OCD! Yes, I get it! While I am thinking seriously about something, especially my right hand remains idle most of the time. Because I am left-handed, the right hand is free and automatically the process begins! This is one of the most important reasons why I try keeping both of my naughty hands engaged. Quilting, making ribbon flowers, glass cutting! While reading or writing, I have to be very mindful as to what my right hand is upto!

Shrikant did not believe in wasting time, especially when it came to his wife. He prepared a resume for me. Also, a list of ten medical agencies in Manhattan was typed by him on the typewriter he owned. The list was handed to me. I don't remember after what number of visits to the medical agency I succeeded in getting a job. On April 15, 1974, I started my first job in this country. It was a Physician's job, from 9 am to 5 pm with a 1-hour lunch break. This included history taking and routine physical examination of the employees of one Garment Industry near the 29th street and 8th Ave or something. Most of these employees were Spanish speaking. This is where I learned many Spanish words and tiny sentences. "Tine, altra pressione?, ke problema higado?" "Do you have high blood pressure?", "Do you have any liver-related problems?"

Trust me, it came in very handy in my later career and actually became one of my sure vehicles to impress some people around me by asking questions to the patient in Spanish! The salary was $15,000.00, a very comfortable amount when the subway tokens costed only 35 cents each. I felt very good and proud of myself then, and even now I had made my Shrikant visibly happy! It reflected in enjoying weekends, going around shopping, including spending time with Lilatai, one very good friend provided by Prema. We bought our first Melamine dinner set for 8! The design had beautiful yellow daisies and green leaves all around. Eventually, a set of two was handed to a few of Shrikant's and my younger nephews who came to the USA as students and it was just a starter for them.

Life was very good in general. Our love (Lust) life was mutually desirable and was looked forward to by both partners whenever possible. Plan was made, definitely decided by Shrikant to leave Brooklyn and move to Queens after the lease expired. I was taking birth control pills, actually, without knowing much about their significance related to taking one of them each night! I must have missed swallowing them occasionally, especially during the move to 52nd Street and Roosevelt Avenue, Woodside, Queens.

Eventually, when I finally became mature in my thinking, I realised what happened next was not surprising at all. Shrikant had successfully implanted his seed in my womb kind of effortlessly. My ovum was fertilized, which in retrospect, was the BEST THING that had happened. The only problem, it was without being aware of its presence. I started having severe upper abdominal distress to the extent I ended up having upper GI series with multiple X'rays of the stomach. There was no diagnosis for the stomach pains except that the obstetrician in my employer's building declared me to be pregnant!

I actually applaud both my sons and especially their wives, how very knowledgeable they were at the same age I was at that time. They planned everything and literally had looked forward to the good news, eventually to be shared with the parents of both of them! I really think I was too stupid not to have the instantaneous natural feeling of being overjoyed. Definitely, in that category, my growth was way too delayed! Luckily I soon realised that the womb, where my baby to be was growing exponentially, was protectively covered by a big lead glove, a normal must-do practice while dealing with women of childbearing age.

By all means, having a baby is the best news to share with others. As soon as both my bosses, Dr. Arshoroff and Dr. Newman, heard about this news, they did congratulate me but at the same time told me that I won't be able to continue working because they won't provide insurance for the delivery and related matters. I would have to resign in due time before I deliver. At the same time, they both made sure to write wonderful recommendation letters for my future use. I had saved them for reference for a very long time, and then they were recycled.

As I said, each and everyone has aided me in planning my future. Both Lilatai and myself were guided to take the FLEX examination. This is the medical licensing examination allowed by some states to take even before starting an internship or residency. It was in October, and we both had flown to West Virginia for that. It was a total of 6 hours of examination with one hour break in between. Before that, while I was working, in the evenings, I used to take classes to aid me in preparing for the examination. Again it was courtesy of Shrikant's to guide me about location, how to reach there 3 or more days a week before reaching home at night, taking the D train, and getting down at Ave J!

This is how I started appreciating the beauty while traveling at night. In the NY City, each and every room of the office buildings were lit with electricity during the night hours. How did these people afford the expenses was one of the constant questions to my own self?

To my surprise, again, I passed that examination. Truly, I absolutely had no idea that this was the best thing that had happened as far as my future medical career was concerned. I don't remember the details as to how I decided to apply or who provided me with the information regarding the vacancy for first-year residency training in Anesthesia at Boston University Hospital starting from January 1st, 1975. Sometime after the results came out and before December ended, I must have gone to Boston for an interview. Dr. Kripke, the director of the BUH Anesthesia department, offered me a first-year residency in Anesthesia without needing to finish one year of internship!

Doing one year of Anesthesia training in India, laced with passing the medical practice licensing examination, was really a very big asset for my future career. Can anyone tell me why Shrikant, my husband, would not be proud of his Suhasini / Pratibha? I had the slightest idea that he had a checklist somewhere in his brilliant mind, and he was able to check marks, kind of cross out the items from "The things to do" list for his wife once they were accomplished. I don't even remember if I had any morning sickness. If at all it was there, there was absolutely no time there for me to be fussy! Everything that happens to a girl, to be transformed into a wife, then into a mother, all that is supposed to be a natural phenomenon!

Here I must thank Sanju, Shrikant's cousin, the general surgeon. She was the first one to encourage me not to miss this opportunity. Usually, the residencies start from July 1st of every year. Those starting from January 1st are not common at all. I never became confident to live life by myself independently. I thought I was always sheltered, till finally a time came one day.

The management where I live now approached me in 2018. They asked me why I didn't become a resident of this Brookdale facility instead of staying here as a respite. They had to explain to me this new term "Respite". Apparently, they had allowed me to live here under that category much longer than they usually do. In 2017, I had stayed at this facility for 8 months in one stretch. The first time when I came here straight from the psychiatric hospital was in June of 2016. That stay was only for 2 months. The maximum allowed, as a respite, I think, is 3 months at a time. In June of 2018, I signed the contract with Brookdale facility, Battery Park. Finally, I got my permanent address! It took two and half years and a few days after I was forced to leave my sheltered life at 58 Greenwoods on Christmas Eve 2015 afternoon.

Shrikant and I boarded the train with a couple of my bags. It was New Year's Eve 1974. It was an overnight journey to Boston, Massachusetts.

Chapter 13: Life In Boston, Mass.

Early morning of January 1, 1975, we arrived in Boston as if this proved to be my introduction to the future closeness to my Massachusetts memories. Anand, our first son, joined Harvard University for his undergraduate studies in 1993. His girlfriend, fiancée, and then wife is from another town called Attleboro, same state. These and a lot more memories are attached to my introduction to this area in general. I don't remember whether we had prearranged my stay with someone before when I had come here for the interview. But I did move with one Philippino girl named Venus Baleva.

She was a senior resident in Anesthesia Department at BUH. Possibly the town she lived in was Brookline. I'm not that sure, but I definitely remember that we used to take a bus to come to the hospital. It wasn't that difficult for me to mix in with the rest of the residents of different ethnic groups and some of the staff members who were of Indian origin. This is where I came to realize that passing that medical license examination was a really big plus. Some third-year anesthesia residents there were not able to clear that exam. They couldn't be a staff member and practice anesthesia without it.

I don't remember having any difficulties getting along with my roommate. Here, I don't mind repeating it again in the next several other incidences. This is mainly because I really have never expected anything much from anyone, including my now ex, my children, or others. "The only thing I wish in return from you is FRIENDSHIP" was the frequent sentence I used to write in many Birthday cards to several of my friends. There was parting with some of my beautiful creations or monetary gifts if I thought it was necessary instead. Baleva's was a one-bedroom apartment. I used to sleep on the sofa, not a sofa-come-bed. I recall absolutely nothing significantly unpleasant that occurred, which needs to be shared with the readers, except one thing for sure, I definitely missed the closeness of Shrikant on a daily basis, especially at night.

My due date was June end, 1975. I don't recall if I actually was or at least was aware of the fact that my baby was growing in the womb when I had first come for the interview. But definitely, when I joined the residency, it was the actual FACT! I had to let my director know about it. Increased incidence of spontaneous abortions and some rare fetal anomalies were linked to anesthetic agents, especially nitrous oxide, N2O. There was documentation in various Anesthesia journals and occasionally in newspapers. To avoid the hospital being sued by me, I was told to sign an agreement that in such an event, I would not sue the hospital. The problem was solved mutually and instantly! I don't recall much teaching being done to the new student, which was only myself. I was assigned on-call duties every third night. Luckily the next day's work was light, and I was able to go home and rest or do laundry, etc. During one of the night duties, I met one radiology resident who turned out to be our thoracic surgeon Dr. Tilak from Aundh Hospital, Pune! I was pleasantly surprized and was able to carry on talking and sharing conversations. Later on, in my private life, he turned out to be the close relative of one of my nieces-in-law!

My anesthesia training in India was one of the best things that had happened in various ways. First, detailed training for me was not needed, but most importantly, I had saved one whole year for Shrikant's future dream for me to come true! I didn't have to do one year of internship. My teachers on the staff (they are called Attending Anesthesiologists) seemed comfortable letting me manage most of the cases. But there was one senior teacher named Dr. Norton. All my colleagues used to make fun of me that if I was assigned to do a case with him, I might go into premature labor! The only case of most significance that I remember was the procedure called "Retropubic Prostatectomy!" It meant prostate removal by accessing it via a lower abdominal incision. I will never forget the massive blood loss during that one particular surgical procedure. This important lesson alerted me every time later on in my career to be prepared in advance for the procedure. I would make sure that I will have enough access for multiple blood transfusions if needed.

By the middle of April, I was 7 months pregnant. I'm almost sure that Shrikant had pre-planned all his strategies. He had already started collecting residency applications for me from NY City area hospitals. During the first couple of months, I traveled to NY by Greyhound bus and spent weekends together, including cooking, etc. When it became a bit difficult for me to travel then, Shrikant used to travel to be with me. At least, I don't recall at all him attempting to find a job for himself in the Boston area. But then it became my duty. It was my first "White Lie" when I had to inform Dr. Kripke, the director. "Because my husband is unable to find a job in Boston and due to the need to be together for the arrival of our baby in due time, it is necessary for me to resign and find residency in the NYC area!" Dr. Kripke took absolutely no objection. I got a very good recommendation letter from him. After all, I was a very sincere student. Being pregnant was never used as an excuse to avoid hard work!

The colleagues said good-by and good luck. Venus Baleva, my roommate, gave me a tiny silver piggy bank for the upcoming baby. This was my first gift for the baby to be born! She used to receive Christmas cards from me every year in Montreal, Canada. We had kept in touch for a long period of time. Only after 4 months, I left Boston by April 30, 1975. The future was unknown to me this time, also!

Sanju paid a special visit to me one weekend prior to that. I was actually craving seafood! She took care of that for me.

Chapter 14: Springs Summers and Winters That Followed

In this chapter of my life, I mention about something that will be hard for anyone to believe. I write this while being part of someone's marriage celebration in Coppell, Texas.

The person who got married for the second time, he is actually my niece's ex-husband, a doctor by profession, went through almost exactly the same ordeal, followed almost exactly the same sequence of unfortunate events. My younger sister's beautiful daughter, aided by my own mentally sick younger sister, filed for divorce about 5 years ago. Similar pathological lies of hers, like my own ex's, got him arrested, handcuffed and thrown in prison overnight. He went through the same mental torture for a much longer duration. Luckily he had his close friends, his own mother, and his stepfather to soften the torture.

In early 2014, he had approached me for the first time even when I was his now ex's relative, an aunt! Soon after that, my own saga started shaping up! He had absolutely no idea what had happened to me. At the same time, his story was brewing in the background. After more than five years, in 2019, we got reconnected. We exchanged our stories for the first time. Lucky for him, the Hon. Judge in Texas had thrown away the case in my niece's face. He didn't lose his medical license! He is doing totally fine. Over fifty of his friends, their spouses and their young adult children, and close relatives of his and hers were among to witness the union of two souls. My nephew-in-law and his new beloved wife were both the victims of someone's severe but unnoticed mental issues.

Because in reality, I actually didn't belong to either his or her close family and introducing me as the groom's ex's aunt to the whole audience didn't seemed desirable. I remained kind of an unknown entity throughout those 4 days-long celebrations. Definitely, it didn't hurt my feelings in any drastic ways, but I still definitely felt the pang somewhere deep in my heart! My nephew-in-law's assuring words through WhatsApp just before the actual ceremony started were, "You are the person who I can have an amazing personal relationship with and have a heart-to-heart talk!"

Over 30 years of my medical career, the whole month of May 1975 was the only time I really had to work hard to find a job! Multiple interviews were already lined up. Again it was courtesy of Shrikant, my concerned husband. He had already filled up 7-8 applications or even more that I really don't remember. They were duly signed by him using my name. Later on, he continued signing my name on occasions using my letterhead provided by the Department of Anesthesia at Valhalla, NY! Of course, among many other things, I was not aware of this practice of his while it was actually happening.

The only thing I know for sure is that I had travelled by subway by myself to various areas of Brooklyn and Manhattan & even the Bronx. These were the places where I did not dare to go again in my life so far. Imagine, I was over 7 months pregnant. One interview was at Harlem hospital. While talking to one of the residents after the interview, he said everything was fine about this hospital except its location! In those days, it was one of the very high crime areas.

A similar situation was at Downstate Medical center, Bellevue Hospital, Brooklyn Jewish Hospital, Jacobi Hospital, Flushing General Hospital, or maybe more that I don't remember. One of them was Metropolitan Hospital, 96 street, and 1st or 2nd Avenue in Manhattan. But I think the Interview took place at Flower and Fifth Avenue Hospital. Dr. Bizarri was the Chairman of these two and a few other hospitals that were under the umbrella of New York Medical College located at Valhalla, N.Y. This is all acquired information that I came to know about in later years. His secretary's name was Miriam. I remember him asking me a question about Succinylcholine, a quick-acting muscle relaxant!

I think I have already mentioned about its use for intubation while doing my Anesthesia Training at Sassoon Hospital in Pune, India! His question was, what can happen with repeated use of this particular muscle relaxant? I am sure he was pleased with my answer. The same afternoon, I got a call from his office. "Dr. Bizzari has accepted you to start the residency from July 1st, 1975!" Apparently, he had called Dr. Kripke, my Director from BUH, right after the interview was over. Within the next day or two, I had to call his office to tell my second White Lie! There was a mistake in calculating the due date of delivery!

My actual due date told by the obstetrician apparently was June end and not May end 1975! The reply from the Chairman's office was there should be no problem. I was allowed to start my first-year residency in Anesthesia from August 1st, 1975! I was told that the whole month of July would be considered a vacation. This means for the next 11 months, till June 30, 1976, till the end of my first-year residency, I was not allowed even a single sick day! Later I learned about the rules specified by Anesthesia Boards. Residents were allowed only 20 days per residency year to be absent from the training. Otherwise, they were required to repeat the lost days before getting the certification.

I think the month of June 1975 was relatively free and fun-filled for me. Lilatai had invited us for dinner in her apartment, possibly for something equivalent to a baby shower, except that the gift was not for the baby to be born. It was a gift for the one, which was me, who was going to bring the bundle of joy into this world. I don't remember what the actual traditional gift she gave was, but there was something that she did which will be in my memory forever. She was the one honoring my request, gave me my First Haircut!

My first shoulder length haircut.

Again, the before and after pictures are there, I promise, in one of the first albums, a real big fat red wine-colored album. One just has to try looking for it! There is a picture of me wearing a beautiful and colorful soft silk sari facing the mirror so as to show my thick and long single braid of curly hair. Also, there is a front-facing picture of mine after my first shoulder-high haircut. I think the reader has no choice but to guess the real picture from June 1975! Now even the shoulder-high length has been the history of the past for a really long time.

Some time by the end of my career, I took one silent oath, I would never grow my hair again and will never make the chapatis (Indian flat bread made out of whole wheat flour)! So far, I have been true to my own promise to myself! This is the only rare one which is not like from tomorrow, I will sincerely walk at least 5,000 footsteps!

Possibly according to some, may be there is absolutely no reason why I should be describing my hair story in so much detail. To this my answer is "Why not!?" It so happened and continues to happen even at this late stage of my life, and people continue complimenting me positively about my now salt and pepper color hair. My physiology teacher in medical school, my chairwoman Dr. Elizabeth Frost during my career over here and as recently as a month ago, one unknown middle-aged person in the Shop Rite grocery store are just a few of them praising my hair and not my looks! Besides, because of the Covid 19, I have actually started doing my own haircut out of necessity. It so happens that I have actually started saving some money! Now even some of the grouchy seniors in my building actually have started admiring my additional skills besides mending their torn pants etc. Many of them have developed age-related arthritis of the hands. These hair-cutting skills of mine are strictly for myself except for there is another wonderful resident of Indian origin in my building. She occasionally requests me. But her haircut is 1-2-3! Her hair is very soft but very thick and straight, tied together in a pony tail. The charge for her is "100" zeros! I get the kick out of it when I am able to make the slightest difference in someone's self-image. It is very easy to remember. When I realize that it is about time for me to take charge of that specific scissors bought from a dollar store in order to give myself the most needed haircut, her's is usually the next! It is usually repeated roughly every 2-2 1/2 months.

On June 27, 1975, my first bundle of joy stepped onto this Planet Earth. My obstetrician was Dr. Paranjape, with the same mother tongue as mine. Later on I really felt sorry for him and hopefully had apologized right away. He actually tried his best till almost the end that I delivered this baby naturally. The labor pains were so severe that I uttered all the bad words I could think of in Marathi! He finally gave me intravenous Demerol to decrease the intensity of the labor pains and the screaming, a very common practice. The baby's head was disproportionately big. Soon after that the continuous fetal monitor indicated fetal distress. Emergency c-section took place under general anesthesia. It is just impossible to try forgetting anything that happened next. An attempt was made with the aid of the nurse on duty to breastfeed my 8-pound baby. Between the sore nipples, the bikini incision for the c-section making it difficult to hold the baby and the lack of expected visit from Dr. Paranjape to comfort his patient, all of these were some of the contributory factors for the failure. Anand, my hungry and vigorous baby just couldn't stop crying.

Finally, the decision was made to start feeding him the appropriate baby formula. And it became necessary to retard and eventually stop the lactation. It was very important to avoid the occurrence of Lactating mastitis. It was one of the most difficult both emotionally as well as physically painful experiences. Not sure if I should look at it as a blessing in disguise.

As agreed upon, I started my Anesthesia training on August 1st, 1975. The contract was for Metropolitan Hospital. But for the first 5 months, I was placed at Flower and Fifth Avenue Hospital at 105th street and fifth Ave. This was one of the busiest hospitals for private practice. Surgeons with a variety of specialties were allowed to schedule any procedure at any time of the day or evening. Their own convenience was allowed as priority No.1 irrespective for those including the patients themselves. As far as I know, even now, Anesthesiologists are very often considered secondary by some surgeons especially if the anaesthesiologist happens to be of origin other than being born as White American! At least for me it always remained the truth, the fact!

By the end of May, my mother had already come from India to help us just in case. Again this was a very common practice and continues even now. Usually it is the maternal grand parents or just the maternal grandmother who is expected as the number 1 priority by both the baby's parents. This turned out to be the first out of a total of four of her visits to the USA. Just recently while completing the self-analysis, I was able to revisit some of the significant events pertaining to me. It was going to be okay for my mother if I decided not to marry if that is what I wanted. But "Pratibha, I will like you to show me America in the future!" These were her words in 1972 beginning. She stayed about a month or so after I started my training. She did stay with my older sister in Columbia, S.C. for a month or so and flew back to India from N.Y.

At least I was not aware of any facilities available to pump and safely store breast milk during the 1975 period. This is what I meant by the blessing in disguise. Anand's growth chart as per the pediatrician was above average with the baby formula. We found a very good baby sitter in our building on the first floor. She was a Spanish speaking house wife and a mother of four. Anand was happy in the company of four children and the dog as a bonus to play with.

I had to leave the apartment by 6:15 am. Subway #7 was actually two minutes away. The fire department was just in front of our building. We definitely felt very safe in that area. I had to reach the hospital by 7-7:15 am. to get ready for the surgical procedures starting at 8 am. Soon I realized why I was posted at this hospital even as a fresh first-year resident. Again there were no daily lecture series that was supposed to be the requirement as per my sincere thoughts. My prior training both from India and now from Boston was conveniently considered advantageous for the Attending Anesthesiologists at this private hospital.

It was left up to Shrikant to get our baby ready with all the necessary things for the whole day, place him in the baby carriage and wheel him down through the elevator to the first floor where the baby sitter waited for him.

Chapter 15: Story through Different Seasons Continues

This in general, was the routine that lasted for the next three years. But still, there was some variety even in that routine. I was placed on call duties every third night. Invariably I was assigned to answer all the calls from the obstetrics section. Being a private hospital, obviously, the pregnant ladies were also kind of private, meaning they needed to be attended to even for normal delivery!

For whatever reason, they somehow wanted to push out the baby at all the odd hours of the night. Basically, I was kept awake the whole night and actually, in many cases, used to end up giving only oxygen by mask. Occasionally I ended up adding some N2O for partial pain relief. But I had to make sure that the patient didn't step into the La La Land while inhaling this Laughing gas called Nitrous Oxide!

This is because then one may not get the patient's cooperation to push the baby out. Only once do I remember adding an anesthetic agent called cyclopropane. This actually is NO, NO! First of all, my attending on-call should have been present in the room. This agent is extremely flammable, especially in the presence of Oxygen or something. It is long discarded from anesthesia practice. Anyway, everything went fine.

I don't see any reason why I should not mention it here. This experience as a first-year Anesthesia resident also has contributed to a great degree that I never liked the practice of anesthesia for Obstetrics.

Most of the C-sections were done under spinal anesthesia during those days. Of course, the patient must be agreeable to it. General anesthesia was avoided whenever possible unless it was an emergency C-section. I was fairly comfortable using the thinnest possible gauge spinal needle to avoid a post-spinal headache. Now epidural anesthesia is the commonest form of regional anesthesia practiced even in developing countries for pain relief. If needed, an additional appropriate local anesthetic dose can be added through the same indwelling epidural catheter. Unfortunately, I never gained confidence in much of the regional anesthesia practice.

How can I ever forget the name of a pediatric surgeon named Dr. San Fillipo? For whatever reason (I actually know why!), Dr. Nadgir, one anesthesia attending, and myself were assigned to his pediatric procedures, including the ones needed for neonates. Sometimes there are at least "love-hate relationships". Between Dr. San Fillipo and myself, there was only a mutual "I hate you" relationship. At least for me, it never changed over the next total of almost 30 years till the end of my career! Instead of being cooperative, he had always proven to be the biggest hindrance, especially during the initial phase before he could safely start the planned surgical procedure. I got exposed to almost all types of surgical emergencies related to neonates. This was all within only my first 5 months of training.

One good thing for me was, Dr. Linda Hernandez was an anesthesia attending who used to like me. She was one of the seniors, and I used to get assigned to work with her very often. Her usual assignments were for a surgeon named Dr. Lees, whose speciality was in breast-related procedures. The only thing was that she used to hate if anyone ate their lunch in the ladies common room that smelled obviously garlicky or onion smell or something! As long as I avoided that, it was totally fine! It was in this room that I did most of my studying that was needed to face the written anesthesia examinations.

The basic concept of private anesthesia practice was introduced to me in my early months of training. This was especially regarding billing the patient or his insurance for receiving the anesthesia for the surgical procedure. We were required to fill up certain information even prior to starting to write the special Anesthesia chart meant for that particular surgical procedure. This chart is used as proof to ensure all the proper guidelines are followed. It is a must that the chart is duly signed by the anesthesia resident in training, and below that, the attending anaesthesiologist assigned must sign it as well.

The routine was extremely strenuous. Once, I actually had, I believe, herpes Zoster or maybe simplex whatever! It was extremely painful being in the inguinal region. I was feverish. I was not allowed to call in sick. Another incident I specifically remember is that I was on call the previous night. As usual, I was up the whole night. The next day at five o'clock in the evening, I was desperately looking forward to going home to my own infant. I was told to start another major thoracic procedure with Dr. Sernik or someone.

Dr. Strauss was the surgeon. I really had it. I went to look for my chairman Dr. Bizzari, but he was nowhere to be found in his office.

Finally, I was able to talk with him on the phone. He was at Metropolitan Hospital. "Dr. Bizzari, don't you think I am a human being!?" I had worked for 34 hours! In response, he requested Dr. Sernik to pacify me by offering me candy.

I started the anesthesia with the Attending on call that evening and finally was able to rush to my baby, who was at least an hour away!

It is very difficult to figure out what could be the driving force behind how each and everyone in this type of routine can keep up their sanity and keep up the enthusiasm. I remember making use of each and every moment at my disposal of awake time at home in the evenings and weekends. We both tried our best to take care of all the necessary chores, including cleaning and vacuuming, and laundry, so that on those weekends I was not on duty, all three of us could enjoy outdoor activities. Yes, life, in general, was fun! No doubt about it.

Chapter 16: Completion of Residency and More

In January 1976, I started working at Metropolitan Hospital. This being a city hospital, the residents were exposed to a much more variety of cases.

Trauma was No.1 that kept us busy many times throughout the night. Unfortunately, I couldn't escape the obstetrics anesthesia here also. For the first time, I met the rest of the residents from my batch of first-year residency. They were five of them, all men, all speaking the Korean language. Here I also worked with second and third-year residents. I still remember the names of some of them, Dr. Villafania, and Dr. Sadeghi. There were two new residents who had just joined at the first-year level from January 1st, 1976. They were Dr. Narendra Majithia and Dr. Gajapathi. It was Narendra who kind of startled me by saying "कसं काय, काय म्हणत आहात?" meaning how are you? How is everything going on? Obviously, I was happy to hear someone saying something in Marathi, my mother tongue! It so happened he was married to the love of his life who happened to be a Maharashtrian girl! Even to this day we have been in touch and have exchanged multiple visits and auspicious occasions. In age he is actually much senior to me but he always refers to me as his "GURU!" his teacher. I was only six months senior to him. Dr. Gajapathy was our neighbor for many years after we both moved to Old Tappan, NJ.

There are too many memories but it will be difficult to write about all of them. Something I distinctly remember is that we, the residents ourselves had to make sure that the anesthesia machines were well-equipped with everything we needed for daily use. We were required to fill the liquid anesthetic agents like Trilene, Halothane, and Ethrane! We needed to replace the oxygen and N2O tanks when empty, etc! Now it sounds so strange because till I decided to write just now, I had actually totally forgotten about it. Again here there was really not much teaching or the presence of the Anesthesia Attendings in the operating rooms that I can recall! Usually the senior residents were teaching the junior ones! So I had already developed the skills of an Anesthesia Attending (A teacher) by the time I finished the third year of my residency.

During the first year, the six of us were driven for a few months once a week to Westchester Medical Center, WCMC. Here in the NYMC, we were taught again to dissect the human body. I really don't remember how invasive it was required to be. But I clearly remember Dr. Laterri, reminding us "No chop, chop!" meaning we were expected to do a nice and clear dissection. We six used to make fun of him in his absence. During these travels, all five Korean colleagues of mine used to engage in conversations in their own language. With practice and with the aid of occasional English words in between, I had become an expert in decoding the Korean language! We did have fun. Later on I remained in touch with one of them named Dr. J. U. Lee. He had moved to Los Angles after residency. Every time I attended the Pediatric Anesthesia conference in L.A., we used to have lunch together. One thing I can never forget is the incident during one of the luncheons! He had offered me a piece of chewing gum. Within the first or second act of chewing on that piece of gum, my tooth cap had come out! Without him noticing, it was shoved in my pocket book! Needless to say, since that day I have NEVER chewed on a piece of gum! For many more years we both had regularly exchanged New Year Greeting cards.

During my second year of residency, I kind of achieved the favouritism of one most important Anesthesia Attending, Dr. Samuel Hernandez! He turned out to be the husband of Dr. Linda Hernandez from Flower and Fifth Hospital. They didn't have children. For me, I had personally nothing to do with him. In fact I used to get disappointed with the way he used to treat other residents. It was obvious emotional abuse and discrimination by any standards now. He would always talk of Dr. Sadeghi as one of the stupidest residents! I really used to feel sorry for him. If you keep saying to someone "you are stupid "repeatedly, obviously that person may finally start believing that he is really stupid! It used to remind me of my honeymoon period. The way Shrikant used to present his mood swings, I sincerely believed that may be something was wrong with me. I also found Dr. Hernandez to be a jealous human being. We had a junior resident named Dr. Devanesan. His brother was a surgeon in our hospital. For whatever reason, he was getting verbally abused by Dr. Hernandez so much and for so long that during private conversations, Devanesan used to day dream that there was a plane crash during the flight from the Philippines. Two bodies among them were burned beyond recognition! Incidents like these are impossible to forget!

Because I was kind of a favorite second-year resident, I was allowed to attend a big Anesthesia conference, called ASA, in San Francisco. It was October 1976. Biennial centennial year for the USA. Shrikant, Anand, our 1&1/3-year-old son and myself, we really enjoyed the time together. It was fun. I still remember the pictures of Anand standing at the driver's seat, holding the wheel and beautifully smiling. I could sense the victory on his face appropriate for his age. After the return, I had to present my report about the conference at one of the Thursday meetings in front of a large audience! The beginning sentence of mine was, "I found most of the people in downtown San Francisco to be weird!" I think my second year of residency can go in the history book as one of the Okay years during the training period. That time the written Anesthesia Examinations were held in June. The dates were changed later on. For whatever reason that I don't remember, I was allowed to take my written boards at that time. The results came when I started my third year of Anesthesia training.

I had actually passed my written boards in Anesthesia during my third year of residency. Whatever studies I did were mostly during some free time in the hospital. It was just impossible to close the door and study in the apartment. I remember Anand banging on the closed doors and crying loudly. It will be hard for anyone to believe but I passed my written boards only by reading one book, Dripps book of Anesthesia! It was a blue hard covered book, about an inch and a half in thickness. I actually used to remember which important sentence was written on what page including its location on that page! We were required to buy the huge book of Churchill Davidson. It remained brand new till the end. Same thing with the Anesthesia Journals. I rarely referred to anyone of them in my almost 30 years of career. I hope you understand that this is written mainly as the memories of the facts and not as an Ego factor 🙏.

I am not sure if it was acceptable or not from the Anesthesia Board standards point of view. But my third year of training in Anesthesia was considered as a specialised year in Pediatric Anesthesia. I doubt if any Anesthesia attending was actually officially trained in Pediatric Anesthesia. But it was Dr. Samuel Hernandez who was the one in charge of my training. By this time, his level of favoritism for me had dropped drastically and obviously way at the bottom. No one will believe me but it was because of the presence of a new, much more kind of sexy student named Dr. Kasad! I never understood the necessity of showing off the long sexy legs in such obvious way! Even for my own eyes, it was something that could not be ignored! The way the conversations were carried on between the two of them, it actually was truly pathetic!

Anyway, I cared the least except for the fact that he started treating me way beyond my simple, non-complex mind could accept. One particular incident took place right in the beginning of my third year of training that I can never forget. It was a bilateral inguinal hernia repair on a premature baby. It goes without saying that the surgeon was Dr. San Fillipo whom I hated the most. After the baby was Anaesthetised (Anesthesia induction), I had to start an intravenous using a 24 gauge butterfly needle. No doubt it was difficult.

Succinylcholine was given through intravenous. But unfortunately the IV was infiltrated. Intubation was not successful right away. Baby started turning blue. Don't remember the details but eventually everything went smoothly. The baby was transferred to the recovery room (RR). I gave the report and checked the baby again. Everything seemed okay so I returned to the operating room. There was an emergency call from the RR. The baby was not breathing! I ran to the crib side. Baby being premature, quite often can get into "Sleep Apnoea". I stimulated the baby. Explained to the nurse how to take care of the baby till she was more alert. She needed to be kept in warmer conditions. The baby was finally discharged to her room under the care of her parents. For absolutely no reason Dr. Hernandez started shouting and yelling at me in front of everyone. I tried explaining to him that this is not uncommon because the baby was Premature. Anyway there was another incident. He used to sit in a small enclosed area right in between the two wings of the ORs, between the two passages. I used to call it a yellow cubicle. Something had happened and he told me to get out of that cubicle. It was at this time, I had passed my written boards. I decided to give back, "You get out of this room!" I yelled at him, I did what I had long planned to do.

Few more things of importance that I remember. Our department was approved for a Nurse Anaesthetist Training program of two years duration. The male person in charge was Mr. Bethea. He was apparently gay. I absolutely had no idea what it meant. But used to wonder why he often used to accompany one nurse anesthetist student and walk up the stairs in an unknown area! The name of the lady nurse anesthetist in charge was Miss. Freedman.

During my second year of training, I did go to the Flower And Fifth Ave. Hospital for one more rotation. But it so happened that whenever they were kind of short of staff in that hospital, I was sent there occasionally without any explanation. Also in the same year, I had to rotate to WCMC, Valhalla for Cardiac Anesthesia training. It was a really long commute. I used to stay there the whole week and come back Friday evening when not on call on the weekends. Dr. Keshav Kubal used to give me a ride to and from the hospital to the train station. Here the on-call rooms for the residents were far away and we had to walk through a tunnel. Just like many others, I often used to get scared. Sometimes we used to joke that one must carry a syringe loaded with succinylcholine just in case any prisoner escaped and we had to confront him! We had the prison on that premises. They used to come for surgery occasionally. My husband had kept in mind such conversations among us, the doctor friends and had actually made use of one of them as his conspiracy theories in late 2015. His idea was to make sure my restraining orders became permanent.

By June of 1978, my three-year training in Anesthesia had almost come to an end. Because I had done 4 months of training in Boston, I was able to get the approval for a medical license to practice in N.Y. State. I had already passed that exam from West Virginia in October of 1975. The reciprocity process was not difficult at all because the required 3 years of residency training was already complete. Obviously it meant that the time had come to apply for Attending

Anesthesiologist job at some hospitals. Dr. Guifrida was the director of Metropolitan hospital. He, Dr. Lagman, the chief of OB anesthesia and maybe a couple of others had given me the recommendation letters. But the idea was they really didn't encourage me to go for any interviews at other hospitals. They actually wanted to retain me as the Junior Anesthesia Attending from July of 1978! In fact the director's attitude was, how dare I go for interviews in any other hospitals! The only interview I actually went for was at Bronx VA hospital. I was rejected! Last few days of June 1978, I had gone on vacation to Florida with my relatives. I did not have a Job in my hand even after I returned. For me, I was more than happy to be a stay home mom. It was not to be so. The paperwork was completed. The NY City Hospitals commission had approved one position at Metropolitan Hospital. The position created was to provide anesthesia for ABORTIONS.

So from July of 1978, I became the Attending Anesthesiologist at Metropolitan Hospital, N.Y. Eventually in the next couple of years, the ever-so-busy Flower and Fifth Avenue hospital was turned into a place for chronically ill patients.

Here I will like to make a note. My chairman Dr. Bizzari was the one who had completely understood both the sides of my coin. He had long known that this Dr. Joshi (he used to call me Josh!) was a very hard-working, sincere, good girl who was least interested in money. Actually in the third year of my residency, I was doing everything in the capacity of a chief resident. It was the only year, there was no designated chief resident! The $1,500.00 City budget was engulfed by some of the superiors from the department. Dr. Bizzari also knew that this same Josh will be dangerous if the residency inspectors came to talk with me. Many of the TRUTHS could be revealed! They never allowed me to be interviewed by those inspectors!

I became an Attending Anesthesiologist without signing any written contract! One person, my Shrikant was very happy without any doubt. He already had his future plans ready to be implemented. Simultaneously, his belittling of his wife, Suhasini, became more and more apparent. Thinking back, I am pretty sure that I had noticed it. But for whatever reason, I had not started reacting to it. Had I already become the enabler so that he became more and more emboldened in his psychopath behavior? It is quite possible that those in his favor can easily question why is it that I didn't open my mouth right away? May be it does make sense. But do I repent? Absolutely not! I was totally happy with the family of three of us that we had created together!

Chapter 17: The Best of the Dream Come True

Till June end 1978, I was an Anesthesia Resident and a student. From July 1, 1978, onwards, my job title changed to Attending Anesthesiologist, a teacher. Dr. Suhasini Joshi was the same. I was already used to teaching the junior residents being a senior resident. Nothing had changed, including the same hospital. Not sure about the seniors on the staff, but I see no reason why I should not feel good about myself, why I can't congratulate myself! I started the residency on July 1975, continued my career, and ended it at the peak from the same Institute of New York Medical College! I officially retired on January 2nd, 2003, 9 days shy of my 55th Birthday.

As I said, everything remained the same except my signature on the Anesthesia chart was now under the signature of my resident, my student! Once, I asked Narendra, why is it that my salary suddenly jumped to more than double!? He is the one who explained it to me. Now I was responsible for that particular case. If something happened, then I would be the one who would have to answer. I never forgot about my responsibility related to the signature and towards the patient.

With the consent of Shrikant, I would try to bring during summer time someone from my family, one of the sisters, or someone very close, to the USA on a visitor visa. We would send the tickets for one person and her one child. In 1977, my second eldest sister Sulabha had come with her youngest son, Sunil. She was from a joint family.

Therefore others, including her husband, Suresh, were willing to take care of her other two older children.

Sunil was about 5 years old. In 1978, my younger sister came with her 3 & 1/2 years old daughter. She is almost the same age as Anand. It was really a lot of fun. Especially for Anand, this was a major change, not having to go to the babysitter for at least 3-4 months. Definitely led by Shrikant, we had started looking for a house in Rockland County. We had a very good friend working in Orangeburg, NY. Shrikant and I both used to love that area. We signed a contract for one of the houses. Sometime during my residency, Shrikant bought our first car, Austin Marina. We all used to travel in that car.

It was time for my sister to return to India. I was worried about Anand. We had to change 3-4 babysitters for him in 3 years. With the new job and especially moving to an unfamiliar area, I was worried about new babysitting arrangements. Not unusual for us, the immigrant professionals, we started thinking of sending him to India to be taken care of by Shrikant's parents. Of course, this was supposed to be only a temporary arrangement for about 6 months. They had gladly agreed. Obviously, the 3-year-old Anand had no say in this matter. So sometime in September, Anand travelled to Pune, India, with my sister and her daughter. My brother had also come that time, for the first time, through his workplace. So they all reached Pune safely.

I learned to drive with the help of our babysitter's husband. My work in the hospital had become much less hectic. For the attendings, the city used to pay additional money besides the salary for overnight duties. This worked out to be the best for me. The rest of the attendings from my department used to take my call assignments for additional money. This meant I could spend more time at home with my family, a win-win situation for me. Sometime in October of 1978, we moved to 192 Blaisdell Rd, Orangeburg, NY. Many evenings and weekends, Shrikant and I would spend time buying things for the house and decorating it.

There were frequent visits to Burger King or McDonald's. I think we were very happy. Once, we met the parents of one Indian couple. Their dress code was such, absolutely no doubt they were our language-speaking people. The young couple, Mr. And Mrs. Anant and Anu Kelkar, remain one of my best friends even today. Especially after they moved to Connecticut, we used to visit them frequently. It had become our weekend home! We did so many wonderful things together. There were trips to see fall colors, Thanks Giving Dinners, visits to the Casinos nearby, skiing, and sightseeing.

There are so many pictures in various albums, unfortunately, out of sight forever. Anu turned out to be a childhood friend of my brother's wife. She is the only one who knows everything, inside and out, about my Family Saga. I doubt she has missed anything! Besides, her memory is really sharp. I don't need to repeat anything. She is the one to remind me if I have forgotten any links! Eventually, they moved to Douglas, Georgia and after Mr. Kelkar retired, they finally settled in Jacksonville, Florida. The last visit to them with my now ex was in February of 2015. This was one of the trips I had kind of forced on him.

Our routine was set. We would both go to work using the car, and I would park the car at my workplace. In the evening, I would pick Shrikant up at a particular place and would drive home together. This was the time I had my second experience of suffering from Alopecia aerate. Again I started losing my hair. There were patches of baldness. Every evening, I came home to the empty bedroom of my son Anand. The walls of his bedroom were decorated with beautiful blue wallpaper covered with sailboats and all. Every evening I used to cry uncontrollably sitting on the empty bed. The bed covers and the pillow had the Superman design. The first time the emotional torture was because of my friend, Alaka. It was in 8th grade.

Obviously, my nature is such that I take everything too seriously. I just can't help the way I express my feelings. They are too serious, beyond anyone, including what I can imagine! This time I ended up having scalp injections of steroids. Eventually, I got my hair back.

I had learned sewing during my school years. We decided to buy a sewing machine. It is a Kenmore brand from Sears. It was bought in 1978 for the sole purpose of stitching window curtains. I had succeeded. In later years, the same machine was used extensively by our housekeeper, Elsa. She was the one who had maintained it well. After I retired, I made use of the same machine to stitch countless bags and over 300 baby quilts. During my attempt to rent an apartment after I was made homeless on Christmas Eve, 2015, this same machine was one of the items I was allowed to bring to my apartment.

It was the courtesy of my husband. The list of the items to be moved from our house had to be presented to the court, duly approved by my husband and his attorney. Then only my children were allowed to help me to move them to the apartment. I rented one two-bedroom apartment starting on March 1st, 2016. After I vacated that apartment in Norwood, NJ, on Memorial Day Weekend of the same year of 2016, some of the items, including this machine, were brought back to the house in Old Tappan, NJ, where I had once lived for the period of 30 and 1/2 years.

The same sewing machine was only one of the very few items I was able to retrieve from the house on March 6, 2020. After the prolonged depression that followed, I restarted using it. It was repaired only once a very long time ago. Since then, I have been lucky to sort out the simple problems with it! Again I have started doing my baby quilts and bags and many more things. This means the almost antic sewing machine is still working!

It was not that common to call India very often. I think we mainly depended on letters from India. We were successful in making new friends in this new area. We were all young couples. The backyards of the three of us, the neighbors, were a big open space. We all got along very well. Eventually, Dr. Amin, one of the neighbors, became our paediatrician till both the sons went to college. All of us were able to spend a little more time in the evenings and weekends because I didn't have to attend to too many overnight duties.

Overall, life was good, except I was missing my son badly. For Shrikant, obviously, his future dreams had begun shaping up. They were becoming clearer. His doctor Suhasini, Pratibha, was definitely on the right track. Our love (Lust) life was still intact. Shrikant didn't have anything better to ask for. For me, everything was okay, being totally ignorant about my husband's future plans for his whole life.

Chapter 18: Destiny Never Stops Surprising

I was happy with this less hectic life at work. But right before New Year, before the annual Christmas party of the Department, Dr. Bizzari called me into the office. Apparently, there was a budget cut from the City Healthcare or something. The position created for me in July of 1978 was retracted. Truthfully, Dr. Laterri was absolutely contributing nothing to the day-to-day activities of the department. He could have been easily forced to retire. But me being the most junior attending on the staff, was going to be the obvious victim. Dr. Bizzari gave me two choices, either I could work at Lincoln Hospital in Manhattan or go to Westchester Medical center at Valhalla.

By late 1978, WCMC had suddenly become very busy. This is after one cardiac surgeon, Dr. Reed, had joined. He started bringing a significant number of cardiac patients for surgery. Following him, a variety of surgical specialists acquired the privileges for working at the hospital. More than the normal number of operating rooms needed to be utilized during the daytime. So in those months few of the senior attendings from our Metropolitan Hospital started moonlighting there. Interestingly these attendings were getting a regular salary from our hospital. At the same time, they were earning income from WCMC!

Undercover activities like this were totally accepted. Actually, dental procedures for mentally retarded patients under general anesthesia were also covered in a similar fashion! None of those who were moonlighting were interested in accepting a regular salaried job at WCMC. They didn't want to work that hard with very little salary. During Christmas parties and on several other occasions, I had already met the original group of Anesthesia attendings at WCMC. In fact, one of those, Dr. Sanchala, encouraged me several times to join the Anesthesia department at WCMC.

Thus in the middle of January or so of 1979, I started working at WCMC. I was not used to driving in unfamiliar places and was very poor at following directions. I did practice 3-4 times and wrote down the directions before actually joining the department. So basically, for the next about 24 & 1/2 years, I crossed that Tapan Zee Bridge almost on a daily basis. When we bought the new car, my only request to Shrikant was that the car should be as big and heavy as it could be. I was never interested in any fancy car. Instead, I was more interested in safety, especially driving on the bridge. I don't think I had any trouble getting used to the routine in this new atmosphere. Besides, the residents under me were very smart, and actually, all the girls eventually became my long-standing friends.

As I had mentioned before, Dr. Bizzari was the chairman of all the hospitals under N.Y.M.C. The director of WCMC, Anesthesia department was Dr. Shibutani. I found him one of the worst discriminating people. He did not like hiring female staff members. The reason given was that they got pregnant and called in sick! He was the typical representative of the Japanese culture in Japan, where women are still considered secondary.

A couple of years ago, there was an article in the NY Times about a Japanese bride who walked down the aisle and stood in front of the mirror. Many friends witnessed. She decided to marry herself! She told the guests, I can take care of myself! Because I was hired as the first female anesthesia attending on the staff, all the members gave me a big welcoming party. I can't tell about others who were trained under Dr. Shibutani. But for me, I really had a very low opinion about him to start with, and unfortunately, it never changed. "Are you done with the family?"

This was one of his standard questions when eventually, more staff was added to the department. He was one of those who did not work in the OR much but was very much research-oriented. Most of his research was based upon disapproving anything that was already published in the Anesthesia journals! He had a very talented Japanese research assistant. I am almost sure that Dr.Shibutani didn't have a favourable opinion about me either. Invariably he would find something to disapprove of my vacation. The reasons given were ridiculous. Anyway, I was stuck with him for many years.

In my private life, I was told and also saw through the pictures sent from Pune that Anand's health had deteriorated. Apparently, my mother-in-law was so stubborn she took him along with her on several travels by train. She used to feed him milk by spoon! He was 3&1/2 years old! Pictures showed obvious rickets, protruding belly, and very thin arms and legs. My sister Sulabha brought him to her house. He was treated by Dr. Shirole, my former professor of Paediatrics.

By the middle of March 1979, my mother had brought Anand back from India. This was my mother's second trip to the USA. My little boy looked fine physically. Maybe I was wrong, but he had lost the mischievous childhood expression on his face. He appeared too serious, too mature. The first few times, he was very shy when Aziz, of the same age, our neighbor's son, came to play with him. Later they became very good friends. Now both families of their own have been in touch with each other on a regular basis.

My mother stayed for a few months. Anand joined a private preschool in Blauvelt, NY. The bus would provide transportation both ways. Things had started to settle down. Both Shrikant and I used to leave the house very early in the morning. He drove to downtown Manhattan, and I drove towards the East, over the Tappan Zee. I do remember that he had started sharing a ride with one lady to save money on gas or something. I had absolutely no time to think about things that didn't matter much or were not that significant.

A serious thought had started peaking in my mind. I wanted to have another child, and this is mainly because I wanted at least one sibling for Anand. Then there was something I noticed, Shrikant was reluctant to have sex! I don't know why, but maybe one can guess now that he didn't want the inflow of money to halt, even though it may be temporary. Now the same husband, after making me homeless on Christmas Eve 2015, I heard him complaining to someone that he actually wanted 4 children and that Suhasini had refused! Anyway, sometime by the end of 1979, I did have a miscarriage. The only thing I remember very clearly is I sobbed for a few days and nights in my bed, holding Anand close to me, and then started going back to work.

By May of 1980, I did get pregnant again. But just like with Anand, before I realized that I was pregnant, I started getting severe epigastric pain and again underwent multiple X-rays! Though this time, I was worried throughout the pregnancy. That summer, Shrikant's parents came to visit us for the first time. I do remember almost two weeks of a roadtrip with them and the three of us. Along with sightseeing, we did visit multiple of their as well as our very close friends. This time I did have time to think about the morning sickness. I was being pampered!

My work was going on without any sick leaves. One most important thing I should have mentioned before. When I joined WCMC, I was given a totally unwanted title. I was given the position of the Chief of Pediatric Anesthesia! Total shock, but I couldn't dare utter a single word against or in protest! The reason was too obvious! Guess whom I had to face again! Dr. San Fillipo had acquired the privileges to operate on Pediatric patients in this hospital also! Besides, he used to live in Chappaqua. Later I found out that, apparently, Mr. Clinton was his neighbor. The unfortunate thing was, not only no one else was interested in facing him or was assigned to provide anesthesia for his procedures, but knowing that he literally used to harass and emotionally abuse the other OR staff and me without failure, no one, including the anesthesiologist in charge, was willing to support me.

They always were catering to these so-called superiors, the surgeons in the operating rooms. I hated it beyond what I can describe. Eventually, after many more years, I heard that the nursing supervisor of the operating rooms had finally reported him to the proper management. Anyway, the reason I didn't want to be the chief was because I never considered that I had adequate training in Pediatric Anesthesia. In fact, I learned much more about it when I actually became the staff member!

By 1982-83, a pediatric cardiac surgeon joined the group. I realized that I may end up providing anesthesia for Pediatric Cardiac Surgery. On June 9, 1983, I wrote an official letter to Dr. Bizzari. I still have the copy in my file! In that, I had expressed my willingness to undergo training in Pediatric Cardiac Anesthesia at Boston Children's Hospital or any other comparable training program for at least four weeks or so. Without such training and some experience, I had requested him not to consider me to handle those specialized procedures. Obviously, the answer was negative regarding such training.

The relative shortage of anesthesiologists on staff remained the constant factor till I decided to retire. In fact, It was one of the reasons for considering retiring at a much earlier age. Besides, soon I had come to realize that I saved myself the huge grief and headache of facing those so-called special group of cardiac surgeons, full of boasting images of themselves.

During 1979 & 1980, few new attendings were added to the staff. One of them was a very capable and thorough gentleman Korean doctor, I think, named Dr. Ho. Very appropriately, he approached Dr. Bizzari after he passed both parts of the Anesthesia Boards. He wanted to know his future. The answer was to let him go! Dr. Bizzari was such that no one was allowed to question him! How dare one can ask such a question about his or her future? There was another, Dr.

Greenspan, a board-certified Anesthesiologist from California who joined the department. I was personally very happy with his addition.

I had failed my first attempt at the oral examination part (part 2) of the Boards. Dr. Greenspan had promised me coaching. Also, he was the one who really did some most needed changes for our department. He started displaying the procedures on the central board. He is the one who arranged the schedule in such a way that the attending on duty from the overnight call was allowed to leave early and all that. The original staff, like Dr. Kumar, Dr. Sanchala, Dr. Kubal, Dr. Her, and myself, were not that gutsy, all of us being immigrants. Of course, Dr. Shibutani was always just for himself.

I believe we definitely needed someone like Dr. Greenspan. I will never forget one incident. Dr. Lowenfels was a general surgeon who scheduled a so-called emergency appendectomy, which actually should have been done ASAP. He scheduled it for the evening at his convenience. I was on call duty that weekend. It was Dr. Greenspan who supported me, saying if it was an emergency, then it must be done within an hour or so and not according to the surgeon's convenience.

Right after I joined the department, some talks started regarding the various departments going private. WCMC was a county hospital then. Dr. Bizzari held meetings with the 6 of us from the original group. Right during the first meeting, Dr. Bizzari casually mentioned my salary to be something like $45,000.00. "Dr. Bizzari, you had promised me $55,000.00!?" To my question, his answer was, "Oh! is that what I said, then ok, it will be $55,000.00!" As I have said before, there was actually no signed contract anytime so far! During my first six months of training, I had already gotten the idea of billing for the private practice at Flower and Fifth Ave. Hospital.

When he started talking about partnership and shares, Dr. Her and I were the only two who dared to take objection. According to me, salaries can be according to the seniority, but I thought the profit sharing should be equal. It so happened I was vacationing in South Carolina in December 1979. I actually got a call from Dr. Shibutani. "Dr. Joshi, Albany is taking objection to approve the Title for the private corporation (PC), Valhalla Anesthesia Associates. This is because the two of you and Dr. Her are not board certified!"

It is impossible to express the massive blow I felt. After coming back, several times, I asked to show me the letter from Albany. It was never shown to me. Again, I still have the copy of that official letter written by me to Dr. Dante Bizzari, requesting for clarification of the New York State requirement to become a shareholder in an Anesthesiology PC! I knew for sure that a few of the Anesthesia attendings at my hospital for training were definitely not board certified, and in fact, many other hospitals had similar PC with some non-board certified attendings. They were all part of the group.

This was one of the first blows and had realized that I would have to fight for myself, by myself, for justice. Dr. Her and I were the only ones who had the guts to open our mouths. But for others, they had gotten what they wanted, and obviously, they deserved it. They were made full partners right from the beginning. They all owned 20 shares each out of 100.

Two things of importance, one, I was surprized that Dr. Bizzari did not fire me at that time and even in the future. I had taken objections multiple times. I would approach him in his office with a written letter in my hand. I thought that I was better at expressing myself this way. The other thing is he did keep part of his promise to both Dr. Her and myself. We were allowed additional money, as promised, for the professional expenses. I knew that the department would show those as the PC expenses for tax purposes. I was able to present most of the gas, telephone, travel, computer-related, and other expenses.

Also, I was able to lease the car through the department and was able to change it every 3 years. I drove the largest and the heaviest station wagons from different companies. I don't remember the details. I never was a car fan. I never had the appetite for expensive cars. Also, till the time I retired, I remained part of the original group and received an additional salary from NY Medical College. My academic title remained as Assistant Professor. I never aimed for or desired an Associate or Full Professor title.

Dr. Greenspan naturally approached Dr. Bizzari for his future. He wanted to be eventually part of the private group. I don't know what exactly happened in Dr. Bizzari's office. The next thing I knew, he was leaving. Unfortunately, I failed for the second time in Part 2 of Anesthesia Boards. It was held in October of 1980 in St. Luis. There was another very talented girl named Hema Chauhan. In fact, she was one of my best students. She was offered the position at our department. She knew it well. In a few words, she expressed her disappointment as to what she was offered and declined the offer. She went to Florida. Just recently, I contacted her.

As far as my children are concerned, they never knew how much their mother had to fight for her rights throughout her career. I doubt they even knew that I was actually the main breadwinner. I never knew or looked at my income in that way to start with, and money was NEVER my No.1 priority. Their father knew everything very well. He was totally happy with the way things were going.

One of my characteristics, this OCD, obviously includes that I will always fight for JUSTICE, including for others. Unknown to my children was the fact about this Warrior Queen of Jhansi, me. They actually thought in recent years, Mother's Day of 2019 to be exact, that I stopped taking psychotropic drugs, which is the reason why I again started behaving the way they perceived my behavior.

The medications were stopped gradually, as per Dr. Yemins, my psychiatrist. He was totally convinced that I didn't need them anymore. Truthfully, none of those psychotropic drugs prescribed to me had ever worked. It was since my first forceful admission to the psychiatric hospital, the Heaven Facility at Westchester, on my birthday, January 11, 2016. They had not worked at all. Except maybe they helped me to go to that predictable and most wanted sleep. The uncontrollable thinking ability of my brain then was subject to those nonstop dreams instead.

Chapter 19: Three Most Wanted Months in My Life

Days and months passed by. Baby must have been growing nice and easy because soon, the need for maternity clothes arose. Yes, this time I did buy a bit better quality, so-called presentable clothes, at least one or two of them. As an assistant professor, occasionally, I had to drive to Metropolitan Hospital to give lectures to the Anesthesia residents there. On one such occasion, I met Dr. Samuel Hernandez, I hope you remember my teacher for Pediatric Anesthesia training. As soon as he saw me with the big belly, "Looks like you are going to have a baby with only one eye in the middle of the forehead", these were the comforting (!) words that came out of his filthy mouth.

One has to realize that these were the types of people the residents were subjected to during their training. The good thing is they were only a couple of them, like Samuel Hernandez. Because of the exposure to radiation during the first trimester, I was definitely worried this time but could not do anything but wait, watch, and pray.

At WCMC, one new surgeon named Dr. Ashikari joined. He specialized in breast surgery. He had given me a new title, "Mother" From that time till I retired, he always referred to me by that nickname! Regular work and on-call duties were going well. It was very rare for us, the girls, to call in sick. The funny thing is some of the male doctors on the staff were the ones who would call in sick much more often. Before we could say that we are tired, it is them who were the first ones to declare about being tired! The girls on the staff used to get the kick out of it! We had a junior female coworker named Uma on the staff. She was the only one who was allowed to work part-time. But the definition of this 'Part Time' was such, she would work from 7 am to anywhere till 3 to 5 pm or so.

The only thing was she didn't take on-call duties. But for that duration of hours, the salary was so little that it was totally unbelievable. Not only my dear husband but even myself, I would not have accepted that type of so-called part-time job. Later on, she joined the hospital much closer to her house. Her husband, Dr. Shankar, is a very good orthopedic surgeon who, in fact, had assisted one of the surgeons when Shrikant needed surgery in September of 2010. The cause and what type of procedure, nothing were known to both the children and myself prior to the surgery itself. Uma, Shankar, and I remained friends for many more years, actually till 2015, till I got stuck with my own destiny!

Once my in-laws found out that I was pregnant, they decided to extend their stay. Getting a doctor's certification to do so was not difficult. During one of my last prenatal check-ups, in the beginning of January 1981, I started spotting blood. The doctor immediately advised complete bed rest. There was a little placenta Privia, which means the portion of the placenta was ahead of the baby's head. Baby's growth was well, according to the obstetrician. Besides, she was going to be out of the country by the time of my due date. Therefore planned c- section took place on January 14, 1981!

It was done under epidural anesthesia. I was awake to see my normal-looking baby, as I was concerned about the effects of radiation. A beautiful bundle of joy, a boy, was shown to me before he was transferred to the nursery. It was the Day of Makar Sankranti, one of the most auspicious days in the Hindu calendar. This time, I myself had requested not to let me produce breast milk, no lactation. Don't remember exactly, but I was given something with Magnesium. A good size baby, easy to handle, was named Atul! It was the suggestion of Sanju, Shrikant's surgeon cousin. Atul means No comparison! Our first one, Anand means Happiness! This time the one-week stay in the hospital was a totally complaint-free stay. The obstetrician had visited me before I could complain!

We were discharged home. I was sanctioned 3 months of maternity leave. This means I was not expected to go back to work till April 15, 1981! The actual official letter was in my possession before I had delivered. By the end of January, very close relatives or friends were able to visit us. There are definitely at least two beautiful pictures lost in those albums. One is with Sanju holding Atul, her husband Amrit next to her, and of course, Anand wearing a red top, a 5&1/2-year-old big brother. The other one is with Madhuri and Raju Kulkarni, one of our best friend couples whom we had met in 1975, and they remain the only bridge-playing friend couple of ours.

They were moving to Riyadh, Saudi Arabia, soon. The duration was unknown at that time, but it turned out to be 14 years! Every year they used to visit the USA and of course us. Now they have long settled in San Antonio, Texas. Needless to say, we have visited them a few times, and vice versa. On that particular day, for lunch, my mother-in-law was in charge of the kitchen. Each and every utensil in the kitchen was out. I can never forget that incident. It was total frustration. Could not do much as my c-section wound had not healed yet enough.

On February 18th, 1 month and 4 days to be exact, my in-laws left for India after 8 months. I still had almost two months before I had to show up at work. I may have said three months, but I was okay at least with two months of one of the most wonderful, most wanted periods of my life. Imagine, I had my husband and the two beautiful babies he had given me. I had wonderful friends around me, and I already had an ongoing job. Can anyone tell me what else anyone may want?

I thoroughly enjoyed being a housewife. We had already planned that my sister-in-law, my brother's wife, and her two sons would come for at least for 4 months by April 15, 1981. The ticket for his second son, my brother had willingly accepted to pay for. Naturally, Atul being the real tiny baby, he needed it, and therefore, I had to pay more attention to it. It was Anand, our older son, who soon complained and was really sincerely crying. According to him, he was not my favorite son! It so happened in a few more years, and it was Atul who had complained that I was paying more attention to Anand!

To this, my own explanation always remained the same. The mother's attention was equally divided, 50/50! To anyone's disbelief, including mine, this impartial attitude is the one that actually was responsible for me becoming homeless on Christmas Eve 2015!

I was enjoying myself being the mother of the two, meeting with other stay home moms in the afternoons. Shrikant would come home in the evening on time. Things were wonderful! And then I got a call from Miriam, our secretary. Dr. Bizzari wanted me to start working from April 1st instead of April 15, as it was said in the official letter. No questions asked! There was one more total disappointment. Just for 15 days, we needed to find a babysitter. It is impossible to forget. We did find one in the neighborhood. Anand would go there from his school. He invariably used to see Atul in the playpen crying and the babysitter smoking. Anand repeatedly told us not to bring Atul there for babysitting. Did we have any other choice? I doubt if any other immigrant professional like me was given any idea as to what is at stake.

On the weekend before April 15, my sister-in-law arrived in NY with two of her sons. Shrikant went to pick them up at JFK.

Later on, I always dreamed of and eventually had actually desperately looked for some break from work like this wonderful period. I had to wait till December 1998. I needed a hysterectomy for a fibroid uterus. I was not worried at all about the actual procedure. I had full confidence in the surgeon and the anesthesiologist. I was seriously looking for a sick leave of six weeks. Dr. Kwon, my surgeon, had given me the official note!

Chapter 20: Back to Routine

It was not that easy to get into the routine. During my maternity leave, I got hooked on "General Hospital!" I think it is an everlasting show on ABC. So if one didn't find Dr. Joshi anywhere between 3 pm to 4 pm, invariably, the nursing staff or anyone could trace me down to the common coffee lounge!

Work at the hospital was getting busier. Being part of NYMC, we had both residents and nurse anesthetist students teaching programs. Invariably just like with other staff members, I had to manage anesthesia for two operating rooms. Only if it was a very complicated case, then I had to supervise only one room.

For me, it always remained my utmost responsibility of keeping the patient safe under anesthesia. But being a mother now of two, I could never imagine working in my capacity if I was not able to provide a safe and comfortable environment for my own family and my children. This is how I started training my mind to handle multiple tasks at the same time. On a daily basis, I would talk to the nursing staff to help me find a babysitter/housekeeper. It was the must for my near and for far future. During the late evening hours, I was able to mingle with the nursing staff much more. And one fine evening, my prayers were answered.

An evening nurse named Hilda, living in Nyack, NY, informed me about Elsa. She had come to the USA as a housekeeper for the Ambassador from Uruguay. Her duties towards him were over, and she was free. The very next evening, Shrikant, Anand, and our 8 months old Atul and I, drove to Nyack and visited Elsa at her friend Edith's house. Elsa knew and spoke only Spanish and had an Ambassador visa. With the help of the translator, we hired her right on the spot! She had already fallen in love with our beautiful baby with blue eyes!

I owe so much to Elsa. She was 50 years old when she came. We would pick her up from the bus stop on Sunday evening and drop her at the bus stop on Friday evening. I can write volumes about her presence in my life, but it suffices to say for the time being, I have always considered myself to be one of the luckiest! And to feel that way, she was one of the most important reasons. She stayed in the capacity of the housekeeper from October 1981 till January 1993. She became part of our family. I think Atul carries her picture in his wallet. I never took any objection. She learned English on her own and became a US citizen. She had taken almost total charge of the household for the daily routine.

My third most important task was to pass Part 2 of Anesthesia Boards. I needed guidance. Just having knowledge definitely was not enough. We had only 3 chances at this. If I didn't make it, then I would have to take the written test again in order to get the other 3 chances at Part 2! Dr. Her, my colleague, was in the same boat. He, unfortunately, had gone through this already. He was very intelligent, but unfortunately may be due to a proper language barrier, he had to take the written examination twice, and only on the 6th attempt he finally got the Anesthesia Boards Certification.

I couldn't imagine myself going through this emotional torture. I had a very sincere student named Dr. Vyankat while at Metropolitan Hospital. He had started to practice in another hospital. We were in communication. He agreed to guide me. Shrikant used to drive me to Long Island to his house on the weekends. My prayers were answered. By October of 1982, I was Board Certified in Anesthesia!

As I said, at each and every major step of my career, I had to fight for my rights. Now was the time to finally ask for the partnership that was promised in 1979. When I approached Dr. Bizzari, his answer was that the new corporation year starts on April 1st, therefore, I will be admitted to the Valhalla Anesthesia Associates P.C.(VAA) from April of 1983. Even when the time came, the original verbal offer was only for 8 shares which actually meant I would get much less remuneration than I was already getting without being a partner. Finally, after back-and-forth visits to Dr. Bizzari's office, I believe I was offered 12 shares from April 1st, 1983.

The work and the responsibilities as Chief of Pediatric Anesthesia were getting more serious. And again, the time had come to approach Dr. Bizzari. I actually have a typed letter to him as the President and to the Directors of VAA, written on April 9, 1984. The request was for an adjustment in my remuneration at VAA. Using the proper language and reasoning, I requested two things, one to include me as a member of the Board of Directors. This way, I would be able to participate in the decision-making process at VAA. The other request was to issue additional shares to a total of 16 shares out of 116 shares issued. In the same letter, I had already requested to allocate more shares to make it equal to the other shareholders from April 1st of 1985. I wanted to be a full partner of VAA, P.C.

I had never recognized it. I was a fighter. But the fight was always genuine and was for justifiable reasons. As a female, non-American-born, brown woman, it never became easy to be accepted by the professionals in the world of some white professionals. But interestingly, it was almost equally difficult to be treated fairly by some of my own skin color colleagues. What I realized was that the conversations between the Physicians were mostly money-related complaints! I used to wonder if so, then what about the nurses, secretaries, the cleaning people? I always felt more comfortable outside of the circle of professionals! I am still in contact with many of the O.R. and recovery room nurses.

A similar thing happened with my own coworkers who were not in the P.C. They were the employees of the P.C. While negotiating remuneration for overtime duties. I always remained on their side. With joint efforts, additional compensation per hour after 4 pm, certain fixed amounts for overnight duties, and weekends became part of the distribution of the P.C. income. I don't remember the details, but there was one major conflict between our P.C. and Dr. Her. At one point, he was forced to be on his own, including case assignment and billing separately for his income. He was a very good clinician, and I did my part in supporting him. I used to request some of the surgeons to have him provide anesthesia for their cases. The conflict was somehow resolved in the near future. Be assured, I didn't expect anything in return. It has been my nature to put myself in the other person's shoes. I always thought of treating others the way I would like to be treated. For many years, whenever I thought that I needed an extra hand while managing any difficult case, invariably, he was the first one I used to ask for help from. After all, it was all for the safety of the patient.

There was a genuine reason why I wanted to go back to my husband even after he had made me homeless on Christmas Eve, 2015. I had recognized some very good qualities residing on his one side of the coin. He was very simple, no smoking, no drinking, and no drugs. He was the one who was helping me to type all those very precise official letters. It would never have been possible to walk up the ladder of conventional success without his assistance. I absolutely had no doubt in my mind.

I believe I was totally content in my private and social life. The stress, difficulties at work, and any daily occurrences in my professional world were only revealed to my husband behind the closed doors of our master bedroom. They were not for the outside world, including my growing children. Because of Elsa's presence, I really was worry-free about my precious children. And they both were very well mannered, respectful & studious.

For a long time during my career, I was able to concentrate almost fully on my duties at the hospital. In fact, it had remained my No.1 duty for as long as I remember. My Anesthesia Department remained my No.1 home. The home at 58 Greenwoods was No.2 in every practical sense.

Shrikant had assumed and actually was allowed, without any doubt, to be in charge of the rest of the duties, including the financial decisions. There were no questions asked by his dutiful wife, Suhasini! For tax purposes and for a better comfort level, he started talking about buying a bigger home in an area of renowned public school systems. We saw houses in Greenwich, Connecticut, and different areas of Westchester. But somehow, we both preferred to be on the west side of the Hudson River.

I had always liked our area. Somehow I was reluctant to buy a house based on my income. I had requested Shrikant that it should be affordable only based on his salary. I was never told, and also I was never interested in knowing his earning capacity. Truthfully I never wanted to work hard at all. But it so happened that our income bracket grew much higher. And finally, we made an offer on the house at 58 Greenwoods Rd in Old Tappan. It was a brand-new house, and the builder was also very young. I knew very well that I absolutely had no patience to plan and build our "Dream Home!"

This house, that we put the down payment on, remained my Dream Home. This is where I had created and hung a big piece of Art saying, Love, Laugh, Dream, and Inspire. Eventually, when I entered my own home on March 6, 2020, with the police, this piece of art was nowhere to be found. Every remaining thing in the house was thrown everywhere.

I think on July 24, 1984, we closed the deal by signing the papers and became the co-owners of 58, Greenwoods, Old Tappan. I do remember being present at that meeting. The house was within 3 minutes of driving from our home in Orangeburg, NY. Now the state changed to NJ!

My Home Sweet Home, bought in 1984, had to leave on December 24, 2015

December 24, 2015 - Our living room and the artwork of mine left behind

Chapter 21: New State and Environment, New Agenda

Elsa was of tremendous help during and after we moved to our new home. Atul continued going to nursery school in Blauvelt, NY. Starting KG, he also joined the public school in Old Tappan, just like Anand. It was, and I am sure still is, one of the best public school systems in NJ. I hardly had time during weekdays, especially if I was on a late call. But all those evenings when I was home on time, I never thought that I deserved any additional time for myself. I was away from my house duties and my children for so many hours on a daily basis. I understood Elsa's importance very well and, therefore, always treated her with respect as a family member. Initially, without any doubt, there were lots of adjustments on my part, but I always adopted the balancing act.

On the contrary, once Elsa's presence was established in our home, it was Shrikant who actually took off! I didn't know that time, but he started coming home late quite frequently. I didn't pay much attention that time because I myself was coming home late many times due to the hospital duties. Not sure, but because he was a NY City employee, he was allowed to maybe attend free courses at NYU. He was very much into investments and financial and corporate matters or whatever.

Between 1985 and 1986, he bought 13 two-family rental properties in NJ. Also, he had rented two offices, one in Pearl River, NY and the other in Fort Lee, NJ. If one asks me even now about the purpose, I absolutely have no idea. There was zero discussion prior to buying those rentals, also, I had no clue when he was actually purchasing them. Eventually, I came to know somehow, many times through our close friends, including Amrit or a couple of his cousins. I believe he used to brag about it with them. This is just the way he had convinced all our friends and relatives, including maybe our children that he was an IBM consultant!

Believe me, I didn't really know, but even if I had known, it would have made no difference in my day-to-day activities! The only connection I had with what was going on in his life was the task he had kind of ordered me to do! There were actually stacks of cancelled checks, and my duty was to enter them in the log book that he had provided. I had no intention of wasting additional time while at home. I always carried the heavy bag with me to the hospital! During night calls, in my spare time, I used to enter them in the logbook. The standing order was that the task needed to be completed on time.

It will be hard to believe, but the fact is, in 2010, for the first time, I was able to solve the puzzle. How did he buy all these properties where my name was included as the co-owner? I had never gone for the closings, nor did I ever go into those 13 two-family rentals. Eventually, after I retired, I did enter one of them at Englewood, NJ. Again, one of my dreams was to get it renovated one of the days while thinking of downsizing! Just like any others, this remained just a dream. By now, I have gotten used to countless such shattered dreams!

It so happened, he had asked me to sign the Power of Attorney once sometime in that period, absolutely without any knowledge that I recall. Also, whenever he was purchasing one, he would ask our 4-year-old son Atul to type and change the date! Two things are very important here. First, the 4-year-old was very smart that he could type, but at the same time was not old enough like his 10 years old brother Anand, who may have potentially asked the purpose behind it. I am able to tell all of this with confidence because later on, I was able to gather all the facts. In 2010, whenever I got any chance in his absence, I searched his office room. I came across so many unexpected, unknown facts that it will need pages to write. More than the criticism, I want to point out that these psychopaths are very smart. They take into consideration each and every minor detail! My employment letter with the fat salary was essential for the purchase of those properties.

I think in the year 1985, during summer, Shrikant's parents came for a visit to our new home. Their first visit to our Orangeburg home was different. Now my hospital work had increased by many more folds. Besides, it was Elsa who was in charge of the household. This turned out to be one of the most frustrating periods for me. On a daily basis when I used to come home, invariably, I had to listen to Elsa's complaints about my mother-in-law. This was to the extent I feared that Elsa might leave!

Shrikant's mother would always give orders or interfere in Elsa's routine. It is better not to describe in detail again, but my father-in-law had given up on her a long time ago and was not that physically fit himself. He had heart problems, so it was me who had to somehow patch up the tension! Their son, Shrikant, my husband, rarely came home on time. This is because he was busy with extracurricular activities! He was taking college courses, managing rental properties or whatever. Initially, my mother-in-law insisted on waiting for her son to come home to have dinner with him. It lasted only for 2 days! Most of the time, the parents were asleep before their respectful son would come home by 10-11 pm!

This was the second and the last trip for my in-laws. Two or three years later, my father-in-law passed away. He had a heart attack sometime after they went back to India. After that, I visited them during my India trip with Anand and Atul. I bowed down, touching his feet and asking for a blessing. It was my definite thought that this would be the last time my children and I would see him. That was the time he had asked me if I had any objection if all his estate goes to Shrikant's younger brother, Sanjay.

Of course, I had no objection. Not sure if he had asked this question to his older son, Shrikant. Later in life, one thought did come to my mind. Would he have asked the same question if our living conditions were not comfortable during their visits to the USA? After all, we were living in a six-bedroom house on a one-acre lot. Both of us were working to earn money. We had a housekeeper. In later years, I had come to know that when Sanjay, their younger son, got married, my father-in-law had very clearly told his second daughter-in-law that she wouldn't be allowed to take any outside job. Apparently, her duties were assigned by my father-in-law! Eventually, she was in charge of the whole household including the keys to the safe.

Later in 2010, when I was desperately trying to get answers for Shrikant's behaviour, my father-in-law's best friend's daughter had told me something very interesting. My father-in-law had made a statement regarding me to his friend, Mr. Karandikar. I had made it very clear again and again to my mother through the letters and to everyone in Shrikant's close family. I really wanted to retire way long time ago, even at the age of 40-42! His statement was, "What is Suhasini going to do after retiring so early?" My mother used to write similar things in her letters. "Pratibha, both of your sons have yet to finish their education, and they still have a long way to go. You can't afford to stop working!" Little did I know or had thought that my income as a doctor was of so much importance! In 2010, some circumstances arose. I had finally realized that 80% of my total income in 30 years was because of the profession I was in. Before or even after I had finally come to know the reality, my behavior towards anyone, including Shrikant, had never changed.

I had never felt superior because of my earning capacity. In fact, in all our friends' circle, I was described as being "Down to earth!". I would never introduce myself as "Dr." so and so! When asked, my answer always remained the same. Does anyone introduce himself or herself as "Engineer" or "Architect", so and so?

In this new neighbourhood, the distance between the two houses was far enough not to get the chance to say even Hi to each other. Besides, I actually had no time to explore the possibility of knowing them. The only neighbour I knew for many more years was Dr. Gajapathy. At one time, he was my student at Metropolitan Hospital. Elsa knew many of them. In later years, I allowed her to clean the houses for a couple of neighbours. Her work for our house had decreased significantly. Her requests asking for more salary besides providing additional cash for social security money and free lodging and boarding, including all the weekends, were not justified. For many years during her employment, she stayed with us, including on the weekends. She had breakfast, lunch, and dinner with us. But it was assumed that she wouldn't work on those days! In fact, after I terminated her services in January of 1993, 7 times out of 10 years, she had come from Uruguay and had enjoyed anywhere up to more than 2 months as a guest!

Anyway, truthfully, it didn't matter at all, but in the whole town of Old Tappan less than a 2 square mile radius, I didn't know a single Indian family. This remained the fact way till the year 2014-2015!

In my department, a few changes were taking place. Dr. Bizzari had decided to retire. A new chairman, Dr. Lees, was appointed. His presence for the next five years, I had considered as President Reagan Era, at least for myself!

Chapter 22: Next Few Years of My Career

Dr. Lees, a lawyer as well as an Anesthesiologist, appointed as a Chairman was the best thing that happened to me personally. He was the one who decided that after a few years, there was no such thing as junior or senior and made it possible for me to be the full partner of the PC. He was from Maryland. Almost every weekend, from Thursday evening till Monday morning, he would be absent from the office. For many years, it was my responsibility to prepare the "On Call" schedule for the following month.

The cardiac anesthesia schedule was prepared by someone else. I think this is the right time to mention that I never got to practice cardiac anesthesia, including for Pediatric cases. I must say that this could be one of the hundreds of reasons why I call myself lucky in spite of…..! Initially, there were only 2, or maybe at the most 3 staff members assigned for every evening. But by the time I finally left, there were 6 attendings assigned for every evening hour. No.1 on the call schedule was responsible for that whole evening, night, till 7 am the next day. Eventually, even the second on-call also ended up staying in the hospital till the next morning.

Till Dr. Lees came, somehow, I never got the support to fight against the discriminatory behavior of Dr. San Fillipo and some other general surgeons. At least as one of the involuntary key clinical persons in charge of the whole department, I felt the severity of this to a greater extent. Siding with surgeons at the expense of one's own colleagues was disheartening for me. Thank God, I rarely had to face some of those nasty, full of themselves, cardiac surgeons. Dr. Lees was the one who fully supported and held our whole department to the highest. He had clearly mentioned that the first on-call on any given night would be The Captain of the Ship!

Dr. Kubal, one of my senior colleagues, was in charge of "running the floor." It meant he will assign the cases for the next day, will carry the code 99 and special 838 beepers for emergencies, and was responsible for almost each and every affair of the smooth sailing of the daily Operating Room (OR) activities. It was Dr. Lees who had suggested that there has to be at least one more person who should assume the responsibility in Dr. Kubal's absence. No one had consulted me, but my name was suggested. There were at least 3 or 4 staff members senior to me. Maybe it can be considered an honour by someone, but for me, especially in the later years of my career, it proved to be one major factor detrimental to my physical health.

Somehow Dr. Kubal could manage not to assign himself to any operating room while in charge unless one or more staff members called in sick. He could manage handing his "838" and code 99 beepers to me while he was attending any meetings in the early hours or otherwise and also while in charge of one cardiac anesthesia room. But interestingly, I never got the luxury of attending any such meetings. Once a month, there was a common meeting for those involved with Pediatric patients. Even when I was chosen as Chief of Pediatric Anesthesia, I rarely got to attend those meetings. I rarely got to just carry those beepers and not be assigned to any ORs. Frequently

I would manage two ORs, at least one of them invariably a Pediatric case, while carrying those two beepers.

On the paper, the person in charge always remained Dr. Kubal. But behind the scene, many more days of the month, it was this Dr. Joshi who had ended up managing the floor. And maybe being a lady or a mother, or for whatever reason, I had always assumed additional responsibility to make sure each and every resident and attending gets coffee or lunch breaks! This remained the situation almost till the end of my career. We had around 26 to 28 areas to cover on a daily basis where the presence of an Anesthesiologist was necessary!

Along with these responsibilities, quite frequently, I was requested by some parents or my acquaintances at the hospital to provide anesthesia for their loved ones. These were mostly all Pediatric patients, including those as old as one month old, and also one of the most complex surgical procedures. Seemed like others had more confidence in me than me in myself! If there was difficulty in securing the intravenous in a tiny baby, various departments, including radiology and endoscopies would call me for assistance. And to keep up with the confidence of others in me was really a very difficult task.

I don't recall the exact year, but soon a major Pediatric Urology surgical group joined the WCMC. This was the ONLY group that had shown total respect and confidence in me as the Chief of Pediatric Anesthesia. It really was a wonderful group to work with. Once there was a real major case that Dr. Levitt had scheduled. I was requested by him to be on that case. That is the ONLY case I remember that lasted more than 24 hours. I honored him and the parents. Only after transferring the patient to the ICU at the completion of the procedure by 8:30 am the next morning, I had gone home.

This was the same group that Dr. Reda had worked for. I don't really mind telling regarding his remarks about me at this stage of my life. Right after I retired, beginning in 2003, I joined the Woman's Club of Old Tappan. Dr. Reda and his wife Clare were friends with Clovia, one of my friends from the club. "When Dr. Joshi was behind the Ether Screen taking care of the patient, we didn't have to worry about the anesthesia part!" I am the only non-American woman in the club ever, now for last almost 20 years. We all have mutual respect and friendship with each other. Dr. Franco, another one from the group, often used to tell the anesthesiologist in the operating room after I retired. "I wish Dr. Joshi was here to secure the intravenous for the tiniest of the tiny baby on the operating room table!"

My very good nurse friend Tomy was the one who used to keep me well informed for many years till she actually retired a few years ago. Dr. Kogan was another great surgeon from the group. He had commissioned me to make a stained glass frame for his wedding! Also, after I made the stained glass Golf player for his father as a gift from his son, I got a wonderful Thankyou note from Florida! They all truly missed me after I retired at the end of 2002.

Which at least I was not aware of, but Dr. Lees, our chairman, had committed to only five years of service in that position and had then decided to go back to Maryland. So basically, what I called the "Regan Era!" for me, had soon come to an end.

For some reason, in October 2006, I had written a letter to Dr. Lees just as a friend. I thanked him, maybe for the first time after almost 16 years! I had included a couple of pictures of my stained glass creations. I have his letter in my Time Capsule Box from October 22, 2006. It was from Bethesda, MD. He had shared the account of his hobbies as a retired person.

Again there was an unknown future for the department. The commissioner of the hospital, Mr. Stolsenberg, appointed a committee of surgeons to interview and select the future Anesthesia Chairman. Not sure how long it took, but in the meantime, Dr. Shibutani, the director of the department, served as the acting chairman. I think by 1990 or so, Dr. Elizabeth Frost was appointed as the first woman Chairperson for our department. My duties remained the same. In fact, in some ways, the working conditions really got worse at least for me. I have tried my best to shorten the writing about my career, but it seems extremely difficult for several reasons. There is too much to be told!

Anand, our older son as a student, I think, was a high achiever. He was intent on keeping his record of A+ grades, a compulsion created by himself. He was complaining of stomach pain for a while. I was so involved in my hospital duties that I had really neglected his genuine complaints. One weekend while Shrikant and myself were getting ready to attend one Indian program, he actually collapsed in the bathroom. He had bled internally from his stomach and needed to be admitted to the ER of our hospital. He needed two units of blood. Luckily no surgical intervention was necessary. Since I was working in the same hospital, I didn't take time off. In between managing the OR, I used to visit him in the pediatric ICU. Everything was fine after that, but I could never get rid of the distressed look on his face when the NG tube was inserted through his nose, reaching his stomach. This was to rule out additional bleeding.

Sending him to India at the age of 3 & 1/2 and neglecting his complaints about stomach aches in his high school year, these two acts of mine were totally unacceptable. I could never forgive myself for that. In the later year 2010, I did ask for his forgiveness in one of my long letters to both of my sons.

Working conditions were getting more and more hectic. There always remained a shortage of staff members. My suggestion to the whole group was to try to retain the best students after they finished the training. Obviously, the idea was never entertained. In general, the consensus was everyone desired fewer working hours. At the same time, they were unwilling to share a portion of the pie with additional staff. One of my students, Dr. Mandy, was one of the best. In fact, I had actually offered ten thousand dollars of my salary in his name so that he could be retained after he had returned back from his fellowship.

While Dr. Shibutani was in charge, there was the decision to establish a pediatric surgery program at St. Agnes hospital in White Plains. Again I was not given the choice. I was chosen as one of four, including Drs. Kubal, Her, and Raghavan. The deal was that everyday we go there, an additional $100 were added to our income receivable. We had a daily signing-in and out roaster for years. On paper, we were four of us, but in reality, it was only Dr. Raghavan and myself who were going directly to that hospital in the morning. After finishing the schedule of the pediatric cases there, we came back to WCMC in the evening. Our on-call duties continued in the parent hospital, and guess what! Again it was Dr. San Fillipo whom I was facing now in the 4th hospital affiliated with NYMC! Everything seemed never-ending.

When Dr. Frost was appointed as the chairman, she was awarded the exclusive contract to be in charge of the Anesthesia Department at St. Agnes Hospital in addition to her duties at WCMC. It was the period around 1991-92. I don't remember the details, but almost immediately, she fired Dr. Greenspan, who had become the Chief of that department. He was the same person who had supported me and wanted to guide me in order to pass Part 2 of the Board Certification around 1979-80.

Few staff members were shifted to that hospital, creating a shortage at WCMC. When the question of payment arose again, I was left by myself to fight for my rights and justice. Both Dr. Kubal and Dr. Her showed sacrifice by giving back the money to VAA. Obviously, their total contribution was nothing compared to how much was due to both Dr. Raghavan and me. Our P.C. had given a loan to form the new corporation at St. Agnes. My justifiable argument was either VAA writes the check payable to me OR deducts the amount of Loan attributed to them.

Dr. Frost tried to take objection. I had clearly told her that she had nothing to do with this because the deal was made prior to her arrival!

I made sure that I received the payment. Dr. Raghavan accepted the offer to be the Chief at St. Agnes Hospital instead.

Shrikant and myself in 2006.

Chapter 23: It Seemed Never Ending

Staffing shortage, my frequency of running the floor, the unnecessary responsibilities as the so called Chief of Pediatric Anesthesia, making the on call schedule for the next month, everything was getting more and more unbearable for me as if this was not enough! There was one Anesthesia Conference in Delhi, India. A few staff members including Dr. Frost had decided to attend. I think it was on Palace On Wheels. I had absolutely no desire to attend but didn't realize what deal I was going to end up getting into. Since Dr. Kubal was also one of those attending the meeting, I knew my fate for those 2 weeks or so. But totally unaware of it, I received an official letter from the Dean of NYMC. I was to accept the order, whether I wanted it or not, I was named Temporary Chairman of the Department of Anesthesia during Dr. Frost's absence! I was enraged. There were at least 2 may be 3 senior staff members above me! I was ready to retire right that day! Unfortunately this was not going to be the right time for me to retire!

In the year 1992, Anand graduated from NVOT as a valedictorian. He was accepted at Harvard during the early admission process. Atul had 6 more years to go. I was getting more and more frustrated with everything including the working conditions, Shrikant's absence from the house in the evenings continued almost on a daily basis. I started noticing Elsa's behavior. She obviously had started taking advantage of her employer's considerate nature. Here I was leaving the house at 6:30 in the morning, and she was comfortably sipping her MATE!

Especially at night, the ongoing noise of TV from her bedroom had started annoying me more and more in our master bedroom! I do understand that this frustration getting worse by the year, month or day was the combination of so many factors but the outcome was affecting my physical health. Every January, Elsa used to go to Uruguay for anywhere from 4 to 6 weeks. Included in this was 2 weeks of paid leave. In the beginning, it was not easy to hire a substitute to babysit during that period but we did manage it somehow.

Anyway, finally I did mention to Elsa that once she goes to her country from January of 1993, I will not need her services anymore. This had followed by Atul frequently crying in the bathroom. Elsa was there to console him. I had no time for doing any such thing. In 2010, when I was forced to write page after page to both of my sons and my husband on a long paper pad, I did mention being aware of what may be hurting Atul's feelings. But also that I did not repent my decision about letting Elsa go. As I have mentioned before, we remained in touch for many more years. We visited her in Uruguay in 2001 during our trip to Argentina.

During the year 1991, in December, I had visited India by myself for our 25th medical reunion. Because I was leaving the children in the care of Elsa and Shrikant, I had bought a gold chain and a bracelet each as a Christmas gift for both children as if I was fulfilling my duties as a mother towards them by buying those expensive gifts. What a foolish consolation or justification for myself! Anyway, I was not able to enjoy the reunion at all. I developed severe gastroenteritis while in India, and lost more than 15 pounds in 18 days. The severe epigastric pain that followed lasted for years. Each and every possible tests were done with ZERO diagnosis. The doctor declared it as one of the psychosomatic conditions. He prescribed Valium, a calming sedative. There was no way I was going to accept that. I suffered the pain for the whole year. I was getting a bit successful in avoiding those horrible pains by avoiding certain foods etc. Pepcid and other antacids were used regularly. I really didn't have much choices left.

Then at the end of 1992, I found one of the best remedies for this. Jane Bederka, a nurse from the Burn unit introduced me to the Art of Stained glass. Bernie Patashnik, the teacher, remained my Savior for many more years. Till the day before Thanksgiving of 2002, any free time I got even during that hectic career, at least till 11 pm, I would be cutting glass in a variety of colors, smoothening the edges with the use of the grinder, foiling, soldering! I used to modify or even create my own designs. Over 23 years, I had literally created thousands of small and some very big stained glass articles. It always had to be my own imagination, my choice of colors. The art was not for sale. It was not the choice of the consumer! For years, before coming home, I would visit the teacher's studio, use his tools paying only 3 dollars each time, buy the glass in every possible color and texture available in his studio and reach home after 9 pm. Once one OR nurse asked me if I could make a night light for her in stained glass. She was willing to pay me. The thought of selling any of my creations had never entered my mind. But definitely accepted the challenge because I always wanted to learn to make them anyway! I designed one, created and sold it for $10! Since then I have done countless of them. "Dr.

Joshi, when we turn on the NL at night, we remember you!" What other thing was I looking for? This Stained Glass Creativity remained the most significant, integral part of my married life for a total of 23 years. I had plenty of opportunities to give back to the society in my neighborhood, and it was through my ART. After my retirement, the public school, Old Tappan Library and the local church got a bit of money through the sale of my stained glass. The most important part of missing my house on Christmas Eve, 2015 was, leaving my stained glass supplies and unfinished articles at home in that big room in the basement. I had left part of my body, my arms there. This blow was severe enough without any doubt.

By 1997-98, this extreme physical and mental stress had already started taking a toll on my physical health. I developed severe high blood pressure. The medical term for this is "Malignant Hypertension." The only symptom was I would faint. The OR staff would wheel me to the cardiologist's office next door, and I would get treated and then once again go back to work! The BP would shoot to over 250/120, and the heart would race to over 120 beats per minute. I was the perfect candidate for developing a stroke. There was no family history of high BP.

Among other things, while running the floor, I used to get to observe some of the worst surgical practices by so-called famous surgeons for their specialties. Countless times I used to rush to Elicia's office telling her that it was essential to report that particular surgeon! They used to boast about themselves being just one step below the God and in reality were literally playing with the patient's life. I could never understand why anyone could not accept his or her own limitations?

I will never forget one incident. A very prominent young businessman, the father of a young child came for a surgical procedure for his son. The child needed some emergency procedure in order to start kidney dialysis. I believed it was my duty to alert the father to bring his child to a well-known pediatric hospital for a kidney transplant. Elicia was the chief nurse in charge of the OR. We are still in touch. So many wonderful nurses in the OR and the recovery room have visited our house during my career and after retirement. Those are the memories! I think the album containing these pictures may be in my possession. Till the Covid disaster, we used to meet once a month for lunch in a restaurant. They would pick me up at the designated train stop in Westchester for the planned lunch.

By the end of 1998, the pelvic pain related to the fibroid uterus was getting unbearable. Dr. Kwon performed the total abdominal hysterectomy. Appendectomy was the Bonus procedure! At least I didn't have to worry about developing acute appendicitis or ovarian cancer in the future! I took advantage of 6 weeks off following the procedure.

Anand had already left the house for further studies. Atul was doing very well with his studies, a wonderful circle of friends, his love for music etc. Shrikant was just the way he had been. By now, I had begun to understand his motives regarding his wife. I was his chicken, laying golden eggs for him! This is the description about him by one of his best, much older friends who have known him since 1970!

By now I had started reacting to his belittling of me in front of each and everyone who was visiting us or we were visiting them. Either both of my sons didn't notice it growing up or simply did not care. But my best friend starting first grade, Alaka's both children very clearly had noticed their Shrikant uncle's behavior towards their mom's best friend and had mentioned it to me just less than a year ago! Obviously some of the relatives and friends who frequently visited us had started noticing that. Those who came across it during a later period for the first time must have created their opinion. This was 100% different than those who had known me from the time I came to this country. After hearing about the episode on December 24, 2015, one of our very good friends from 1975 said, "I was surprized how you could stay with that Demon for so many years?" My best friend Prema from medical school had this to say, "Pratibha, Shrikant has been behaving like this for 43 years! Why are you complaining now!?" For those who still kept thinking of me as being too naïve, I had no problem mentioning that I am not that naive girl anymore.

Personally, for me, I had a more positive opinion about Dr. Frost, our chairman. She was a single mother of 4 young sons. It is not a joke to juggle all the responsibilities 24/7. She was the person who had appreciated my art and was encouraging me during my frustrations while running the floor. It will get better, is what she would say! She is the one who had often said to me, "You have such wonderful hair, why you don't take care of it?" This was in spite of the fact that during one of the meetings I had said to her, "I am having a hard time trusting anyone including you!" She was shocked but we remained in contact after I retired. She was a very charismatic woman. She had invited some of us for boxing day a few times. For her parents' wedding Anniversary, we were invited to the top restaurant in the United Nations building! One of her sons married Scottish style! We had attended his wedding.

Unfortunately just like many others, Dr. Frost had started taking undue advantage of her position. I had obviously noticed it just like others. For years, I had considered my work place as my almost No.1 Family. I even remember having a conversation with two of my colleagues. We were sitting near OR # 9, and I had said that we needed to have a meeting as a family before her behavior goes out of hand. We may need to get the commissioner of the hospital, Mr. Stolsenberg involved. The minute I mentioned this, one of the senior colleagues said, "Dr. Joshi, if you do such a thing, there will be severe consequences for you!" I was actually shut up! In fact there were so many situations when many of these so-called colleagues would kind of instigate and would make me speak up. I used to think of this behavior of them as being cowardly! I never had any problem presenting the Truth, nothing but the Truth! I have met plenty of these characters over the last almost 50 years in this country. And truthfully my observation is about those including the white, the black, the brown and all the 50 shades in between. I call it the behavior of 99.99% of the people on the bell-shaped curve! Needless to say, exactly one year later, the same colleagues got the support of Dr. Reed, the Big Guy, the Chief of Cardiac Surgery. I really felt sorry for

Dr. Frost. She was literally forced to leave the office on the spot by the Security Guards from the hospital. This was one of the major pieces of evidence for me. I had always wanted sincerely to prevent unwanted and predictable outcomes.

Exactly the Same Situation arose in 2010. I had called for a family meeting for the first time sometime in September 2010. Anand, our older son had noticed me snapping at Shrikant, his father. For him it was unusual. This was during one of his family visits to Old Tappan after June of that year. During our meeting of four, I suggested that their father needed mental help. He may end up leading lonely life just like his mother. But the first typed sentence from the note in Anand's hand was, "We, meaning his brother and himself are not going to be the mediators!" Unfortunately, the meaning of the word "Mediator" was unknown to me at that time!

A few years later Dr. frost had displayed the Art Exhibit for one of her friend's photographs from all over the world. Shrikant and I were the only couple from our department invited to her house. Later on, I wrote a thank you note to her. I used the greeting card decorated by myself. Because she had always appreciated my creativity, on any appropriate occasion she used to receive stained glass gifts from me.

Obviously, once again it was time to search for a new Chairman. It was not my responsibility! For me there was absolutely no other choice but to wait and watch!

Before Dr. Frost left, in one of the PC meetings I had submitted my Cardiologist's note. I was swallowing 3 different medications for high blood pressure every morning. But there was no sign of it getting under control. The side effects of those medications were obvious. I used to get extremely tired and was afraid of possibly causing harm to the patient if I ended up working late hours. I told them that I would be willing to have less remuneration. The treasurer asked me how much less will I agree to. The answer was $30,000.00 less from my salary coming from me voluntarily was accepted right away. The totally shocking decision came right in the same meeting! The decision was made that the senior staff members working over ?15 ,20? years won't need to take overnight calls. There were few eligible including me. One of the worst discriminative facts was their remuneration was never decreased. I was the ONLY Indian woman and one of the most senior staff members remained the exception.

Two things happened at the end. I continued to take the 3rd,4th, 5th or 6th call. Many times used to go home as let as 11 pm and had to show up the next day again at 7 am! The worst, the most humiliating fact was about my own colleagues. Many of them had started looking at me as being Below Their Dignity or whatever! While walking from the parking lot, they actually used to avoid walking with me! Here I can now say the words from Mrs. Obama, the lower they go, you raise yourself higher or something like that!

Again, after Dr. Frost's predicted untimely departure, I think we were at the mercy of Dr. Shibutani as being the acting chairman!

__Literally, thousands of big and small creations kept me busy 24/7. I just couldn't live without my CREATIVITY!__

Art was my way of giving back to the society after retirement from 2003 to December 24,2015

One of my most favorite stained glass article has around 150 pieces.

Chapter 24: Can It Be the Final Chapter of My Career?

I had finally gotten rid of my unwanted title of being the chief of Pediatric Anesthesia. Sometime during when Dr. Frost was the chairman, there was the addition of a so-called perfect, very well-trained Pediatric Anesthesiologist, Dr. Petrankar! Dr. San Fillipo was thrilled. "Finally we got the most needed, most deserving Chief!" These were his words! I was more than happy to hand over my Title as the Chief. It didn't last long because of multiple anesthesia-related complications as well as complaints. Then another one replaced him. It was Ms. Fitzjames or someone. The best choice finally was Dr. Mandy, the student once under my guidance. He had come back to work with us with a proper fellowship in Pediatric Anesthesia from Philadelphia Children's Hospital. He truly was finally The Right Choice!

Over the years, may be it was just my observation, but some of the residents admitted to the anesthesia program didn't seem to be that sincere or dedicated. They were supposed to be relieved for lectures at 4 pm. From 2:30-3 pm itself they were getting itchy to be relieved and were checking the time on their watches! When more monitors came into use, the concept of "Clinical Anesthesia" diminished. If the baby's lips seemed blue, it means she is not getting enough oxygen. This is the way I was trained. These new residents needed the pulse oximeter to start alarming to alert them. Sadly I was getting more and more disappointed not being able to teach clinical anesthesia. In general I was ready to retire as early as yesterday!

I was still the full partner of VAA with a voluntary decrease of $30,000.00 only in salary. One more decision made by my partner colleagues was that for whatever reason they excluded me from some decision-making committee. It was perfectly alright for me. I could save many hours for my most cherished hobby of Stained Glass. I was so involved and wanted to create so much, I even started bringing the glass pieces to work for foiling!

My art and myself were inseparable! It was this intense desire to create as much as I could that was the driving force. I needed to make use of each and every minute of my awake time to create something. It definitely did not include my present medical career. I had done my duty! I guess my behavior was so genuine no one from the OR staff took any objection.

Running the floor still continued for a while. There was another surgeon named Dr. Savino, one more with mutual hatred! He was the typical male chauvinist. Not sure if he became the chairman of the Surgery department or was in an Acting position when I was there. He will literally shamefully bark when invariably he himself was the major culprit. No one dared confront him. My frequent argument with him while running the floor was, "Dr. Savino, let's be truthful. You can't perform a single surgical procedure including the one that can be done under local anesthesia. You always request the anesthesiologist to stand by! Therefore let us be friends!" He would raise his voice if anyone came late to start the surgical procedure. But in reality he himself was almost significantly late to start his 8 O'clock case. About him and Dr. San Fillipo I used to come to a conclusion during their bad behavior hours. They must have woken up on the wrong side of the bed! My main objection always was it is necessary to try curbing this type of behavior of anyone as early as possible after it is noted. Otherwise they will continue their behavior thinking that they will get away with it!

Finally we got a new chairman, another female one named Dr. McGoldrick. I had heard about her appointment but for whatever reason, she took her own sweet time to finally join. I had some hopeful explanations of my own regarding her delay in joining. But alas! For me she turned out to be the most useless chairman with no guts, I think she was with no backbone. Or who knows maybe she had her own alter motives planned! Our department had lost the respect from others. I believe it was self-induced. I clearly remember one such morning. It was Dr. Savino's standing order that the patients should be moved to the appropriate ORs after they arrived in the Holding Area and were properly checked by the nurses. Some times it used to be as late as an hour for the surgeon to arrive in the OR. And very often it was him himself!

We couldn't start the anesthesia induction till the surgeon was actually present in the OR. And anesthesia billing would start from the moment the patient went into the OR! Sometimes it was total chaos. That day he started screaming at me in front of the patients and everyone. Instead of confronting him, I directly approached Dr. McGoldrick's office with a pair of scrubs. Her office door was wide open. Her back was to the door and she was engaged in doing something on the computer. "Dr. McGoldrick, please wear these scrubs and come right away to the OR Holding area and face the Mad Man, Dr. Savino!"

By the middle of July 2002, I had finally started noticing the light at the other end of the tunnel! Shrikant had turned 55! In order to get the full benefits of my IRA money for the whole year, it was essential that I complete the year 2002 and then resign. So on August 30, 2002, I wrote the retirement letter effective January 2, 2003. I approached the Chairman's office with the letter, CC to Dr. Sanchala and other members of the PC. Along with that was the request to allow me to use my unused vacation as the terminal vacation.

I had another specific letter already prepared for the Chairman about 3 months before. I had actually numbered the reasons for my disappointments regarding her delay in accepting the offer from the hospital. I was sincerely hoping that she would start improving the situation in our department. It turned out to be just another broken dream of mine. Fortunately, I had NOTHING to do with this new chairman.

On April 10.2002, I went to see Dr. McGoldrick with a copy of the typed letter. I still have the actual letter. It was like this—— "Dear Dr. McGoldrck,

May I present to you the following Facts, Clarifications and Analyses:

Today, VAA faces the following challenges and difficulties-1) a very low (almost zero) rate of new hiring of Attending Physicians, 2) a High attrition rate, 3) Understaffing as a chronic problem, 4) a Lack of strong unified support to offer attractive packages to candidates, 5) Low morale and difficult working conditions within VAA and lack of respect from surgeons and other operating room staff, 6) Total disparities in working conditions, relative compensations, work load distribution towards the attendings working on general side VS cardiac side."

I had ended the typed letter by saying:

"I had sensed the hopelessness of the situation due to staff shortage and overall deteriorating conditions at least 2 years ago. Finally after 15 years, I relinquished the responsibility of running the floor. Now, 3-4 different staff members are trying to share the same responsibilities instead of me. I do appreciate the difficulties they are facing." As I had said before, on paper it was Dr. Kubal as may be acting Director, but in reality, I was the one who was left to face the daily difficulties of running the floor. My suggestions to improve the efficiency in the operating rooms and to support and backup our own staff was never given serious consideration.

On April 16, 2002, I gave a handwritten copy to Dr. Moscatello, an ENT surgeon in charge of the OR committee. Of course, I was never allowed to attend those meetings but I am pretty sure that Dr. Kubal attended them regularly. I used to get so frustrated listening to the same nonsense complaints again and again regarding the delays in the operating rooms for years with almost zero improvements. In fact, one nurse named Su McCluskey, had written a thesis on causative factors regarding OR DELAYS and had earned the Masters Degree! My handwritten letter which I still have a copy of in my possession has provided a detailed categorical listing of multiple causative factors contributing to OR inefficiencies. The listing includes those by the anaesthesiologists, surgeons, OR nursing staff, recovery room, and by some other factors.

While on this chapter, I decided to refer to some of these notes in my file. This helped me to reconfirm my sincerity regarding taking each and every task very seriously! After all, these tasks were not my choice but I had accepted them open-heartedly. This is exactly what one of my students had concluded from my palm reading, "Dr. Joshi, you think too much about other people!" This being my inborn quality, however I try, it is just impossible to get rid of it!

So, the day before Thanksgiving of 2002 was going to be my last day of work. In fact, this year in 2022, I finished 20 years of being off from the OR list. I refused to be assigned on any on-call duty on the Wednesday 27th of 2002, day before the Thanksgiving Day.

As many times as possible, I used to be assigned to OR # 104 on Wednesdays. On that day, the children used to undergo anesthesia of a short duration related to their chemotherapy for cancer. It was our mutual love. The children used to call me The Sticker Lady! I used to allow them to choose any sticker of their choice prior to going in the OR. One parent was allowed to be with them till their precious one fell a sleep. They used to have the IV port already established for long-term usage. The drug invariably used was called Propofol. Being white in color, I used to call it The Milk Of Choice! It might be hard to believe for anyone who have not seen these children who receive this medicine almost once every week. I had noticed that they actually used to look forward to feeling kind of "High!" under it's influence! It is very hard for me to forget that expression! Those who are familiar with the story of Michael Jackson, he wanted that milk of choice, that propofol! And quite possibly he died of an overdose from that anesthetic agent.

Anyway, on my last day of work on Wednesday of November 2002, before Thanksgiving, I had requested Dr. Bairamian to assign me for those procedures in OR#104. Luckily he honored my request. Just due to this fact, my stress level had gone down 50%!

Right from the day I had given the letter of resignation, I was really a total wreck! Truly I really didn't want anything to go wrong especially in those final days of my career. It would have haunted me for the rest of my life and I would not have been able to enjoy my retirement. And there was a valid reason for feeling so. One of my senior attending, Dr. Linda Hernandez was about to retire a very long time ago. Just before that there was one tragic mishap in Metropolitan Hospital. A patient had died during a routine appendectomy. I have never forgotten about it and just couldn't imagine having to face it myself! Truthfully, I did not mind at all if one had labeled me as being not sure about myself, it was most important that the patient ALWAYS remained safe.

During Dr. Frost's days at one time a select team of 3 from the staff was assigned to rate the rest of the staff members. It consisted of

Drs. Frost, Gordon and Kubal. Will prefer not to disclose the shameful act of one of the three. But it was way beyond disheartening that my overall score was even lower than one of the most incapable attendings from the staff! The surgeons really used to request not to assign her on their cases. Except that she was of white skin color! She was assigned to only those cases that were easy to manage. When I questioned if that was a mistake to one of those 3, the answer was "NO!" This same person had trusted me to run the floor for so many years. He had trusted me enough to help establish an Anesthesia department for Pediatric patients at St. Agnes Hospital in White Plains, NY. In a way it had made me realize how low the mentality of one my own could reach! I had looked at him as my senior brother! Anyway, I did go to Dr. Frost, she had at least admitted the mistake and therefore did correct it.

In truth, I had no need to change my behavior anyway just for the sake of those improved scores. I was always going to be the way I was. For me, patient safety always remained #1. I was the one assigned to those most complex Pediatric cases. I was forced to be the Chief of Pediatric Anesthesia. I had ZERO interest in publishing the papers and engaging in phony research. Dr. Shibutani was never my Ideal! I always wanted to remain down to earth in my behavior towards the humans whose life was supposed to be in my hands while under anesthesia.

On my last day, an attempt was made to ask me to start another case after I was finally done with my cases assigned to Room #104.

This time I refused. I was finally done with my medical career. No one was going to force me back to enter that field!

During my last few days or so, there were more than a few send-off parties from various departments including Lithotripsy, Burn Unit, and both Recovery Rooms. Pediatric ICU. On my last day, I made sure that I stopped at each and every department to bid the final goodbye. And the best part of all was Tomy, one of my favorite nurse friends, who surprized me by following me at each and every place I visited, ready with her disposable camera 📷,

"Smile please, great! Ready, 1,2,3 & click! The final click was the stop at Elicia's office. Here the "Good Bye, Dr. Joshi!" cake was waiting to be cut after blowing out the candles. These OR nurses were the most important part of my journey for almost 25 years of my career at WCMC. My wish was never disclosed while blowing the candle at that time! This was all followed by Hugs and Kisses and a spontaneous flow of warm and salty tears!

Farewell Cake From the OR Nurses on November 20, 2002

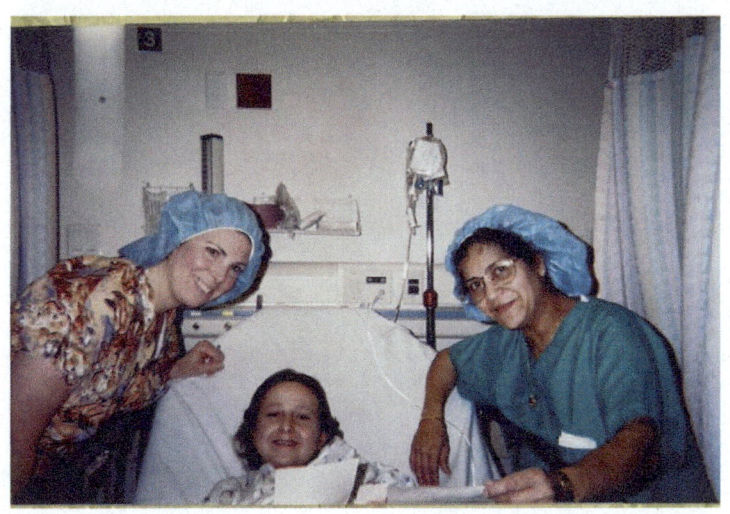

Allowing the patient to select one sticker of her choice before going for the procedure in the OR.

Picture with the Lithotripsy group prior to my retirement

Chapter 25: Farewell Cake Wish

I was not expecting any Good Byes or anything from my own Anesthesia Department. A Send-Off party plan was in the wings sometime in the spring of 2003. I had every intention of looking forward to it. It was going to provide an opportunity for me to give a speech! I already had some vague ideas about its content! One thing I have not mentioned so far. I don't have much stage fear! I love to compose my speeches! By no means they ever have been perfect, great, or anything. Nevertheless, over the years, I realized that I didn't want to miss a single chance to express my feelings!

For our older son's wedding, I was not able to invite all of my big circle of friends from the hospital. So we arranged a 3 in 1 celebration in an Indian restaurant closer to the hospital. Anand had finished his MD, MBA from Columbia University, and was engaged to his beautiful sweetheart, while Atul was going to spend one semester in Argentina. It was part of the 3-year program at Huntsman, a division of Wharton at U.Penn, where only 40 students all over the world are accepted each year. One of the first sentences of my speech was, "The only credit I can take for our children's achievements is that I had provided part of my Genes towards their creation!" While finishing the speech, the end was like this! "Last but not the least, I would like to thank my husband, an engineer by degree, and then an all-honorary lawyer, real estate manager, military commander, and doctor, I know everything kind of person! "etc, etc.

When the OR nurses requested me to make a wish, I had two wishes in mind. One was that I hoped that my colleagues were wrong! They were all baiting that Dr. Joshi was going to come back to work. My wish was, I hope they are 100% WRONG! The other wish was for my mother, whom I had looked at as my God, continued being protective of me the way she had been so far, including throughout my career.

I have absolutely no doubt in my mind that my mother was watching over me throughout my career. I believe there always was that divine connection between her and her Pratibha, a wireless, long-distance connection over the seven seas! I can't avoid mentioning at least a few of those reasons why?

I was requested to provide anesthesia by one Indian doctor for his son's Right eye procedure. As usual, I was running the floor, managing 2 ORs, including this one. The patient was under anesthesia. The OR table was already turned 90 degrees to the anesthesia machine. The surgical area was prepped and draped. Something didn't look right to me! By mistake, the left eye of the patient was kept uncovered for surgery. This intuition of mine, through my inner connection with my mother, my savior, had done the trick! Everyone, especially Dr. Mooney, thanked me profusely!

We had a nurse anesthetist program. The student had a 10cc syringe labeled "Brevitol" ready for a patient who was supposed to have some urology procedure. This patient had H/O asthma. So Sodium Pentothal was avoided. I casually asked the student how she prepared that particular syringe of Brevitol? Her answer was that she didn't have to prepare it. It was already in the bottle. Brevitol was never supposed to be already prepared. It is supposed to be in powder form to be dissolved in saline just before using. It is an anesthetic agent which facilitates Anesthesia induction. I asked her to show me the bottle, and it said Bretylium! This is liquid medication for Cardiac Arrhythmia. I believe if my intuition through someone watching over me was not there, we would definitely have to answer the consequences of using that wrong drug! Possibly the patient would have suffered cardiac arrest!

One Saturday, I was on call. Dr. Stern, a neurosurgeon, had scheduled the procedure called "revision of Ventriculoperitoneal shunt. The patient's CSF, the liquid that keeps the brain lubricated, was not draining properly. For a change, the patient was an adult, the daughter of one prominent professor. The general surgeon, Dr. Menon, was also present in the OR. Dr. Valente was my resident. Dr. Menon had a prior consultation with the doctor on call from infectious diseases.

He was suggested to give a certain dose of K penicillin, the antibiotic (K stands for potassium chloride as the vehicle to dissolve the antibiotic powder.) Dr. Menon had prepared the syringe himself and handed the big 30cc syringe to my resident. I had stepped out of the OR to get a temperature monitor. Upon return, I saw my resident engaged in injecting something from that syringe intravenously. Looking at the size of that syringe, I thought maybe he was injecting a diuretic called Mannitol to decrease the intracranial pressure. By the time I came near the patient who was under anesthesia and, for whatever reason tried to check the pulse at her left wrist, I could not feel her pulse! It was immediately followed by cardiac arrest!!!

Without any moment's delay, along with the surgeon, we started the CPR, which included hyperventilation with 100% oxygen and injections of calcium chloride, sodium bicarbonate, and adrenaline. I don't remember how long it took to resuscitate the patient, but it felt like forever. I was trying to analyze the causative factor in my mind while simultaneously engaged in resuscitation. The 5 empty bottles of K Penicillin on top of the anesthesia machine immediately helped me to diagnose the situation. The antibiotic dose was for a total of 24 hours!

Dr. Menon, the general surgeon who was supposed to complete the abdominal part of the procedure, had handed the whole 24-hour total dose to my resident. The patient had cardiac arrest due to "Hyperkalemia". This means from a very high dose of potassium chloride. Its total content of 5 bottles of the antibiotic had potassium chloride as the diluting vehicle had caused that arrest. I can never forget this incident. Luckily the treatment for that is exactly the same that we had followed without knowing the cause. These types of cardiac arrests are actually very difficult to be successful. But the patient had made it. The surgery was completed. The patient continued to have some cardiac arrhythmia in RR for a while but then recovered completely without any residual effects.

Again, I was running the floor and supervising at least one OR. Jim Masiello, a certified nurse anesthetist, had just transferred a patient from OR #5 to RR. The patient had undergone lumbar laminectomy. I was sitting on a two-step stool in a passage leading to the RR to conserve some energy. "Dr. Joshi, for some reason, the patient is dropping her BP. We have been pumping fluids and have given some small increases of epinephrine, but she is not responding?" I walked to the RR, and the patient looked as white as a white-washed wall. I vaguely remembered that she had a history of recent trauma.

My immediate thought was that maybe she had some Spleen injury at the time of the accident and had a blood clot over it. Maybe the clot got dislodged in the prone position, and therefore, she may be having massive bleeding in the abdomen. I paged, "Dr. Savino, stat to the RR!" He came right away. The patient was wheeled back to the OR. Yes, she had bled internally! My gut diagnosis was partly correct! She had suffered from one of the rare complications from the laminectomy procedure.

The internal iliac artery was nicked accidentally during laminectomy when Dr. Mangiardi was pulling on the fascia surrounding the lamina of the spine. Everything went okay! Dr. Mangiardi had long left to perform surgery in another hospital. Later on, the chairman of Neurosurgery, Dr. Kasoff, had proudly told hundreds of times to so many doctors, "it was Dr. Joshi who saved my patient! "Being the chairman, he was responsible for the entire Department of Neurosurgery. The OR nurse Salvatore, on the case, and Jim, my certified nurse anesthetist, still have so much respect for me, along with the others. Even now, Sal reminds me whenever we meet or connect on Facebook! He had come to my house twice, along with other nurses. We used to talk about this incident again and again, along with all the other memories.

One of the surgical procedures performed on babies born with a condition called "Craniostenosis" still continues to give me nightmares. These babies are healthy and require a corrective procedure to open up the sutures in the cranium that are prematurely closed at birth itself. They usually present around the age of about 5 months. This is a very uncommon congenital anomaly, and intervention is the must for brain development. The size of the baby, the relative amount of blood loss, very difficult access to reach the baby's airway, the need to replace the blood loss cc by cc, on top of it being requested to provide anesthesia, the sense of that beautiful baby's life being in my hand, please anyone can tell me if I was right in requesting additional help at the beginning of the procedure? Was it not a precautionary measure? Did I ever think about the score I was given by someone while evaluating my performance?

During the last one year or so of my career, many times, we ended up doing cases by ourselves with no residents. To me it was totally fine. This way, I was responsible for myself. Once, I was assigned to a case of Laparoscopic Splenectomy. The patient was suffering from hypersplenism means an enlarged spleen. It needed to be removed. Dr. Rajdev and Dr. Bhuta were the surgeons. Anticipating major blood loss, I secured 3-4 intravenous accesses with large bore catheters. Sure enough, during laparoscopy, the spleen started bleeding. There was a rush, a kind of chaos, shouting and screaming from the surgeons towards the nurses in the OR! Obviously, the abdominal incision was performed, and the bleeding was controlled. Then Dr. Rajdev asked me how come I was so calm? My answer was obvious. I had anticipated and therefore had secured the 3-4 ports for blood and fluid transfusion!

I will never boast, even at present while telling these stories. Whoever wanted to say whatever about me, I really didn't care. But the number of mishaps over the period of 30 years of practice were really negligible. Also, they were not due to any wrongdoing or negligence. There was one case of Lisa Weiss. She had undergone a gastric bypass for obesity and had come back to OR as an emergency for post-surgical complications. Dr. Lingam was my resident. In spite of taking all the precautions, the patient aspirated during induction of anesthesia and eventually died a few days later. There was a case filed against us and also the surgeon involved. No negligence related to anesthesia management was found.

There was another case of a prisoner, Robert Hines. The eye surgery could have been easily done under just local anesthesia, but because he was Schizophrenic, again it was Dr. Mooney, who decided to perform it under general anesthesia. I still remember my resident's name, Dr. Park. I know that it is not an excuse, but yes, again I was running the floor and managing 2 rooms. This patient never woke up from anesthesia! This particular case haunted me for so long! Every day for a very long time, I used to visit him in prison to notice if there was any improvement. I don't remember the end result, but this, luckily, the ONLY ONE experience had been more than enough for me to be humble and remained grounded with zero sense of Ego in my attitude in general.

I really feel so content about what I have or have not achieved during my total of about 30 years of service as Anesthesiologist. I have absolutely no regrets. Many of our so-called family friends, who literally had nothing better to do, used to criticize me for ending my career so early. Even now, some of them continue asking me as to how come I retired so early? "How come?" I have long stopped wasting my time and energy explaining it to them. Shrikant's comment, whenever he got the chance after I retired, was, she retired because she couldn't take the heat! I had nothing to say in response because the truth was told repeatedly by me to all the grown-ups. I really never wanted to work hard.

But even then, I did my duty towards my career as well as towards my family, to the best of my ability. Only I knew that I was the perfect candidate to suffer a stroke due to uncontrollable severe hypertension. I also knew by that time that Shrikant's interest in me was always connected with the potential money I would be bringing home. This was exactly the reason why he wanted to marry only a doctor! I must say, so that I succeeded for his own wishes to come true, he had made all the efforts! Another common statement of his was that I would drive him crazy! He was so wrong! First, he was never home to start with, and most importantly, I had actually planned my retirement. I knew exactly what I wanted to do! Therefore for me, none of those things really mattered anyway. Money was and still remains secondary to me.

In the future, maybe I was defeated in keeping my beautiful family of 10 intact. But was I supposed to know what I was going to be gifted with? I always remained the way I was but was paying attention and keeping in mind all my life experiences!

Later on, I got enough opportunities in various ways to continue giving back to society. It continues to be so through my art and now more so through my smile and just being there for those elders who feel so lonely. I truly feel blessed, without any doubt.

If I have not mentioned before, Shrikant, my husband, had actually retired a few months before I did! He never thought that it needed to be disclosed! Interestingly because I didn't know about his plans, I had already started daydreaming prematurely. I had thought, just like any other Indian housewife, that finally, I will be there when he came home from the office. We could have tea together, go for a walk either outside or in the mall, or have dinner together, which I believe we never had in those almost 30 years! Among other things, he was extremely secretive.

When he signed the retirement package, he had requested to get the maximum of his pension money while he was alive. Apparently, he didn't see the need to have anything for his widowed wife. Looking back may, be that is the best thing that happened. We really didn't have to tap into our savings and especially my IRA accounts.

Shrikant was so fixed on his ideas! But to me, those ideas of his were coming from his totally messed up mind! He obviously had married me for the money. At the same time, he saw no reason why the wife should have the right to her money! The explanation he had shamefully offered to a banker in Capital One was that the wife gets to own the money anyway, including hers, after her husband exits this planet! Basically, he was dreaming of controlling me as well as my money. I was not supposed to be asking any questions.

Thus, from the Wednesday before Thanksgiving Day of November 2002 onwards, I got lucky not to be at the mercy of the Alarm Clock anymore, definitely not for stress-inducing reasons!

Slowly but surely, the content of my dreams changed again. First, there were some dreams about appearing for exams unprepared. Then they were replaced by nightmares of not being able to secure the baby's airway and the baby turning blue. I assure the reader these unwanted dreams were very rare. It didn't take that long for them to be totally replaced by just the most wanted ones.

Later, for years I would go to bed totally satisfied with the day's unique creations and the most wanted events planned either by myself or in the company of my friends. I would wake up the next morning only with the wanted thoughts about new creative ideas for that day. The undisclosed truth was, this was already the beginning of life for me as a divorcee or a widow. Shrikant's presence in my life had taken the form of a ghost way before the divorce was announced! His hen had stopped laying the golden eggs, and her use for him was almost over except for occasional lust-related desires, which over time, had ceased solely due to his inability to perform! And again, for that too, this Suhasini of the weaker sex was to be blamed!

Chapter 26: Retirement with Specific Goal In Mind

When I finally submitted my retirement letter, the request was to grant me all of my terminal vacations. So after the weekend of Thanksgiving, for the next two weeks, I would go to the local public library with all the letters from my mother saved from at least for the last 10 years and a writing pad. Hema Palewal, a very good writer friend of mine, had encouraged me because she thought my mother's life was worth more than the 24-carat gold. My father wanted me to be a doctor but it was my mother's pension as a Freedom Fighter made his dream come true. I had to thank her while she was alive and it was going to be my Tribute in the form of a book. The original was in Marathi, in my mother tongue which meant "My Mother, My God." This OCD of mine had a specific reason.

Once while doing a case in the Burn Unit with one of my favorite nurse anesthetists, Debbie Hayes, I made a statement. Why do people wait to say good things about a person after he or she leaves this world? Why can't they express positive views while the person is alive and well? Later this beautiful Debbie died in a car accident while returning home from attending the funeral services for one of her relatives. The book was printed in Bombay, India. Only when it was time to pick up the copies did I let my brother and a brother-in-law know about it. The signs of fulfillment by her Pratibha were all over my mother's face. "You have paid off all your debts towards your parents in this life!" I can't think of any treasure worth more than this statement! Everyone who came to visit her or me got one copy from my mother. She was in charge of the explanation!

This was the first time there was no hanging sword on my mind. I had retired. Was I trying to entertain the idea of spending more time in India? The unanimous answer from whatever number of minds I am capable of conversing with was Big NO! It was impossible for me to get acclimatized to the dust, noise, mosquitoes and unexplained loss of electricity much more frequently than on rare occasions. So after 18 days or so I flew back to my comfort zone at 58 Greenwoods! I had a few copies of the book for my Marathi-speaking friends here. In fact, the last but one copy is still with Ken! I doubt it will be returned to me!

Along with the two previous life time decisions, one not letting my hair grow again and the other not making the Indian bread called Chapati anymore, I decided on one more. I stopped writing a diary. Got up at such and such time, created this and that, met with this or that friend, this truly was my routine. There was very little interaction between Shrikant and myself to start with and it became more apparent. This for me was perfectly alright especially because his eating habits were so simple that I could concentrate more on my creativity! The 24 hours of the day were not enough for me!

I started reading the community news papers for the first time. I used to get second-hand information from my friends when they called me to congratulate me. This is when both our sons frequently made the news for athletic and scholastic achievements. These simple newspapers almost became my Bible! I saw the ad for the Woman's club of Old Tappan. I joined the club at the end of the first meeting as a guest! Next year I will be completing 20 years of WC Membership. Each and everyone welcomed me without any reservations, possibly because of our both sons. They were the friends of the children of many of these women. These women have been supportive of me through and through. Needless to say, I am the only non-American in the club.

Some girls from the WC formed a book club. I used to love reading but with all the other creativities, it had become kind of difficult. The first book we read was "Middlesex." I still hear the positive remarks about me being able to contribute my medical knowledge towards the book discussion. I used to go back to the front page and write down the important sentences from every single book. The girls used to love my sincerity.

Our library was in the middle of a renovation. They were looking for funds. I approached Susan Meeske, the supervisor. They sold some of my stained glass creations and got 50% of the sales. An article of mine promoted by Susan in the local community newspaper helped me to create more friendships. One of them is Fred, his ex-wive Camila and their only daughter. For a big Gala fundraiser, I allowed them to auction some of my bigger creations. It may be a drop in the ocean but they all appreciated it. Betty Lee became a very good old friend of mine. She used to create and sell stained glass art at Trinity Church before Christmas. I soon joined her. There was a big table reserved for us in the corner every year for one Friday, Saturday and

Sunday. Frank Lee, her husband was the cashier. I would give away 50% from the sale to Trinity Church. Harrington Park School, every year had the Holiday boutique sale. The children used to wait for my stained glass articles. Using their pocket money, they used to buy gifts before the holidays. The enthusiastic class mothers would come to my house, get the boxes with multiple of those articles with labeled prices and would return the empty boxes. The school would then send me the check for 50% of the total.

Going to garage sales was one of my most favorite tasks! Eventually I started bumping into the same group of enthusiasts. The articles bought were may be someone's Thrash, but for me they became Treasures! So the Logo for my Unique Tag Sale became "SOMETHING FROM NOTHING!" It may sound a bit of an exaggeration, but truly even now, I myself get surprised as to which part of my brain may be responsible for this CREATIVE MIND? With almost 24 hours at my hand, hundreds or may be even thousands of big and small articles were created in those 13 years of my retired life before I was forced to get out of my comfort zone on Christmas Eve 2015. Obviously these articles needed to be taken away so that there will be room for new creations. Beginning of every April, I started displaying the street signs "Unique Tag Sale" with appropriate arrows for the directions. Through this yearly event, some more friendships got created. One of them is Dale Klineman. She came with her dog "Dudley,"

This was the first time that any 4 legged animal had visited us! But then for many years at least once or may be much more, it became a frequent occurrence. Dudley will only look for water. Both of us, Dale and myself would play ping pong in the basement while chatting nonstop! For whatever reason, she felt me to be so close in the friendship and offered me her free miles. I used some of those miles to fly and visit my best friend's mother and sister in laws in Cleveland area. Their frequent complaint used to be that I visited Prema so often and never stayed with them. I know for sure they both loved me. Tai told me during that visit, "Pratibha, I don't want to die because I don't know what surprise lays in that other mysterious world!" Lilatai's spiritual teachings always remained in my mind to rely upon. I am glad that I visited them. Soon both of them left this world one by one.

As planned before, my retirement party did take place in the Spring of 2003. Doctors from my department, some surgeons, OR and RR room nurses, residents, secretaries some cleaning guys, they all were there. Anand, Jyoti, his wife, Atul and of course, Shrikant, my significant other were there to witness the occasion. Atul was in tears because of being emotional. I had requested him to go over my speech. Tomy, one of my best nurse friends, couldn't make it because Craig, her husband needed to go to the ER. He was suffering from bladder cancer. She made sure that the Memory Book she had created for me for all the photos she took on my last day of work was handed to me. This of course is one of my inseparable treasures!

My speech consisted of some heartfelt truths. I summarized as to how and why I became a doctor and chose Pediatric Anesthesia as my career. I admitted that I had no specific goal in my mind but never repented about being a doctor. I had realized that everyone was made happy by this Dr. Joshi. Most were happy for me because that is what I wanted, I wanted to retire. Also some were happy to see me leave! And I was happy because I didn't have to be at the mercy of that Alarm Clock! I did admit that I missed being with children, missed the fluctuating levels of stress-related increase in epinephrine levels in my circulation! This phenomenon was related to taking care of a variety of difficult pediatric procedures and also facing some challenging personalities. Most importantly I missed the daily gossips, exchanging jokes, discussing sports, listening to and if possible offering a helping hand to so many of those nurses, cleaning people, and secretaries.

I missed showing off my art work. WCMC was not just the work place for me. For all practical purposes, NYMC was my #1 home for a total of almost 30 years! Interactions with everyone, their support and understanding helped me to apply my principles towards the profession and fight for the betterment of my work place. Some of my colleagues used to call me a Lucky Lady! Of course, I was and still am and why not? I had each and every one of them as my friends. I thanked them for their confidence in me while anesthetizing patients including their loved ones. I thanked all of them for their presence that day and well wishes. I remained eternally grateful to all of them.

Some designated doctors, nurses and residents etc. also spoke a little. Dr. Cerabona, a surgeon reminded everyone about the fact related to Dr. Joshi. During bad weather days, I used to drive to the hospital NPO, meaning I won't eat or drink any thing, just in case I would get in an accident. I wanted to make sure that I didn't aspirate the stomach contents during the Anesthesia Induction!

They had a beautiful gift of a necklace and matching earrings for me. This now is the memory gift for Lila, one of my granddaughters. The other two, Anisha and Kira, got one gold bracelet each as their "Aaji's" memory. Khelan, my grandson, has a beautiful pearl necklace to be given to his serious girlfriend in the far away future. It was given to me by my mother-in-law.

As predicted, I did receive a call from Ms. McGoldrick's, the chairman's office. Dr. Kubal called to ask if I would be willing to work at least part-time at St. Agnes hospital. I knew my answer but did visit the department to say "NO" in person.

Soon after I left, the VAA P.C. was dissolved. Some external private company including some anesthesiologists, took over. For over 25 years, I crossed that Tappan Zee Bridge almost daily. I had witnessed so many changes in its infrastructure before finally the decision was made to replace it. The engineer in charge of the design and construction of #13 support of the new bridge was a friend of mine. To anyone's surprise including me, I have never driven on the new bridge by myself! It may be driven by someone else a couple of times but now the crossing of the bridge is ONLY via Metro-North Rail!

Tribute to my mother in January of 2003 in Marathi. English version was done in 2006 after my mother had passed away.

Chapter 27: Retirement Years Continue With Some?

Except that I had stopped bringing the money, which I had long realized to be the most desirable expectation of Shrikant's from his wife, my daily routine had become the most desirable period of my life! Atul had finished his education. He had won the Fulbright Scholarship and had decided to go to Mexico for one year and was encouraging us to visit him there. Soon I started noticing the obvious resistance and unwillingness from Shrikant. Not having time, too busy with the rental properties were the most common excuses by Shrikant.

The same Shrikant, while both of us were working was also handling the 13 rentals, 2 Family houses mean 26 tenants at a time! He had bought them without my knowledge during the period of 1985- 1986. He was still able to come on each and every trip with 3 of us during my conference time. Every summer, we used to spend at least one week together traveling. I would try to select an Anesthesia conference at a place that we had not explored before. It was usually one of the most memorable time periods for me till I think before Anand went to college when we four visited Quebec. I still remember proudly watching all 3 of them enjoying water rafting. Again the pictures most likely have disappeared with those albums. The reason why Shrikant was not much interested in traveling anymore turned out to be very obvious! I used to get compensated by VAA for the expenses that occurred. Especially because I was very careful not to abuse this luxury, except for the plane travel if any, there was very little to no additional expenses towards the fun-filled vacation/ conference time.

We did go to Mexico in early 2003 and first-hand witnessed our baby!, our Atul turned into a wonderful young and independent, social, respectful young adult just like his older brother, Anand. Being raised by the Nanny from Uruguay, he was fluent in Spanish and appeared totally local for that region. I tried to encourage Shrikant to get more engaged in Toast Masters' club etc. He enjoyed poetry and creative writing. In our retirement, I do remember accompanying him to attend some programs, especially because he wanted to. I was interested in exploring anything that I was offered. I enjoyed each and every of those extra curricular experiences. But I guess he preferred the closeness with all the handymen or cheap laborers. May be he quite likely thought them to be more loyal, they would do whatever without asking any questions! With the luxury of creating a very big friend circle of various ethnic groups and all, I did start going on various short and long trips. In addition, Old Tappan had and still has wonderful programs for seniors.

As I said, I enjoyed each and every moment of my retired life. I arranged luncheon and dinner parties and spent time with friends, mostly Americans but some very close Indian friends also. So many seniors who visited me frequently would admit that they forgot their worries for at least a couple of hours! Among several additional friends I made, there was one who then moved to Florida for her job relocation. During one of the frequent visits to Rolling Pin, as usual being very crowded, she asked me if she could join me for lunch at the table for two.

Rolling Pin restaurant, one of the two my most favorite ones

Enjoying being in my favorite restaurant

Since that time, our friendship literally took off! We used to stop at each and every corner of the street, talking nonstop before finally bidding good byes. We still have been in touch. She is on the top of the list among those who have supported me tremendously in my darkest of the dark days.

I think, till 2008 it was not that obvious. Even if we had stopped sharing the bed right after I retired, we still managed to do lots of things together. Our social life was totally fine especially for the outsiders. But our private life was quite different within the 4 walls of our 6 bedroom home with 4 full bathrooms, one big play room / art display room and a big walk-in the basement. Not sure if I have mentioned before, but I had long started living the life of a divorcee or a widow. I was used to it and really didn't have much to complain about. He knew it very well as to how easy it was to please his wife named Suhasini! For me it was more than enough if he just printed those coupons from Michaels and A.C. Moore craft stores.

Now and then, I will ask for cash, and he would gladly give it. I rarely used any credit cards at that time. Somehow I never liked the idea of borrowing! There was an entrance from the basement to come up near the kitchen and the basement had an exit to the car garage. Several times he used to startle me by suddenly entering in from the basement without any prior communication and at any odd time of the day or night. In the beginning I really used to get scared but then I got used to it just like many other things. I had accepted his presence in the house as a Ghost a very long time ago. The purpose of making these statements is in no way in advance of my justification for future events. They are just statements related to the FACTS.

Being a math student, I had every intention of learning about our finances, the additions and subtractions! Several times I had requested him to take me to our Tax Preparer, Mr. Solanki. The more I showed interest in learning, the more he started distancing from me. For absolutely no reason, he would keep his office door locked. Finally, I had kind of forced him to give me the key. It will be very hard for anyone to believe me but what I am telling is the TRUTH. I had made several attempts to enter that office but soon after I entered and saw the condition inside, I used to run for the bathroom! Without failure, I used to get diarrhea! Hundreds of unopened envelopes from the P.O. Box used to be on the floor in plastic bags. It was truly overwhelming. And I must admit that I was not persistent. Again not as an excuse but the fact is, all these especially money matters, were totally secondary or tertiary for me. The most important thing for me was the constant Dream of the Wonderful Intact Family that was still growing till it became the Family of Ten.

I was just totally content with life in general. I was able to CREATE, had wonderful FRIENDS, and a wonderful growing FAMILY! Equally important was the fact that Shrikant was not a demanding person at all! The second most desired expectation for him from me was to leave him alone! He was happy (presumably) with the food I prepared. There was no smoking, no drinking. He was there to drive whenever I used to plan any lunches or dinners with our family friends. My whole outlook towards the world was from mostly within the walls of 58 Greenwoods and may be the 4 square miles area surrounding it. I was totally content in my very own small world except when I used to travel long distances including foreign countries by myself in the company of my friends. This is because he was always too busy. Shrikant had no problem dropping me at the airport etc. And maybe conveniently for me, indirectly I had allowed him to do whatever he most desired, to be left alone!

On March 29, 2008, Atul got married to his beautiful sweetheart Rina. It was a destination wedding. One year prior to that, the moment he had announced his engagement, I had told him that I wanted to give a speech at the wedding reception! Can you believe I knew exactly what I wanted to say one year in advance? There was obvious resistance when it actually was to happen, but for me, there was nothing doing! I must obey my OCD! My friends used to tell me that Anand looked like Pete Sampras. Atul, without glasses looked like Roger Federer! They both happened to be my most favorite Tennis Players! "Atul, among other things, most importantly I am proud of you for the choice you have made as your Lover, your Partner and your Companion for Life!" I meant each and every word of it from the bottom of my heart.

I still claim that I entered my marriage with a totally clean slate. The speech at Atul's wedding was the aftermath of my own thoughts, all created through those 36 years of marriage with Shrikant at that time. While cutting the glass for stained glass articles, listening to the beautiful classical music from Yani, Richard Clayderman, Vivaldi, Beethoven, and Mozart, meditating through the creativity, I was able to simultaneously converse with someone hidden deep somewhere inside one of those multiple minds of mine! These racing thoughts always have been the most welcomed thoughts. Why would I consult someone to make them go away!! Am I that crazy?

Before 2008, may be because the market was favorable to the sellers (an afterthought), Shrikant did sell 7 out of the 13 rental properties. We still had 6 to go. Then I think the market crashed. I hadn't the slightest clue. Nothing had changed in our life that I could pinpoint. This is in spite of the fact that among several reasonably notable incidents, there were at least the 3 significant ones.

I think this was also sometime in 2003 right after we both had retired. We have a very good friend couple, Anu and Anant Kelkar, who had moved to Douglas, Georgia. They were hoping that finally we could visit them. I just wanted both of us to honor their wishes and suggested to Shrikant that we could just visit them for the short duration of 4 days or so. For whatever reason, he refused right away! But then he did buy the ticket for me and I visited our friends in Georgia. I tried calling him late that night but got no answer. May be I thought I would try calling tomorrow! There was no answer again. It wasn't that we were used to having heartfelt conversations on the phone anyway!

Finally 2 days later I got a call from one of our friends, Mr. Naravane that Shrikant had fallen through the attic of our home and was first admitted to the ER at a local hospital, everything was okay except a hairline fracture to the right hip. Since no surgery was needed and there was no one at home to take care of him, he was admitted to

Care One Facility next to the hospital. Since nothing could have been done anyway and in one more day I was to return, I decided not to change the plane reservation and rush home.

Except that I had to figure out how to finally reach home from the airport! Airport to Port Authority, via Coach USA to Parkridge- by courtesy of a friend, finally I reached home. I was very curious to figure out first-hand how it had happened? Being a thin person, he had fallen through between the two uncovered portions of the Beams of the attic to 18 feet down on the stairs to the foyer! There was a huge hole in the floor of the attic. Later, for almost a month, visiting him daily in the morning and evening, with the food and the mail from P.O. Box in Norwood, it seemed like I got some purpose in leading my retired life. He would make me cry every time, out of absolutely no fault of mine! It felt like life in Hell once more after the Honeymoon days. I never came to know what was he exactly doing in the attic at 11 p.m.?

Atul was almost at the end of his year in Mexico and had come to NY to look for an apartment in Manhattan. He was soon supposed to start working at Citigroup. With mutual agreement, totally unexpected for both of us, we cleaned, threw hundreds of recorded cassette tapes, emptied the ceiling-high shelves, 3 out of 6 maybe, and moved them down with the help of someone. This is how I got 2 shelves to organize my Art Display Room! The empty cassette boxes came in handy to sort out my stained glass pieces color-wise, in the basement!

Shrikant was discharged home after a month or so. It was actually him who was reasoning with the authorities at the facility to delay his own discharge. I was actually praying that his wishes came true. During his absence, I was able to think and sort out about our forward life together! On a daily basis, in the afternoon, I will go in the attic & clean. Literally hundreds of things were thrown away or given for recycling with the help of Jimmie, Olivia's friend. Trust me, I was not angry at all but perplexed without any doubt. My mind was filled 100% with the sense of duty towards Shrikant, my husband. I was ready and obviously did bring upstairs his breakfast, lunch, and dinner daily in a nice personally decorated tray! Friends and relatives came to visit and were entertained happily and dutifully by me. Actually lot more can be written further but will go to the next incident.

There was a hornet or yellow jacket infiltration, and the nest was way up near the roof at the back of the house. The presence of these insects coming inside the house is one of THE THINGS that will make me lose sleep as well as peace of my mind at any given time. I suggested calling the proper exterminator and getting the job done. Absolutely to be ignored! He took it upon himself to do the job. He studied, bought the spray etc., and mounted the ladder way high on the deck. I warned him again and again that he may get Atropine poisoning from inhaling the contents of the spray. I provided a mask, surgical gown, gloves etc. From inside the glass door, I was watching his activity. The very bright flood light was almost blinding. He walked up the ladder, sprayed something, got down, and entered the kitchen through the sliding glass door. The next thing I noticed was that he was totally incoherent!

Shrikant had total amnesia!!! I immediately thought it was insect spray poisoning, hoping the situation will improve after a clean shower, dinner and rest. No he was totally confused. I called Anand. He gave some instructions. I took the insurance information and drove Shrikant to the hospital. Jyoti and Anand drove directly to Nyack Hospital ER. It was one of those worst stormy nights. Shrikant was extremely annoyed because of the constant beeping of the EKG monitor. I was helpless as well as speechless! In the morning, he was back to normal. Not sure if MRI was done in the morning but he refused to stay and we came home AMA, by signing the refusal of treatment form. It was labeled as acute cerebral ischemia (?) followed by temporary amnesia.

Later on, once his car was almost totally damaged beyond repair. Shrikant had escaped one or two more near-death experiences. But still he was under the control of his destiny. He still was the commander in chief for the two of us! There was no third one at least as a witness for me. He was the sole P.O. Box keys holder! As soon as he was discharged from the Nursing Home, the P.O. Box keys went back in his possession, never to be seen again???

In between some of these significant events, till June 1st 2010, life for the outside world was perfect! This was for all including our children, their wives and the little ones, in-laws, and all casual and best friends including Prema, and Alaka, it was the perfect, ideal Family Picture that anyone can be envious of. Then……

Is it that time for the spoiler alert? 😜 🫣

Nurses from operating and recovery rooms used to visit my home in Old Tappan while I was working and even after I retired at the end of 2002. Then before the Covid we started meeting in one of the restaurants in Westchester for lunch, once a month.

Chapter 28: Finally The Truth Was Revealed

For Atul and Rina's first wedding anniversary in 2009, they themselves had decided to have 3 families get together (hers, his parents, and their own new family of two) at one Mexican Resort. It was really wonderful. For their second one, again, we all had gone to Traverse City, Michigan. I think it was sometime in July 2010. Shrikant and I flew to Atul's in-laws in Indiana and drove together further. There were sometimes some friendly and minor disagreements but they were perfectly within the normal limits of any family get-together!

I was wondering why Shrikant was engaged in conversations with Atul's mother-in-law regarding exercises for shoulder pain. She herself was undergoing physiotherapy for that. Also, before we got together, something had happened in my personal life with Shrikant that was totally disturbing, and I had actually decided to talk to Atul if at all I got at least a few minutes just by ourselves. It never happened. And my disappointments with Shrikant from the prior month of June never reached his ears. The only thing I remember Atul saying about that trip was his Dad was literally talking nonsense during several conversations while on that trip and that he and his wife were actually avoiding his dad whenever possible.

In the month of May 2010, Shrikant made his own decision to do some renovations in our house at 58 Greenwoods. I think this was the first major renovation since we bought the house in 1984. As usual, he was very confident that there would be no resistance from his wife! Roman was a wonderful handyman that Shrikant had found. He must have helped him a lot with the maintenance of 6 of those remaining rentals that we co-owned. He liked Indian food. So occasionally, the three of us would enjoy homemade Indian food by me. The deck was getting totally redone. There was absolutely no problem for me.

Then came June 2, 2010, or was it June 1st itself? I don't remember. Something had happened to Shrikant, which I couldn't figure out for a really long time, actually for months that followed. The behavior of Shrikant during that period can only be described by saying he was behaving like a chicken without a head! He will ask Roman to do something and suddenly will change his mind and start some new project in the house or suddenly abandon everything and command Roman to take care of one of his rental properties. Without any doubt, he was very much restless and didn't seem to be focusing on anything. Most of the time, I would leave him alone, but definitely, for the first time started getting frustrated and annoyed.

After our trip to Michigan, once again, I started facing a very similar situation. Anisha and Kira, our granddaughters, were supposed to be spending a week with us. I was literally begging Shrikant not to stain all those 6 brand-new solid wooden doors he had gotten installed. The smell was unbearable and inhaling it was not good for the health, especially for the girls. He continued to refuse any simple requests. It was impossible to describe the real situation. Once Anand and his family were visiting. For the first time, Anand saw me snapping again and again against his father. He asked me about it and this was the first time I was in tears, I brought him down to the basement so that his wife, Jyoti, and the daughters don't get troubled.

This was the first time, at his age of 35, I spilled all my life story in relation to his dad from the Day 2 of our marriage. I was crying in front of my son for the first time. Never occurred that time that this crying would go on repeatedly hundreds of times in the near and far future! Definitely, Anand was visibly shocked, and in the evening, he shared this news with his younger brother Atul.

For the first time, I accepted the offer of Anand and Jyoti to enjoy a week in Manhattan in their apartment when their family went on summer vacation. In fact, it was Shrikant who drove me there. I told him repeatedly that now I had no choice but to let my children know everything, from how we met and all that! During this week, for the first time, I wrote page after page using that long, yellow pad. I was writing day and night. I literally had nothing better to do! I was oblivious to the outside world except for enjoying myself while eating at Baluchi, an Indian restaurant nearby, and some others.

They were 2 different topics. My whole life so far with Shrikant and the other regarding my whole family story starting from before the marriage. The writings were addressed one to Shrikant and the other to Atul and Anand together. First, I wrote ALL the positive points about every individual, including my parents but mostly my 5 siblings and their second halves, followed by not-so-positive points. The first sentence while describing myself was, "It is very difficult for me to forget and forgive!" Similarly, I wrote about Shrikant and his parents, first the positive points and then some totally unacceptable ones.

The week went too fast. Again Shrikant picked me up the following Friday, and I think we went directly to one of my colleague's retirement party in a big restaurant. I met several of my friends and colleagues from the hospital. We were supposed to attend two special programs, both Saturday and Sunday of the following weekend. It so happened there was no Lord Krishna birthday celebration or the wedding ceremony of my friend's daughter that we could attend. The moment we reached home, Shrikant told me for the first time, "I will need your help to drive me to the hospital on the following Monday. I am going to have surgery for the rotator cuff Tear of the right shoulder." He provided me no further explanation as to when and how all this had happened.

Equally shocking was the statement he made. The reason he expected me to drive was because it was my duty as a doctor to do so and not because I was his wife! I had to inform both Anand and Atul regarding this new development. Atul volunteered to come directly to the hospital at Peekskill. Dr. Shankar, my past student Uma's husband, was going to assist the main orthopedic surgeon. The Anesthesiologist was my past student, Dr. Petruso. As Shrikant was being wheeled into the OR, the only sentence he uttered, looking in Atul's direction, was, "The police did this to me!" We both were left to analyze the statement by ourselves!

Atul went to work after he met his dad in RR. I stayed overnight at my friend's place in Peekskill. The next day I drove my husband back home. Very little to almost no conversation took place during that hour-and-a-half ride home. This incident provided me with my second chance to prove that retirement had laid out the real purpose for me! The purpose was to take care of my husband. This time everything was really miserable for me. In order to change the dressing of the wound on his right shoulder, I literally had to rip off the old dressing and the adhesive tape. I just couldn't do that!!

I was not ready to inflict that pain on Shrikant, my husband, whom I truly wanted to care for. I really don't remember much in detail about his physical improvement, but he had completely distanced himself from me one more time. I still didn't know how, why, and when he had injured his shoulder. I had never stopped my duty of cooking and cleaning for him.

Shrikant arranged rides for his physiotherapy and other chores. Oscar, a young one of his loyal workers, was also driving him to various places, including the library and post office. Writing checks was no problem for Shrikant. Oscar was at his master's command. Roman, his handyman, started becoming irregular in his duties. The unpredictability in our house renovation project still continued, and finally, one day, I had to tell Roman not to come again.

The arguments between Shrikant and myself did not remain between just the two of us anymore. It had caused a tremendous negative effect on my physical health. For 8 years after retirement, my blood pressure was finally totally under control with a minimum dosage of medications. One morning, I had to place an emergency call to one of my friends, Usha Tate. We had to rush to my cardiologist across the Hudson River to WCMC. I had severe palpitations, and my blood pressure was way off control. Dr. Sorbera, my cardiologist, for the first time, knew what was happening in my private life. My work-related stress was known to him very well.

In late September 2010, I requested a family meeting. Both Atul and Anand came prepared. Anand had a typed paper in his possession. The first sentence of the draft said, "We are not going to be the mediators!" Truthfully I didn't even know the meaning of being a mediator! Along with every other thing, I told our children, now officially in front of my husband, that their father had never discussed or revealed the fact that he was buying or had bought those 13 rental properties. He had never mentioned why he had rented two offices. I had discussed this issue with one of my friends before. I really didn't know or remember how he had managed that. During the meeting, I just uttered the word "Power of Attorney", and Shrikant suddenly became angry and very restless, and nothing materialized. Finally, I just left the house. There was the Lord Ganesha festival being celebrated in one of our friend's homes. I preferred to be there instead.

One thing, when I delivered the copies of the pages I had written during my Manhattan stay to Atul and Anand, I had clearly mentioned that it was up to them if they wanted their wives to read and know about the family situation. Both Atul and Anand had decided to let them know. For me, it became much easier to communicate with all as a family during the immediate and the far future. After all, for me, I had accepted my daughter-in-laws as my family members the moment they had entered my children's life.

Occasionally I tried to communicate with Shrikant. I was willing to help him to organize his office come bedroom. He could just give the instructions while sitting in his comfortable chair. He had literally nothing to do with me except that he had no problem being served his breakfast, lunch, and dinner. He was actually miserable because of the situation he had gotten himself into. I still didn't know what had exactly precipitated all this unrest in my most desired retirement life.

During his absence from home, I started going through the mess in his office. Among everything else, 3 important things were discovered. One, he had reading material regarding Bipolar Disorder. The other most important revelation was the Record News Paper from June 1, 2010! There was front-page news. Shrikant Joshi from Old Tappan was arrested after a police encounter. They were called by the laundromat owner from Cliffside Park. We had one rental property in that town of NJ. One of Shrikant's shirts at the laundromat was damaged, and Shrikant wanted the owner to pay him 4 dollars for the shirt. Mr. Joshi, my husband, apparently couldn't be controlled, so the 911 call was placed by the owner.

It was the police who had twisted and torn the right shoulder ligaments of Shrikant! The blogs written in the newspaper by the readers were so disappointing. They had referred to my husband as some illegal Mexican immigrant, and they wanted us to leave the country right away! It was totally demoralizing and shocking beyond anyone can imagine. It so happened, it was Mr. Ronald Schwartz, our real estate lawyer, who had bailed him out. Atul and Anand were obviously very sympathetic towards their father.

No doubt, what happened to Shrikant was totally unacceptable, and I did feel for him. But it was equally true and important to note that it was his complex personality disorder that was the origin for this incident. Among many things, he believes himself to be the person in command. Extreme Ego, inferiority, superiority complex, and extreme secrecy are some of the components. For me, I had diagnosed his behavior as being genetic in origin from his mother. No one believed me. When I say no one, I mean only my two children. They both thought I was the one who needed to see a therapist. Trust me, just because they said, in 2010, I had seen two experts. One of them discussed anger management issues with me! The other, an Indian psychiatrist or Psychologist, engaged himself in discussing assets management with me. For that, I wrote a check for at least $250 or so for his services!

There was no one who believed in me that, finally the volcano had erupted. It was not dormant, the volcanic activity, the churning of the emotional torture-related activity, had been brewing in the closed compartment since day 2 of my marriage, since our first honeymoon night!

The 3rd most important thing was the actual PROOF. Shrikant did have in his possession my signature for him to be my Power of Attorney! Mr. Vijay Gokhale was the lawyer. I found out that Shrikant would ask Atul, our younger son, who was only 5 years old to change the date by using the typewriter. Atul was smart enough to know typing but was not old enough to ask any questions. Anand, our 11-

year-old son was not fit for this job! He was smart enough to ask questions!

Then some events took place that turned my life totally upside down. I had always tried to maintain my sanity by creating a variety of stained glass articles, doing baby quilts, and meeting friends. But one afternoon, it was my Angel, my mother instructed me to walk up the stairs leading to Shrikant's office/bedroom. The door was closed as usual. Was it locked? I don't know. Just the fact that he was at least talking to someone was comforting for me. Because once again, his mouth was sealed as far as his relationship with his wife of now 38 years was concerned. My Angel, my mother, forced me to listen to the conversation he had with the other party on the phone, unknown to me. There is no doubt that Shrikant's mentally sick, type 2 personality was engaged in that conversation. It was ALL related to my family and me. According to him, he was made aware of all the so-called facts way before he came to visit me as a prospective husband. The worst disheartening sentence he uttered was, "Suhasini's mother killed her husband (my father) by not providing him enough food!!!" I was already in night clothes. I burst into a loud cry. He didn't hear it, though. He had been hard of hearing for a long time due to the job he was in when I first came to the USA in 1973. It was progressive hearing loss. I ran into our master bathroom and continued crying, simultaneously thinking about what to do next.

During this new episode of his mental illness precipitation, he was actually spying on me. He could figure out whom I was calling on a daily basis. He could do this with just the click of the key on his computer. He knew Olivia, my dear friend in Old Tappan. I could not risk going there. He was extremely suspicious and was behaving almost like a wounded wild animal. This behavior was ONLY towards me! It was impossible for anyone to believe in me. I decided to drive to Blauvelt in night clothes, rang Dale's doorbell, and explained to her why I needed to use her phone. I called Atul in Manhattan. We decided to meet at Fort Lee the next day to buy a separate phone for me. I drove back safe and sound. Shrikant didn't come to know my whereabouts. He didn't notice my brief absence from the house that night.

I had jotted down all the horrible, totally untrue statements about my family that had come out of my husband's mouth. He claimed that he was aware of how bad my family was way before he had offered his hand in marriage. To this day, I don't know what made him oblige me almost 50 years ago? I soon got to know who the other person was at the other end of the telephone line. It was Mr. Naravane, one of our so-called best senior friends. I had looked upon him as being my honorary older brother. His wife, Ajita, was a good friend of my older sister in India. To me, she was supposed to be my older sister.

This was just one of those countless sleepless nights for me. The next day I had lunch with Carol, Peggy, Maurine, Cony, and a couple of others in one of my very special Thai food restaurant. I had to leave a bit early. I still remember them talking to each other just as I was leaving the restaurant. They all liked my transparent nature. They all appreciated the truthfulness of my conversations. I met Atul at Fort Lee. I used my credit card to buy a phone that Shrikant was not supposed to know about. This same phone had come in handy for Elsa to use when she visited us as a guest a few more times.

This turned out to be the first scene of Act II of my life story. TWO TRUTHS were finally revealed. One, for me, there was no doubt in my mind that Shrikant was suffering from some mental illness, just like his mother. The other fact was he had not married Pratibha, he had married the Doctor in her. He literally had no feelings for me.

Chapter 29: What Followed The Life Train Derailment

It turned out to be an almost impossible task to correct the derailment. I was totally left alone to figure out how to take each and every step. But the CONSTANT always was the DREAM OF INTACT FAMILY OF TEN. That was my driving force.

First thing, I demanded that I must have the second set of keys to the P.O. Box in Norwood. Since 1978, all our important mail had been going in here. Shrikant never had any intention of me having access to even my own hospital correspondence, including the salary checks or anything. While working or even after retirement, whatever important letters needed to be looked at were the only ones he handed to me. Of course, no excuse but I never even thought otherwise. I must have always trusted my husband.

When I visited the post office, I had to show proper identification before anyone was even willing to listen to me. There was one female worker there. She helped me. The card that was filled out by Shrikant when he opened the account for the P.O. Box didn't even have my name on it. Don't know when he changed the information, but only Atul's name was there, along with Shrikant Joshi's. Once I got the keys, every single day, I would drive to pick up the mail. Before the year's end, I was able to secure two files with the necessary financial information. One was meant for Shrikant and myself, and the other for both our children in case something happened to us.

During those multiple sleepless nights, I studied all the tax returns for the last 37 years since 1973 till 2010. It will be hard for anyone to believe, and I totally agree with it. I never even knew Shrikant's salary! When I calculated and added all the W2 forms, 80% of the total income was generated due to the profession I was in! I studied his real estate activities. A very large sum was wasted on just the mortgage interest.

Especially after we both retired in 2002, the tax bracket was so low that no additional deductions were going to be beneficial to bring the tax bracket lower. When our joint account had more than enough money that was getting only 0.1% in interest, any mortgage interest rate above 0.1% was a waste of money, in my opinion. By 2011, I forced him to pay off all the mortgages, including for our own house. I was more than 100% sure about what I was doing even though I had no support, even from our children. Shrikant's rental real estate was not generating any income at all, even if one considered the advantage of showing the losses. It was always negative. Who knew? Only if and when we sell those rentals, then maybe the negative income would have come in handy.

In our Woman's Club, once there was a lecture on estate management. I expressed my intention of parting our fortune with our grandchildren. Shrikant really was not happy at all with the idea of giving away the money. But after a brief meeting with Anand and Jyoti, both Shrikant and myself started handing over the maximum allowed amount of monetary gifts to our grandchildren. Initially, we had 3 grandchildren, and in 2014, Atul and Rina brought another bundle of joy into the world, a daughter named Lila! Khelan, their son, our grandson, was born in May of 2012.

During the months that followed Shrikant's shoulder surgery, I finally started searching for answers for his behavior. As a concerned wife, or maybe his friend or a doctor, I wanted to know about his childhood. What may have been the causative factors for his behavior? I did know about his mother's mental illness, which had been presumed to be just having postpartum depression. She was actually hospitalized in a psychiatric hospital for some time. In India, even now, there is very little awareness of Mental Illness.

Later on, her behavior was accepted and ignored by avoiding being with her. This is what her own husband, my father-in-law, had been doing. He rarely stayed in the house after retirement. Unfortunately, it was just like dealing with an alcoholic, the people close to him or her end up modifying their behavior. The alcoholic himself mostly remains an alcoholic unless he or she willingly seeks help. I asked Shrikant's friends from childhood in the USA. One of them was Amrit, he told me that Shrikant is extremely secretive, but he guaranteed that Shrikant is very careful with the money. Amrit had repeatedly called me naïve over the 37 years that I had known him. It was sometime during the period 2010 to 2015, that I finally had to tell him I was NOT that naive anymore.

The other person was Surekha Adya. Hers and Shrikant's parents were very close friends. She didn't know much about Shrikant's growing up but did provide me most appreciated conversations between her's and Shrikant's fathers. Also, she had heard a lot about Shrikant's mom from her own mother. I called Sanjay, Shrikant's younger brother in India. His answer was they just thought of Shrikant being schizophrenic and left it at that! In 2012 and 2014, Shrikant and I visited them in India for two of their daughters' weddings. Sanjay never bothered to find out if everything was okay with his brother. He was presumed to be okay! What I find is, there is zero to very little communication and conversations between couples or close relatives. Many of my American friends have asked me over the years if this is cultural, and my answer is always YES, without any doubt.

Mr. Naravane, the senior friend Shrikant was communicating with, had open heart surgery in late September. When he was well enough to have visitors, I decided to check on him as a junior but concerned doctor friend. The main reason was to confide in him regarding Shrikant's mental condition. The one statement, in conclusion, he made in front of his wife was one of the most humiliating, shocking analyses of the conversations he had with Shrikant behind closed doors.

A person at the age of 80 who just had heart surgery, said that the bottom line for the clashes between my husband and myself was there was not enough sex!!! NO! This pathetic advice was not what I was hoping for. I knew much better than that about my husband. Shrikant was in his Alternate Personality behavior. It was again precipitated due to the recent police encounter. I had personally witnessed his behavior of finger-pointing at the weaker sex several times by now.

From day two of our marriage, it always happened to be me! And I was unable to prove it. I tried seeking help from one more senior friend couple with whom we were very close (at least that is what I thought!). Mr. and Mrs. Jategaokar are professors. Again it was a total disappointment.

Frank Lee was the husband of Betty Lee, who was much older than me. I had mentioned his name in connection with the stained glass sale at the church. In later years, after I met her, Betty developed Alzheimer's. He had been taking care of her single-handedly for a long time. He was the one whom I used to visit every two weeks or so. I will take 3 McDonald's sandwiches, and he was to keep the tea ready, covered with handmade Tea Cosy for both of us! He was the first much senior American person to whom I was able to vent out my frustrations. He totally understood me.

By November 2010, there was a definite improvement in Shrikant's behavior. He had started driving. Jyoti, our older daughter-in-law's parents, had invited us for Thanksgiving. They live in Attleboro, Massachusetts. This time I did most of the driving. It was definitely the most needed change for both of us. I still remember, at night in the bedroom, Shrikant said sorry to me without me ever asking for it! He couldn't provide the reasoning, though! I kind of knew that he had the capacity to analyze his own behavior, he definitely was aware of his dual personality, but I had no proof to present. My children would not have understood me. Even now, it has proven to be beyond my reach to convince both of them that I truly cared for their father. I absolutely had no hidden agenda.

In 2010, before the June 1 incident had taken place, a friend of mine had suggested a tour to Egypt. By now, I hope I have made it clear I love to travel! I was hoping Shrikant would join, but the answer, as usual, was No! But he did help me with the technical part of booking the trip. The trip was booked in May of 2010 but was scheduled for December of that year. As soon as I returned home, the first thing I did, maybe for the first time, I hugged him and told the truth that I had really missed him!

The year 2010 came and was finally history. Nothing much changed in 2011, 2012, 2013, or even 2014 from what I had described before. During one trip to India with my colleague and his wife, I happened to get 100% validation for the life-churning statement of Shrikant behind closed doors in late 2010. The statement made at that time was that my mother killed my father by not giving him enough food. The origin of that statement was from one of my brothers-in-law! He, in turn, had apparently heard it from the doctor who had treated my father in his terminal illness. Dr. Mistry had no clue about my father's past history. The FACT, the TRUTH, was my father had developed something called Dumping Syndrome after his surgery for a perforated duodenal ulcer a long time ago. He was not able to absorb proteins.

Any plans initiated by Shrikant always ended up with me raising my hopes up to the ceiling about an intact family! He planned two trips during this period. One was to Spain, and the other was to Turkey on the way to India for his nieces weddings. I always overlooked or neglected his strange, somewhat unpleasant behavior towards me during those trips.

Anyway, my Destiny was getting ready for scene No.2 of Act II of my life drama. Shrikant's behavior was stuck in only one pattern. There was almost zero communication. We were just two strangers living under one roof. He would be out of the house totally unpredictably for reasons unknown to me except taking care of those 6 rental properties. He would drive me to each and every lunch or dinner appointment arranged by me. He was always there to greet when family, friends, or relatives visited us multiple times.

We had made a couple more Indian friends right in Old Tappan for the first time. For every Christmas dinner party of the Woman's Club, Shrikant was there sitting next to me but totally engaged in conversations with others. This was no problem for me. The outside world had no idea about my life with my partner within the walls of 58 Greenwoods Road. I distinctly remember the 2015 Christmas Dinner on December 14th, arranged by the WCOT I think I was not able to hide my frustrations, disappointments, and maybe even the resentments towards the person I was married to for almost 43 years!

There was almost NOTHING of closeness in reality in my personal life. We were NEVER the LOVERS, and we were NEVER the PARTNERS. We were NEVER the COMPANIONS. The speech I had given at Atul's wedding reception was ONLY the DREAM that I must have been carrying on and on and on. This is the DREAM I always continued to wish for all others from the time I had come to realize its existence in my own creative mind. The original LUST I had witnessed on my first Honeymoon Night and its aftermath had unknowingly transformed into something beautiful. It had created the most wanted, the most cherished for, THE DREAM OF INTACT FAMILY OF TEN!

In fact, I realized that I had started caring for my husband much earlier than I had thought. Who knows, maybe it was the instant end result of the SAPTAPADI, the seven Feras, at the wedding ceremony on December 30, 1972. The Holy Fire was one of the witnesses. Finally, I realized at the end of 2014, after 42 years of marriage, that this feeling of caring for my husband was TOTALLY one-sided. Shrikant had no such feelings at all. The complex personality disorder he was suffering from had made it impossible for him to have any EMPATHY for others.

October 2014 was the last time for which I had the photo in my possession of our intact FAMILY OF TEN. We had a joint birthday celebration for Anisha and Kira. By this year, with a somewhat reluctant but voluntary agreement, both the girls' private school fees in somewhat larger amounts replaced the maximum allowed yearly monetary gifts for them. More than the amount of money, I was more concerned about the age-related inequality between the 4 of my grandchildren regarding the monetary gift.

December 30, 2014, was one more year of our wedding anniversary, 42nd to be exact. Shrikant wanted to go to our favorite place, Cheese Cake Factory, for dinner. This time I refused to go. The whole afternoon I entertained myself by creating a beautiful garden space for reading in our huge bathroom area, which had a picture window and a skylight. There was plenty of sunshine for gloomy days! Finally, Shrikant cooperated in decluttering his space in our walking closet. This was then followed the next day by the dinner for two in the planned restaurant.

One of us ordered Bang Bang Chicken and Shrimp, and the other ordered Tomato and Basil Pasta. This is where we always were in 100% agreement! The doggy bags always came in handy for the next 2-3 lunches or dinners!

Chapter 30: Scene II Act 2

During my career, when Dr. Savino or Dr. San Fillipo used to be in foul moods, I would just say loudly to my nurse friends, Oh! Well, they must have gotten up from the wrong side of the bed! In my case, on January 1st, 2015, I had gotten up from the same left side of my king-size bed as usual like for at least the last 13 years. I used to be the only one on that bed anyway. This year numbered 2015, turned out to be something I have no words how to describe! I never regretted then and even now what my OCD, my gut feelings, or maybe my Angel, My God, my mother, or my own conscience had been guiding me throughout the year that followed.

By now, I had realized that for Shrikant, I didn't exist at all except accepting my daily chores of cooking, keeping 10 pealed almonds by the corner of the kitchen counter, soaked the previous night. The daily pattern for him had remained the same as described before. He would exit and enter the house the same way, via the staircase leading to the garage and out through the garage. I never knew for how long?

Some time by the end of January, Arun Adya visited us. He had lost his wife Surekha, who had become one of my very close friends for venting out my frustrations. I complained this time to Arun about Shrikant's behavior in front of Shrikant himself. I had finally started reacting to Shrikant's belittling of mine at each and every opportunity he had gotten for the last almost 43 years. On his own, Shrikant was planning nothing that would bring the two of us together at all. Maybe because I complained, he agreed to visit our friends in Florida. We visited 4 sets of friends during February of 2015, two in Jacksonville, one on the East Coast, and the other on the West Court of Florida. I made all the calls to make sure that our trip was convenient for all 4 of them. We really had a good time, and of course, we definitely needed a change again.

By now, both of us had retired for 13 years already. I used to go to garage sales frequently. During conversations with the owner, one most common understanding was that their parents had passed away, and now they were trying to get the things out of the house in order to get it ready for sale. Our own Woman's Club used to have a big-time garage sale for fundraising. Many of the people from ours and neighboring towns would bring items for that event. Similarly, my idea was, since I enjoyed working in the house and also there would be one less headache for the children to get rid of our belongings as we get older, I proposed one idea to Shrikant. My simple suggestion to him was I would give 2 years for both of us. I will clean all the stained glass-related clutter of mine by creating as many articles as I could. He could get rid of all 6 rental properties, and then we can downsize.

Truthfully, Shrikant had no intention of selling any properties because it had created the best activity for passing the time and showing others, including maybe his children, that their dad was working so hard and their mother was the one doing nothing! Shrikant had one role model growing up. He thought and often expressed in front of many friends and relatives that once he passed away, then it would be the headache for his children! He didn't realize, though, that if he passed away before I did, I would end up with the headache of selling those rentals bought so many years ago without my knowledge. Besides, I doubted very much if that would be one of the top priorities for the children for a very long time. Finally, Shrikant agreed to sell two of the six and started upgrading 2 properties. Of course, the choice was his. I absolutely had ZERO knowledge about any of those rentals. In fact, because I am so naive or simple or whatever and will be afraid of just the word "COURT," was the reason given to Amrit, at least, that Shrikant had decided to keep me in the dark regarding the purchase of those 13 properties.

This was as soon as we had come back from our trip to Florida in February. For months that followed, there was no sign of Shrikant displaying "For Sale" signs for any of those 2 rentals! I had no way of knowing besides asking him occasionally. Finally, he at least got in touch with a realtor named Pina, who, according to Shrikant, was one of the best ones. I decided to get in touch with Pina to learn about the process involved in the sale of those properties. The whole idea that I had started taking everything seriously, I think, was being perceived by Shrikant that he was losing control over me, my money, and everything in general. His cooperation started getting worse to almost impossible.

In July 2015, Anu and Anant Kelkar, our friends from Jacksonville, Florida, visited us. Without showing any interest in welcoming them, Shrikant left early morning to do whatever he needed for the sale of those 2 rentals. I revealed everything to our friends during their visit this time. I showed them Shrikant's office come bedroom. Anant was visibly shocked to see the condition of the room and felt sorry about the whole situation. Unfortunately, no one thought of communicating with Shrikant as a close friend. I was the only one who had a real interest in my husband, more as a close friend than being a spouse, I did care for him. But I also knew that I was getting more and more frustrated and was raising my voice. In order to avoid that, I would write a note to him or will record and sit next to him at night or whenever I got the rare chance for him to listen. Nothing worked out.

I think Shrikant's SUPEREGO was being crushed badly, and I was blamed for being the culprit again. Maybe the children thought the same for whatever reason. On July 1st or 2nd, I requested another family meeting. Because the children were going to come after work and after taking care of the responsibilities towards their own families, I had written down the points to avoid wasting their time at night before they could go back to Manhattan. I wanted my children just as the witnesses while I asked and cleared some points with Shrikant, my own husband! The minute I asked the first question, there was an interference, I believe, from one of my children! My chain of thoughts got derailed completely! Nothing came out except I think I had already lost the support of my children a very long time ago. I didn't realize it at that time.

I wanted to attend our 50th medical reunion in January 2016. I was hoping to have Shrikant with me to kind of SHOW OFF that he is that handsome man who helped me to create the most beautiful, one of a kind of FAMILY OF TEN. I was supposed to be that LUCKY LADY! Till the end of November 2015, he didn't give any definite answer. Because I really wanted to attend and meet many of my classmates, I talked to one of my friends Ramsing, and he bought the business class Tickets to India for the three of us, his wife himself, and for me. Akalpita, his wife was happy that I was going otherwise, she would have been bored, she had said. Following the unsuccessful meeting, Anand came up with another agenda for both of us to follow. He had sent an email to both of us to that effect. There were separate instructions for both of us. Unfortunately, Anand was so busy in his career and the household responsibilities he never got to check if anyone of us actually followed those instructions! I had actually tried each and everything I was told to. My husband Shrikant, their father, made it impossible for me to succeed.

I was instructed by my children for the second time after 2010 to contact a marriage counselor or a psychiatrist. With Shrikant's permission, we visited one. Without going into detail, it was a total failure. I contacted another one and requested if I could at least come once to see him by myself before I drag my husband. He agreed. "why are you here? There is nothing wrong with you!" This was his first reaction. He wanted the whole family to get involved. It NEVER materialized.

I actually had almost 24 hours to do whatever I had always aimed at. Seems like I was always a GOAL ORIENTED person. I came to know this reality in August of 2022! This was from one of my friend's own observations about me during the year 1966 college year!

I started removing the unwanted, unused collections from each and every closet and cabinet. The contents went for recycling and donations, very few went in the garbage. Hundreds of things in the garage were bought by Shrikant many years ago and were never used. Shops like Bradley's and Caldor were not even in existence for years! The things I was not sure of, I would keep them aside. I would wait for Shrikant to come home, then let him rest for a while & check his emails, and have dinner, and only then would I go to his room after knocking and asking if he needed those things or to find out what to do with them.

I love turning the pages of the Photo albums. Both Atul and Anand helped me to label them. I knew there were too many pictures. I sincerely started the task of going through them, getting rid of the unwanted or excessive. I organized them according to the categories. My artwork, my friends, our trips, Atul's and Anand's pictures right from their birth, mine and Shrikant's relatives, joint friends. The end result was well-organized albums. In fact, that was the best thing that happened, which I came to know a few years later after my homelessness.

For Shrikant, the ONLY THING he was constantly complaining against me to our children was that their mother was throwing away things. It was not worth justifying my actions to my children. They were too busy. One of the suggestions was why should I clean the clutter if their dad was not interested in it!! Maybe both the children and possibly their wives had already concluded their opinions about their mother-in-law. I had already distinctly noticed the change in their behavior towards me, but NEVER even in my dreams I thought anything otherwise about their intentions or the reasoning behind that.

Everything my both children had suggested from 2010 onwards till the end of 2015, I tried my best to follow. For me, the ONLY WAY to communicate with them was mainly through emails, handwritten notes, or discussions when we met on special occasions. I remember writing desperate handwritten notes for all four of them before Christmas. The children, their wives, and grandchildren had come to our Breakfast with Santa event sponsored by the Woman's Club of OT.

I bought the tickets myself for them. I believe I had actually pleaded with them in that note. Being the festive season and due to plenty of wonderful contacts of mine, Shrikant and myself had gone to 10-12 different functions during just the last 3 months of the year 2015. None of those 2 properties he put on the market were getting sold. He was asking for too much money according to Pina. Finally, he refused her services. There was total chaos in our interpersonal relationship.

The reader will come to know later on why I believed that my mother was always watching over me. Chase Bank was offering a very lucrative deal if we established any direct deposits in their bank. Later on, Shrikant himself helped me to open a couple more individual accounts because of the better deals offered. Shrikant had tried to convince me to sign the 6 or 10 blank checks which the banker gave us before leaving the bank. This time my answer was NO!

This is how my first individual bank account was opened. Because I was sincerely reading the Community News Paper, just by chance, I came across 2-3 good CD options. I requested Shrikant to make some money available from the parent joint account to open 2-3 CDs with much better interest than 0.1% or 0.01% interest. Luckily he agreed, and with his permission, I opened 2-3 CDs. Since he was not available to come with me, they got opened in only my name, and his name was added as the beneficiary. The reason for explaining in detail is purposeful. It is because of what was destined to happen before the 2015 year's end. My IRA accounts obviously were only in my name.

During the month of October, we celebrated our older granddaughters' birthdays together as usual. Because we had fulfilled our voluntary promise to pay their tuition for private education, I just bought two useful gifts, and that was supposed to be more than adequate. Shrikant, my extremely secretive husband, without letting me know, gave additional usual monetary gifts. The only reason I found out about it was because I saw a copy of the two checks being withdrawn next month. The worst thing was yet to happen.

In spite of the total detached relationship between the two of us, I tried my best to keep normalcy. On Christmas Day, Atul invited us to their apartment in Manhattan. Besides small gifts for everyone, I had wrapped a gift for Shrikant, his favorite pastries. This year in 2015, we were unable to celebrate Khelan's 3rd birthday in May. He had fractured his hip, and the birthday party needed to be canceled. Even now, I get the feeling of disheartening for his parents, Rina and Atul.

It was Christmas season. The decorations were on display.

The morning of Christmas Eve, 2015, I came down to the kitchen as usual, peeled & kept the 10 almonds for Shrikant at the counter corner, and prepared the cereal for breakfast for the both of us. Shrikant came down in the kitchen, and as gently as possible, I asked him if we could give Khelan the monetary gifts from both of us as planned for the last couple of years. We were supposed to see them the next day for Christmas Celebration. His shameful refusal and totally unacceptable justification angered me beyond what I couldn't describe.

I was more frustrated than angry, advanced towards him, and started pinching and shaking his shoulders. I couldn't contain my anger. I did bring both my hands towards his neck. But he held both of my wrists and told me to control myself. I NEVER got to touch him again. This time he had succeeded in what his pathologically sick mind was planning for a long time. His provocation, instigative techniques, and raising the platform for me to lose my control at the click of a moment had finally paid off. I continued venting out my frustration by just banging both my fists on the countertop. He called 911. I seconded by saying, "Go ahead, I was going to do it anyway for the emotional torture I have been going through since day two of marriage!" I was in night clothes when the police came, the two of them. One was a male officer, and the other was the female one who had lectured us recently in the Woman's Club of Old Tappan.

They immediately separated both of us into two rooms. Shrikant was brought into the dining room, and I stayed in the family room. The police interviewed us alternatively. I told them exactly what had happened. Shrikant's refusal of the monetary gift to our grandson angered me. This I told them was in the background that he had given much larger amounts himself to our one set of grandchildren. Money given was not my main objection, but his unfair treatment towards our grandson was the reason. It never occurred to me to tell that he had been emotionally abusive for a very long time, 43 years! I had absolutely no idea as to what statements Shrikant gave the police.

I was handcuffed. I requested them to take my picture. My pocket camera, the 60th birthday gift from children, was right there. I told both police officers that I wanted to show this picture to my 4 grandchildren when they grew up. Both Shrikant and myself were supposed to be picked up by our Indian friends from the town. We were planning to see an Indian movie. This was the first time I had planned some outside activity for the two of us with our friends. I had tried hard to show my husband what the normal retired life meant.

The police officer told me not to worry. I should be back home in time to go see the movie. I did jot down our friends' numbers, just in case. Early morning of Christmas Eve 2015, I left my beautiful home in these nightclothes.

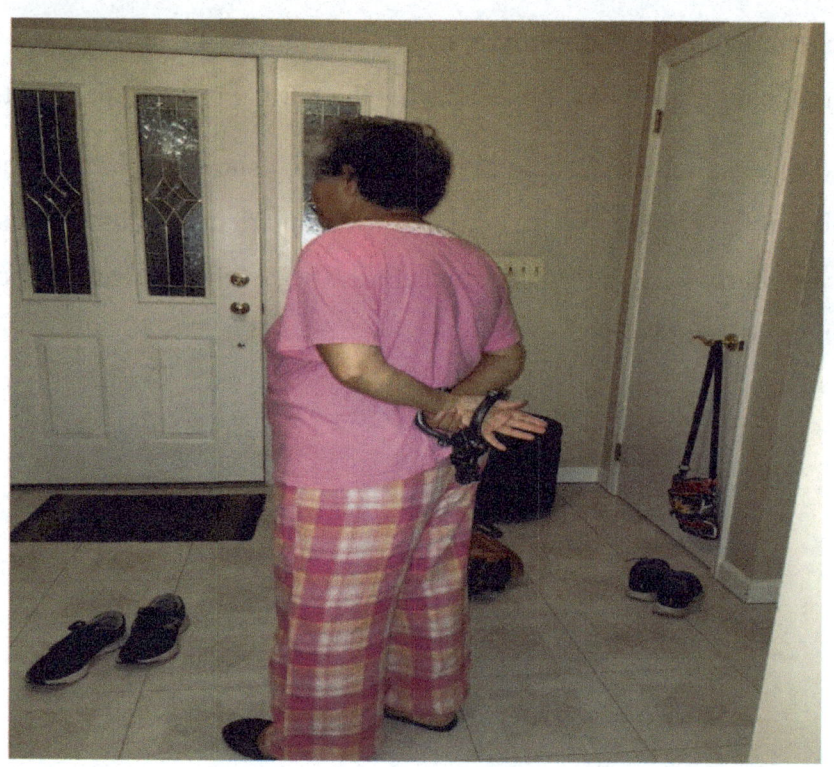

I never got to eat my breakfast, one of my favorite daily meals. I was shoved into the back seat of the police car, my hands tied behind my back.

I was told by the police that they were not allowed to take pictures. Again my OCD would have nothing to do with it! 3 years later, I requested Shaila's daughter to take my picture. I was in the same night clothes from Christmas Eve 2015. It was the Halloween season. My creative mind suggested me to buy fake handcuffs. I had to have this picture of mine in my possession for the future writing of my memoir!

Chapter 31: Trip to the Police Station

It is impossible to tell what was going on in my mind during that ordeal. Definitely, I was not scared or crying or thinking, "I wish I had not done this or that." I never blamed myself then or at any other time. Even now, I never thought I had done anything wrong.

Once in the police station, I was seated on a bench. Now my right ankle got chained to one of the legs of the bench I was sitting on. I was totally unaware of what was going on. What was my dear husband up to?

During those 4-5 minutes before the police entered our house, I was sitting on the sofa in our family room, totally perplexed. I was watching Shrikant's actions. I distinctly noticed him looking at his left hand for whatever reason. So while the policewoman was guarding me at the police station, I mentioned to her that I hope my husband doesn't say anything about me scratching him or causing bleeding or anything. I distinctly remembered showing her both my hands and telling her that I had cut my nails just yesterday.

Obviously, there is no record of anything like this me saying. But definitely, in the report that I read a few days later, they did mention that I requested them to take my picture!

It felt like hours before I noticed any activity. I did request restroom usage, but I am not sure how they made sure that I didn't run away. My husband was finally able to contact Mr. Schwartz, who happened to be our Real Estate Lawyer whom I had met once before when Shrikant had driven me to his office. This is the same lawyer who had bailed him out on June 1, 2010. I had read it in the Record Newspaper. Shrikant was finally successful in getting temporary restraining orders against me. Anand, our older son, was called by his dad to bail me out. I still don't know whose check was used for the Bail amount of $2,500. I was told to sign some papers before I was released.

For a long time, I had no idea about the details of those release forms I had signed. The only thing I knew was that I was very hungry, I had no handcuffs, and I was being driven by my son to my home. The police car was following us. I was given the whole 20 minutes to enter my home, grab whatever I could, and leave home! While driving me home, Anand asked me what had I done now to his father?

The drive home was not even 5 minutes. I was not sure where Shrikant, my husband of 43 years of marriage, was. But Jyoti, my daughter-in-law, was there to help me pack a few things like clothes. As soon as I entered my home, I rushed upstairs to my master bedroom. The first thing I grabbed was one out of those two files related to our finances. Those were the two recycled empty old files I had recovered in 2010 from Shrikant's thousands of collections in his office. This file then turned out to be my lifeline. Also, if you remember, the 2-3 CDs opened before, and at least one Chase Account opened only in my name in the last 5 years remained only mine.

It was my Angel mother who had guided me through her premonitions! The few other things I grabbed were the Telephone list, my car keys, my pocketbook, and most importantly, the container where in I transferred the rest of the oatmeal cereal I had prepared for both Shrikant and myself that morning.

Apparently, I had taken less than 20 minutes, and the police actually commented, admiring my efficiency! This turned out to be the last time I got to sleep and get up from either the left or right side of my king-size bed. I drove my Toyota Camry with my belongings in the trunk. Anand followed me. We stopped at the BiState Plaza of Old Tappan. There were ZERO words of sympathy towards his mother. Instead, I heard my son, with MD, and MBA degrees, engage in conversation with someone regarding me. Maybe it was one of the psychiatrists he had talked to during at least the whole last year of 2015.

I did request him saying if the conversation is regarding me, let me at least hear it myself! Anand was visibly upset or disappointed or may be angry, who knows maybe because now he would have to hear from his loved ones about spoiling their Christmas Eve. I did request Anand to feed me at Mcdonald's nearby. I could barely swallow anything. I believe I cried there. Once near the cars again, I had to figure out the next steps. I was left to make my own decisions again. I called Shaila Naik, one of the very close friends I had made after retirement. I explained the situation. I drove to her house in New Milford, NJ. Anand did offer me to go to their apartment in Manhattan if nothing else could be arranged. I think I made the right choice.

I had my car at least to drive me around to familiar places. Before Anand and I parted, I made sure to hand him over the gift I had wrapped for Shrikant, my husband. They were going to celebrate Christmas the next day.

Later on, several times, one question came repeatedly to my mind. If at all, my grandchildren had asked their ABBA grandfather the next day, the Christmas Day get-together. Did they ask him where their AAJI, grandma was? I still didn't get an answer from my sons. I doubt I will ever know the answer to it like many others.

I reached Sheila's house safely, as usual within 35 minutes. It was Shaila who was surprised and pointed out several times later on, how come, my children, didn't even bother to find out if their mother had reached her destination safely? Were they not concerned about their mentally unfit mother? They must have been so angry with her behavior, she had done so much harm to their most tolerant father! That night I emailed Andrew Bolson about something totally unexpected that had taken place on that day, the morning of Christmas Eve, 2015.

It so happened, for a very long time, I was very much worried about the possibility of being forced to handle those 6 remaining rental properties, especially after the June 1st, 2010 incident regarding my husband's arrest. I didn't even know their locations. I had zero capability of driving to those, and I had zero clue in general. I just couldn't imagine wasting hours and days and years just in the name of managing them. After all, I didn't even entertain the idea of being an owner of those rental properties. I knew for sure if something happened to Shrikant, the whole headache was going to be mine.

My husband had made use of my hard-earned money to keep on paying those excessive amounts of mortgage interests, anywhere up to 15% in the beginning years, and in turn, I got the heartache and potential headaches. I had tried several options as to how to convince him to get rid of them. I had talked to my friend Connie's lawyer husband, and I had discussed this issue with Poornima, my lawyer friend. I actually sent a handwritten letter to Mr. Schwartz, our real estate lawyer, just a few days before the December 24 incident.

In fact, Andrew Bolson was my first lawyer retained as the mediator sometime in December 2015. He had actually prepared and sent an official letter to Mr. Schwartz on my behalf. I was finally so desperate to make sure the rental properties got sold before anything happened to Shrikant. Just the remote possibility of needing to manage them single-handedly was the ONLY THING that had kept me sleepless for so many months past 2010. It was just impossible to get any visible cooperation from Shrikant, my husband. I had exhausted all the different approaches to communicate with him. I had literally failed. I was defeated!

I stayed with Shaila for the rest of December 2015. Except during the holidays, I drove every morning to pick up the mail from the P.O. Box. Her son had come on vacation to his own home. I requested her to explain to her son why I had to come and stay in their house. I was actually HOMELESS! I didn't want him to feel awkward in his own house.

On Christmas Day 2015, Shaila was working in her Biochemistry Lab at Cornell Hospital. I was experiencing one of the worst palpitations again. She decided to get my Cardiac Enzymes checked. The one and 3-hour reports both came normal. I knew that I had the best, strongest genes from both of my parents!

I did not want to spoil the holidays for my friend and her close family. On the day of my Wedding anniversary, I took all 4 of them to Cheese Cake Factory. During the long wait, Shaila's daughter gave me a lot of practical instructions regarding iPad technology and changing the password. I still am so much poor in knowledge, especially in this computer technology.

Right after January 1st, I drove to Andrew's law office in Montvale. He helped me to retain the senior Divorce Lawyer, Steve Rubenstein, from their Law Firm. I had a brief meeting with him right there. Andrew's plan for helping me with mediation related to rental properties stayed at the back burner. He then ended up being my real estate lawyer in the very near and then very remote and unknown future. By December 4, 2015, one of the rental properties was finally under contract for sale. Sometime in the first 3 months of 2016, Andrew represented me when the deal was closed. He helped me to transfer 1/2 of the proceeds from the sale to my own account at Chase. That time I was allowed to communicate with Andrew with difficulty from the Five Star Psychiatric Hospital (Prison), the Heaven Facility in Westchester County!

On my iPad, while residing at Shaila's place, I noticed one email response from one of our friends, Pramila Sarva. It said, "Thank you. Happy New Year to Both of You Too!" With a bit of difficulty, a totally shocking, startling TRUTH got revealed on its own! On

January 1st, 2016, my dear husband wrote an email, must be to hundreds of our friends with just a click of a button! "Happy New Year to You and All Your Family!… by Shrikant and Suhasini Joshi!" Unfortunately, he failed to add one thing by mistake! He had finally won! He had just succeeded in getting rid of Mrs. Suhasini Joshi. He had made her homeless on the Eve of Christmas 2015. He didn't know and didn't care about her whereabouts, though! He forgot to inform about his victory in that email to all.

Chapter 32: First Visit to the Court

I was ordered to appear in Hackensack Court, NJ, on January 4, 2016. I guess everyone was ready to get back to work and start enforcing the Rules Of The Law!

The official complaint filed in Old Tappan Borough by the plaintiff Shrikant Joshi was, "the defendant, Suhasini S. Joshi, did commit simple assault by purposely, knowingly or recklessly causing bodily injury to Shrikant G.Joshi, specifically by strangling him, choking him, scratching his face and forehead and slapping him in the face!"

Finally, I had read the details of the papers that I had signed on Christmas Eve afternoon when Anand had bailed me out. Oh! No! In reality, I had done NONE of this! Before the police came, Shrikant must have scratched himself wherever he had described he had been scratched by me! No wonder why he was looking at his left hand that morning! The wicked mind of my mentally sick husband was planning his next move constantly. I had known that he always had his left pinky fingernail grown up to about 1/2 inch. The reason given by him to the whistleblower was "Just In Case!"

Later on among many more things, one of Shrikant's relatives told me about its purpose. During my future saga, for a very long time, she had become my whistle-blower. When she came to this country, apparently, I had become her Role Model! She was keen on knowing my side of the story! She really tried her best to kind of mediate unofficially. Unfortunately, she couldn't succeed. My creative mind had surely noticed Shrikant looking at his left hand just before the police had arrived that day. Finally, I was able to figure it out now!

On January 2nd, 2016, from Shaila's home, I wrote an email to Andrew Bolson, "Andrew, I am scared, hopeless, optimistic, frustrated, angry, but still trying to be in command of my thought process!" I explained to him exactly what had actually happened that morning of Christmas Eve 2015. 58 Greenwoods was the only home known to me that was bought because my earning power had increased significantly by 1983. Even if I was the co-owner, I had no pride, no attachment, only unimaginable heartache from those 13 rentals bought without my knowledge.

Andrew promised to notify Steve of my side of the story. He wished me that, hopefully, 2016 would bring a much-needed fresh start. In reality, my DESTINY had its own plans, major twists, and turns. I bet even an experienced reader may not be able to figure out what happened next.

Sunday evening, Shaila asked me about my choice for food for supper. I had 100% moral, emotional, and physical support from her, her family, and her friends. Her question about the choice of food formed an impression on my severely traumatized but creative mind. I thought of it as my LAST SUPPER! I was to be crucified tomorrow outside of the court! All the spectators, including my loved ones, were going to be the witnesses.

The next morning, Shaila arranged for me to be dropped off at Hackensack Court. Atul, the younger son, came directly from his apartment in Manhattan. The fact that he had to take time off from work for his (unworthy) mother hammered a severe blow into his mother's heart! Steve met me in the court. The next court date needed to be changed because of my pre-planned trip to India for my 50th Medical Reunion. The decision was made through Steve regarding the date to allow me to get my Passport and travel bag from our home. My children's presence was a MUST, according to the law. I don't remember the details, but I think I was photographed and fingerprinted. The screaming and shouting of the guard just because I requested him to wait for a second, the humiliation was way beyond what my simple inexperienced mind could take. Again, unfortunately, I could do NOTHING about it.

Sunday, January 10, 2016, Atul picked me up from Shaila's home, and Anand came directly. As soon as I reached the premises of 58 Greenwoods, the first thing brought to my attention was my dear husband, Shrikant, had changed the locks of the front entrance!!! Truly, my hats off for his efficiency and quick thinking! I wanted to SCREAM, but I couldn't! Within 20 minutes, we were out of the house. I requested both my sons to spare a few minutes. I went to visit Pat Royal, a neighbor, my senior friend from the Woman's Club of Old Tappan. She had a recurrence of breast cancer and was undergoing chemotherapy and radiation.

Just recently, I had promised her to give company while she visited Columbia Hospital in Manhattan. I entered her house alone to explain the unexpected situation I had gotten myself into. As she walked out with me to bid goodbye, we spontaneously hugged each other and burst into tears. Yes, I did cry uncontrollably. What to do with these excessive emotions of mine?!

Anand went directly to his apartment. Atul drove me to his apartment. While on my favorite Palisades Parkway South for the first time, Atul revealed to me his knowledge from his father's own mouth, in his own words. This was possibly sometime in the beginning of November 2015. In my absence, my dear Shrikant had provided both the sons and, most probably, their wives a detailed description of the physical abuse inflicted on him by his wife, me, my children's mother. It was TOTALLY SHOCKING beyond what I could describe.

I was totally speechless for two reasons how the pathologically mentally sick person's mind works constantly and plans its next move, next strategy. The technique of GAS LIGHTING, the pathological lies, is so powerful, so amazing, and so creative! Also, what was equally shocking to me was how my well-informed FAMILY of 4 adults had kept it from me!? For five years since 2010, they all 4 kept adding to the list of all their mother/ in-law's wrongful actions. They all four just sat on it. They were equally comfortable accepting the voluntarily given monetary gifts for their children from the same mentally sick, ungrateful mother/in-law. They NEVER confirmed the validity, NEVER bothered to find out the TRUTH, NEVER warned me against doing those gruesome actions, NOR did any four of them remove their father/in-law or me to avoid any further events.

In fact, later on, not too long after the Dec. 24, 2015 incident, Jyoti was surprised and therefore had asked me wondering if what the Uncle (Shrikant, my husband) had been telling them was possibly false, untrue? This clearly showed that everyone of them, who knows, maybe their parents, had totally believed in my husband. And that is why all had come to the conclusion that something like what happened on that dreadful day of Christmas Eve 2015 was bound to happen!

In fact, I still had no idea exactly what Atul was talking about. The only thing I knew was during the months of November and December 2015, Shrikant had accompanied me several times, at least 12 times, if not more. He used to drive, and I sat next to him every time we went anywhere. Then in his written certification for the Judge, he stated that he was afraid for his life during those times of November and December 2015! This was also when he had continued to stay willingly under the same roof of 58, Greenwoods!

Before our next court hearing, on February 1st or 2nd, 2016, Shrikant had amended the list of Domestic Abuse that he suffered from his wife of 43 years. His whole idea was to get permanent restraining orders against me, barring my entrance to my HOME, for good! He was bent on teaching me the lesson. Did he succeed? You bet he did!! On December 24, his complaint against me was, my actions were purposeful, preplanned, and knowingly undertaken.

In fact, the opposite was the TRUTH. His mentally sick mind had been planning his moves for a very long time! After all, at one time, he thought of me to be an easy target to be controlled. But now, I was defying his hold on me. As per my husband, I deserved punishment, a big-time one. That is what he had thought.

Chapter 33: Detour To 5 Star Prison Instead

Today is January 11, 2023, my 75 birthday. Memories and words are flowing very easily! 7 years ago, on this day, I was forced to get admitted to a psychiatric hospital. Absolutely no justification was given by the two wonderful, too-concerned children of mine. I absolutely had no one who was able to understand me. I felt totally helpless. Hence, the following is the TRUTH that got typed very easily!

Steve Rubenstein was the choice for Andrew Bolson to represent me at the NJ State Court. I had already been to that court on the 4th. Michael Austin was another of Andrew's best friends from another Firm who was going to represent me for the charges filed against me in the town of Old Tappan, NJ. I was supposed to be present there at 4 pm on January 5th, 2016.

Michael had already succeeded in getting that trial postponed. So I had 5 more days before being escorted to my home to get my passport next Sunday. I was consistently hopeful that Shrikant would get rid of the restraining orders and that I would be able to go back to my home. Being concerned about my safety, Shaila drove me to Nyack for my next session with the psychologist, Dr. Kaplan. I had continued seeing him, especially after the recent new developments.

During the daytime, I did go to the bank and post office. Dale, whom I had befriended for a few years, decided not to continue the friendship. At least she was gracious to admit my story was going to create a negative impact on her already not-so-positive life. I totally understood her. For the first time, at the hairdresser appointment, I requested her to color my hair along with the haircut! This was in preparation for my India trip for the reunion. I treated myself by visiting Rolling Pin Restaurant. Visiting this and one other Thai restaurant was always THE MUST before I went on any foreign trips! Just in case something bad happens, I did not want my Soul to remain unsatisfied and keep wandering around as per the Hindu Mythology!!! I still love these two restaurants.

Friday, 8th of January, 2016, was the last HOPE that Shrikant went to the court in person to remove the restraining orders against me. It didn't happen. I was totally devastated, totally depleted of my adrenaline storage. That Friday and Saturday, for 48 hours, I was totally sleepless before Atul picked me up to get the passport and travel bag.

So on the 10th of January, while in Atul's apartment, trying to pack things for my pre-planned India trip, I just couldn't contain my feelings of HOPELESSNESS. I started crying, actually more like sobbing. I didn't want my two of the most adorable grandkids to witness their Aaji so unhappy. They had not seen me for a very long time. The decision was made by their concerned parents to keep me away from them. As I was being driven to Anand's apartment, I requested Atul to bring me to the E.R. to rule out a HEART ATTACK.

This was the 3rd time since Shrikant's own arrest in June of 2010. I was driven to Cornell Hospital. I believe I must have received special treatment because Anand is a Vice President at that hospital. The heart attack was R/O. There was a 3-hour wait before the second enzyme report came out. For whatever reason? Cat-scan? MRI was done. I was made to lie down on the stretcher under very bright lights for hours. The only thing by this time I wanted was to go to the apartment of one of my sons and fall into an eternal sleep! By now, I had been deprived of sleep for almost 72 hours!!

I was forced to get engaged in totally unpleasant, unwanted, and unnecessary conversations with both of my sons, who obviously were very much concerned about my well-being. After 7 years, I still don't know why, but the E.R. Physician in charge that night ordered a psychiatric consult for me. The E.R. being the Mad House, as usual, it further deprived me of sleep.

Finally, a young doctor with a white coat and a stethoscope around his neck visited me near my stretcher. He looked like a kid who had just graduated from High school. After asking whatever questions and listening to whatever answers he heard from me, I was diagnosed and labeled as a Bipolar Disorder Patient! That was it! It was as simple as that! According to my loved ones, this explained everything. Both of my sons must have been relieved at that time. They both must have thought that was the best thing so far they both did for their mother since 2010 after their father's own encounter with the police. They got me diagnosed, and with the treatment, I will be alright.

According to my dutiful sons, their father was right in telling everything about their mother behind her back because, during the meetings requested by their mother, their father always had his mouth shut, zipped, locked!

I was admitted to a room in the psychiatric section and was given some sedatives. Finally, I was able to fall into a sound sleep! The next morning, January 11, on my birthday, I was in a hospital bed. I got up with a totally clear and rested mind. I had nice conversations with a couple of young girls who were admitted there must be for similar reasons. We talked about their potential bright future. This was in spite of the fact that I hadn't the slightest clue about my own immediate and distant future! I felt fine, except I was now totally disappointed, thinking maybe I had not brought up my children properly. I had failed in my duty to instill the core values in my own children. I had not taught them that they MUST listen, pay attention, understand both sides of the equation, and then draw the conclusion, or maybe they had done that!

Sometime in the afternoon, both of my children reappeared. So also another 3rd or 4th very young, definitely another least experienced doctor came to visit. He had a nurse standing next to him. She had accompanied him and was holding a tray with a syringe and some medicine. The plan was to admit me to the psychiatric hospital in Westchester called The Heaven Facility. It must have been well discussed and approved by my two loved ones. I absolutely have no doubt that both of them had discussed this with their wives and both of their in-laws. Just in case the doctor and the staff experienced any resistance from me, their bipolar patient, the plan was to ZAP me with whatever medicine they had in that syringe and forcefully send me to the place of their choice! They all were 100% sure what they were doing was THE RIGHT THING TO DO.

I still believe that with each and every step my children took after they both came to know my story in 2010, everyone of the step had ended up in a wrong turn, actually 200%!

I was totally helpless! Truly didn't know what to do? "If this is the ONLY choice I am offered, then please, there is absolutely no need to inject me with that sedative." I walked to the stretcher. I was driven by ambulance via the Tappan Zee bridge to the Heaven Facility in White Plains, Westchester. It is one of the psychiatric hospitals under NY Presbyterian.

There is no doubt in my mind, what happened on January 11, 2016, on my Birthday, will always haunt my children throughout their lives. I can still envision both of my dutiful children. They both were standing against the wall, unshaven. They both had been visibly deprived of sleep.

Chapter 34: Scene III Act 2

The way all the choices got proposed to me one after the other from the morning of Christmas Eve 2015, I was totally mesmerized! I was numb. I was speechless. This was when I had made only one legitimate suggestion to Shrikant. And the suggestion was to give our usual and voluntarily agreed upon monetary gifts from both of us in the form of a check to our 3-year-old grandson on Christmas Day. He had missed his birthday celebration because of the hip fracture he had suffered at that time.

Without allowing me any input, now I landed in the ER of the Heaven Facility at Westchester. Dr. Mamta Modhwadia was the admitting physician. After hearing my story, she clearly told me that I don't have any Bipolar disorder. I am not in a manic state. I still remember her conclusion. First, I was too old to be diagnosed for the first time to be bipolar. Second, the severity gets lesser with age. Most importantly, she said that what happened to me was very common. Especially true in Indian culture. If the wife is making more money, the husband with an inferiority complex very often shows this type of behavior. In my case, my income was 80% of the total. It didn't matter, even if I never felt superior. I am more than 100% sure that someone was typing the notes. The name of the admitting nurse was Juliane.

Once I got admitted, each and every belonging of mine, except some, maybe if considered harmless, was taken away, including the dental floss! My pants were no good because I had removed the elastic and threaded the ribbon instead to tie. I was left there by myself (dumped) by my loved ones. I had already taken too much of their precious time away from their own family and work. There was no question of expecting anyone to come to see me in this new facility, at least that evening. And unexpectedly I got visitors! They were Mr. and Mrs. Sarva! But how? Possibly, I had called them while at Cornell. They, after searching for me in Cornell Hospital, drove all the way to see me. In fact, it was Mr. Ramesh Sarva who helped me to write the official letter that I should be released after 72 hours. Apparently, once admitted as a psychiatric patient, the hospital is allowed to forcefully admit that person till 72 hours.

No Doctor came to see me that afternoon or evening or at least the next whole day, but I was given various psychotropic drugs still with the diagnosis of Bipolar disorder. I believe something like Depakote or Risperidone.

It must be the usual course of action for everyone. Two days later, in the morning, I had to present myself in front of about 10-12 people! They looked or pretended to be ready to listen to my story.

I had to present myself in front of 10-12 people.

"I am a victim of mistaken identity. I don't have any mood swings. The whole of my life, I always had positive thoughts and attitude in spite of what I witnessed just one day after our marriage while on the Honeymoon! I LOVE my life and will never think of taking my own life or of anyone else's. Being aware that this is the only Human Life I am going to remember while being alive, I want to make use of each and every moment I have on this earth for as long as I can! I know 100% that my husband, children, all the friends, everyone knows that these are exactly what my thoughts are."

The reason I can write all this is because I still have the notebook they provided me on the day of admission. I had written down all the points to spill out in front of the whole committee that day. During the afternoon, Ms. Genoveffa Flagello, the lawyer appointed by the hospital to represent patients like me, came to see me. She was actually ready to represent me when she heard my story and believed in it.

And then, that same evening, for the first time, just a few hours before the 72 hours deadline, Dr. Sanchez-Baranco, MD, paid me a visit. He convinced me that they wouldn't keep me any longer than needed. He wanted to meet with them in person to make sure that my children and their wives would take care of me and not abandon their responsibility.

It was Tomy who visited and brought a few decent clothes for me, including pants with elastic. I kept only one pair and requested her to return everything else. I attended all the required classes, including group therapy, talking with a social worker, Art, Reiki, yoga, meditation, exercise classes, psychiatric rehab, and anger management. Multiple times the blood was drawn to check for ideal blood levels of the drug Depakote. MRI, EEG along with, EKG, and X-rays were performed in the ER itself. I obviously withdrew my 72-hour release request. Both the sons and their wives came to meet with Dr. Sanchez, and Friday January 22, 2016, I was released from the hospital.

I was supposed to see Dr. Kalayam or someone on an outpatient basis, I think in White Plains. This person had absolutely no clue about my history and used to actually sleep during the session!

On February 1st, for the 2nd time while in the Hackensack Court, Shrikant filed an amendment to the original assault charges on December 24. 2015. He had kept a record including the dates in the months of Nov. and Dec 2015. It shows that he was the one who was well-prepared. To me, it was all pre-planned by him and not me! Also, there was no one who really was interested in checking their authenticity.

Between February 5th till Feb 26 appearance in the court, multiple back-and-forth correspondence took place between Steve, myself, and Mr. Ronald Schwartz, who was representing Shrikant, the plaintiff.

Steve tried his best by filing a motion with the court requesting to relieve Mr. Schwartz from representing Shrikant for the FRO (Final Resting Orders). This is because Mr. Schwartz was actively involved in representing both of us for closing a real estate deal at that time. It was obviously a conflict of interest. Unfortunately, the Judge granted permission for Mr. Schwartz to continue representing Shrikant. Mr. Schwartz, the lawyer, had actually lied in the court under oath!

Steve had apparently made a deal with Mr. Schwartz in between. He wrote to me on February 18, 2016, "Sue, your chances of winning after the trial are very slim. The plan is Shrikant will amend his DV (Domestic violence) physical assault complaint to include an allegation of harassment, and you will acknowledge that you harassed him!!! Even though it is still a FRO, I think that having it based on harassment instead of a physical assault that Shrikant is alleging is a better choice for you!!!"

In the same email, Steve warned me that I should separate the assets ASAP, even though I didn't want to divorce him for whatever reason. He didn't trust my husband.

On February 26, 2016, in the court, FRO were ordered. At the same time, something TOTALLY SCARY AND DISAPPOINTING, I called it a horrible punishment for actually doing NOTHING HARMFUL to my husband, was ordered by the Hon. Judge. I was to attend the ADV counseling, which consisted of 26 once-a-week sessions near Hackensack Court, 4-6 weeks after I completed the initial intake with that agency. ADV meant Alternate to Domestic Violence, which apparently meant that I needed big-time training for something, in actuality, had NEVER occurred. I had neither harassed nor physically assaulted my husband. They were all his pathological lies.

On February 27, 2016, I was also allowed to enter my home for the last time with the police escort and both of my children.

After I was released from the Heaven Facility, I traveled back and forth between Manhattan, from my children's apartments to New Jersey. I still had my car parked at Shaila's house. I had signed the lease for a 2-bedroom apartment at Sutton Place, Norwood, NJ. I believe it was for a reason why I had met a wonderful senior friend named Janet just a few months ago. She had once driven me to that area after one of the senior retreats.

The children did follow my suggestion to rent a small truck. Early morning of February 27, I paid a visit to ShopRite to get some huge empty boxes. At 9 am, we all were allowed to enter 58 Greenwoods, where I had dwelled for more than 31 years! A police escort was the MUST to be paid by the defendant, myself! Atul, Anand and I think Rina helped me to move out some of my belongings. I had to provide the list in advance, and ONLY the items allowed by Shrikant could be taken away. They needed to be pre-approved by my dear husband through his lawyer, Mr. Schwartz!

By March 1st, 2016, children had helped me to settle in. We did shopping at Target for the necessary things. I had already ordered the bedroom set from Bobs Furniture. One friend from OT. Woman's club used to work there. Janet, much older than me, was already there as my friend in this new neighborhood.

I think I was totally ready for at least the next 2 years to lead an independent and so-called peaceful life and do the crafts to my heart's content. I had moved most of my craft supplies and the Sears Kenmore sewing machine! On the paper approved by the court, I was somehow supposed to have access to my Stained Glass room in the basement. I didn't think I needed anything more! This is EXCEPT……

It never happened. I had to leave behind everything related to stained glass for good, forever! On March 2nd, 2016, I wrote to Steve, "Can you please do anything in your power after talking to my husband and convincing the Judge to cancel the ADV counseling?" Separately I had also begged my children to convince their father to cancel the same. The terms were very difficult for me to undertake. I was actually very much scared of driving, especially to unknown places. Once started, I was to appear there for 26 consecutive weeks, even during bad weather conditions, including snow. Maybe 1 or 2 breaks in the continuity were allowed. If not, it had to be repeated! And at the end, still, it was up to the counselor if they were satisfied with my performance!

On March 17, Steve wrote directly to Shrikant, maybe because he was not being represented by Mr. Schwartz, who had retired in between. "Suhasini had expressed to me what I believe to be a very sincere desire to try to reconcile with you. She is extremely remorseful both about the event and its consequences. She has every desire to salvage the long-term marriage." This was all because I always had a very simple and beautiful DREAM of an Intact Family of 10!

His presence was supposed to be No.1 for that dream to be complete. The other, EQUALLY important, was my belief with 110% accuracy. All his actions were indicative of the stronghold his genetic and mental disorder had on him. His behavior was exactly like his brilliant mother. Except that she was a female and didn't have control over the money her husband had generated over the years through his business. At least from the 2010 episode of his own encounter with the police, I was finally desperate that he gets treated. I didn't want him to be left alone, especially because I was a doctor and his concerned wife.

Shrikant, my dear husband, had nothing to do with this. The only 2 things he was looking for were permanent restraining orders against me and that I must undergo the punishment of 26 weeks of ADV counseling. He had actually succeeded in Brainwashing everyone, including my loved ones, the lawyers, the judge, the police, and many of his relatives both in the USA and India. Especially regarding the last on the list, I was totally unaware of it for a very long time!

On January 2nd, 2016, Michael Austin had already submitted a "Not guilty" plea at the Municipal Court in Old Tappan. There was no need for me to appear in the court of OT on January 5th, 2016.

On February 3rd, 2016, I wrote to Tomy, "I will fight Shrikant's crooked mental disease, and then only I will lose the battle if I have to!" Only then was I going to accept my DEFEAT.

On April 5, 2016, I appeared in the Municipal Court of Old Tappan. That was the first time I actually met Michael Austin, my best lawyer recommended by the only TRUSTED lawyer of mine, Andrew Bolson! Michael was ready and all set to fight for me that evening. But unfortunately, by this time, I was so exhausted mentally and physically. I requested him not to, and I was ready to accept whatever charges my dear husband had against me. He had 99.9% lied to the police on Christmas Eve 2015. I had signed the papers that evening without reading them. My children had already seemingly disowned their mother. It was too little too late by more than 5 years since 2010. I had actually given up. I paid the clerk whatever fees I owed. I never saw Michael again. Anand drove to his apartment, and I drove to mine in Norwood.

On April 7, 2016, Shrikant appealed against allowing me not needing to attend the 26-week ADV counseling.

On April 15, 2016, Steve requested the Hackensack Court to vacate me from the provision which required the defendant, me, to attend the 26 weeks of ADV counseling sessions. He had already submitted my certification. This time I actually had lied under oath! "As a result of the hospitalization and my ongoing therapy, I have learned that the incident which occurred on December 24, 2015 was inappropriate! I have learned to work on controlling my frustration and anger!"

I still believe that anyone in my position would have reacted the same way. Shrikant had emotionally abused me for years, right from day 2 of our marriage. He had continued instigating me, provoking me for the longest period of time, especially from January 1st, 2015. Eventually, I came to know exactly what I was meant to him for years. He had married me ONLY because I was a doctor. I was just a money-making machine. I was the golden egg-laying hen! Because I had finally opposed his control freak behavior towards me and my hard-earned money, he was bent on teaching me the lesson of a lifetime.

He had succeeded in raising the bar for me to react! How come no one, including my loved ones, the lawyers, the police, or the Judge, noticed it? His amended complaints were for ONLY November and December of 2015. How come my alleged behavior was ONLY towards him, and that also for only those 2 months? During the same months, he allegedly convinced everyone, especially my children, that he was afraid for his life being with me. He had accompanied me several times while driving in the same car. Why didn't he move out for safety? Why my children or their wives did not think of preventive measures? Why did they not remove one of us to safety if they were made aware by their father-in-law? The answer to Shrikant's behavior was very clear. He had realized that he had lost control over me and my money! Truthfully this never meant that he had wasted money. He was extremely secretive, among many other things.

On May 13th, 2016, along with continued FRO in effect, "Defendant's motion to be terminated from ADV is granted by the Judge as the defendant (me) is currently under the care for psychiatric issues, and the court doesn't see the need for ADV counseling."

Obviously, I was not present in the court that day. It was sometime in June of 2020 I contacted Steve after a very long time. I had never seen the proof. I had to have it in my possession for the record as per my OCD!

During the same period of 2020, I tried hard to get the phone numbers and addresses of the admitting physician, Dr. Modhwadia, and the lawyer Genoveffa Flagello. I wrote certified letters. Unfortunately, I didn't get any response.

The reason why I was not present in court on May 13, 2016, was obvious! The drama continues…

Chapter 35: There Is No Proof But...

It was the beginning of March. The chilly, cloudy weather was not comforting my mind, full of racing thoughts. The reality struck me hard the moment I hit that brand-new bed for the first time that night. I had never felt that lonely anytime before in my life. I was made homeless by the person with whom I was hoping for everlasting, sustainable companionship! Also, somehow I had lost the TRUST of my children somewhere in those last 5 years. I was not able to pinpoint any particular reason. Reluctantly because they were trying to convince me that the psychotropic medications were going to make me feel better, I started taking them sincerely.

Nothing was really helping my mind. When the children called, I told them the truth. Anand is one of the big shots in Cornell, and the decision was made to try outpatient therapy. I joined the outpatient program at Cornell for the next 3 weeks. The commute from Anand-Jyoti's place was within walking distance. The therapy schedule was the same as in the Haven Facility. In the evenings and nights, I was able to spend time with my family and especially the granddaughters. Again sorry to say, but whatever teachings and coping mechanisms were taught there, in reality, NOTHING was getting registered anywhere on any of my brain cells! Some more medications were added, and I was to see the new team of psychologists and psychiatrists, Mr. And Mrs. Laura Bhatt, in downtown Manhattan.

After spending 1-2 weeks more between the two sons' apartments, the decision to go back to my rented apartment in Norwood was honored by both couples. There were very little to zero improvements in my mental condition, but it was of no use revealing it to my loved ones. Once I got into this situation, without any doubt, they all were doing their best and did everything in their capacity to support me. The decision was made that my older sister Chimi from Columbia, SC, would keep me company for a while. I was to commute to downtown Manhattan to see the doctors by bus and subway. I had talked to a couple of my very close doctor friends. One of them was Dr. Nara and her doctor husband, Nagarjun. From the beginning, they both disagreed with the diagnosis. It was situational depression, according to them and not Bipolar.

My mind was plotting something else. I was totally convinced by now that I was of no use to others as well as to myself. In 2010 I had lost the trust of my children. I had failed to instill the simple core values in them therefore, I didn't deserve them. I had already lost them and therefore, I decided to end my life. The blow related to the feeling of losing closeness to both my children was so severe that I just couldn't take it! There was ZERO doubt in my mind about my decision. Plan was to swallow as many prescribed pills as possible at night. I had 2 or 3 Tylenol #3 (with codeine) in my possession after the recent dental procedure. There was absolutely no hesitation.

I kept myself busy the whole day by decorating 25-30 greeting cards. The night arrived. I had dinner, used the restroom, wrote the suicide note, and kept it in a visible spot on the nightstand. Don't know why, but I locked the door from the inside. I did swallow a very large number of pills and went to bed with the idea of not meeting TOMORROW. I did lie down on the left side of the bed and turned on my left side after the final prayer to God.

I was hoping for the very much wanted and anticipated eternal sleep and peace. Instead, the next morning the flip phone on the nightstand next to me rang, which sounded from a very far away distance. It was Anand who was calling from Texas or somewhere. I guess the babbling sound coming out of his mom's mouth said it all! "Aai, what did you do to yourself?", was the question that I couldn't answer. I vaguely remember sliding down on the floor and having passed away again.

Then some noise and activity was coming from around me. I was being wheeled by ambulance to a nearby NJ hospital. Till now, I have not bothered to find out which one! Luckily they didn't have to pump out the stomach contents! I don't recall anything more than that, but I was wide awake sometime on that whichever hospital bed. Anand had instructed the staff to get me moved to Cornell Hospital. Both Jyoti and Rina were there. Again I don't remember much, but I distinctly remember the room this time definitely looked and felt like a prison cell with a very small cot to lie on.

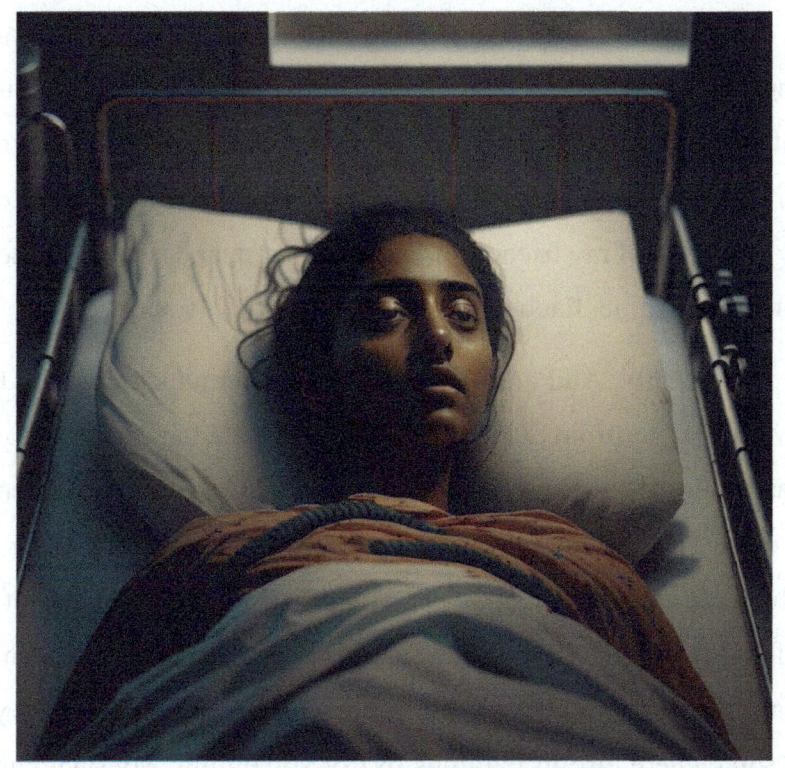

The room this time in Cornell Hospital definitely looked like a prison cell with a very small cot to lie on.

The next morning I was transferred back to the same Haven Facility, this time for legitimate reasons. I remember writing a check for $10,000 this time. Being designated as "SUICIDAL", there was much more guarding outside the room. This meant no sleep because the guards were engaged in talking most of the time, and the door was purposely kept open! As I was entering the hospital, I had decided that I would refuse to receive any brain shocks called ECTs. (Electroconvulsive treatment) while in India, I used to provide anesthesia for the same procedures.

In reality, I had in all agreed to 11 of them, I think, twice a week. The doctor's idea was to facilitate recovery from the depression along with the drugs. In reality, NOTHING worked. I refused the 12th ECT. To some extent, I was feeling and behaving actually like a Zombie! By now, few of my friends had heard about it, and several of them had come to visit me. Each and everyone was visibly shocked!

Apparently, Atul and Anand were in communication with Chimi, my older sister from SC. She had already landed in a nearby hotel and was visiting me every evening. Several heads must have been engaged in discussing together the future plans for their invalid mother or any other relation. This time they had plenty of time to figure it out. I was offered two choices, either to go to Brookdale Battery Park in lower Manhattan (where I have been living now for last more than 7 years!) or somewhere else in Paramus, NJ or something. My own choice of going back to my house at 58 Greenwoods was not for discussion. I did choose the first option obviously because this building is right in front of where Atul used to live at one time.

This Apt. 606 is a furnished apartment. Being mostly under the influence of those psychotropic drugs, I was able to comprehend everything but was not able to react that easily or not at all. Unfortunately, my sister's presence was not really helping either. But we were doing some activities together, including a daily walk along the River Hudson.

Now onwards, my life was not in my hand. It was being handled by loved ones and others, excluding me. Chimi eventually had to go back to her home. The plan was, I will pack up whatever little belongings I had and fly to S.C. to be under her care. Andrew Bolson visited me in the apartment and prepared the Power Of Attorney papers for me. It was essential that I vacate the rental apartment in Norwood.

On Memorial Day weekend, with the help of Shaila, Chimi, and myself, it was vacated. After providing a proper explanation, I was released from the 2 years lease. This is the time, once again, my mother and my Angel came to my rescue. A gentleman named John Franco from the neighborhood paid a visit when he saw me going back and forth from the garbage dumpster. For extra income to support his family, he was used to cleaning the apartments in that development after they were vacated. He got plenty of brand new things from my apartment, including especially the whole bedroom set, in exchange for taking care of my apartment after we left. He was of tremendous help. I left a few belongings at Shaila's, and John dropped my sister and me at Brookdale. I paid him $100 cash. Since then, I have requested John's help several times, and he has been compensated appropriately. We are still in touch.

Last week of June 2016, Chimi went back, and I spent one week with Anand and his family at the vacation home they had rented. Just before that, with Atul's recommendation, I got my iPhone for the first time. I absolutely had no clue how to use it. A few of my belongings were moved to Atul's weekend home in South Hampton, L.I.

The psychotropic drugs prescribed continued doing the magic trick on me. This was to the extent, half an hour after taking the Depakote, the totally dependable sleep would take me to my La La

Land. Unfortunately, the dreams were never pleasant. During day time, I had absolutely NO DESIRE to get up from bed unless forced to. My conscience was definitely at work 24 minus the most wanted sleep hours, but I couldn't do much more than try my best to avoid crying in front of the grandkids. Given a chance, at every awake moment, the ONLY ONE THING that was occurring spontaneously was the CRY! We were actually inseparable.

Obviously, the medications were not really doing their job of improving my mental health. After all, it was actually Situational Depression. The basic situation had not changed at all for me. Somehow the arrangement was made for my mail to go to Anand's apartment in Manhattan. My situation remained in limbo as before after becoming homeless. I kept moving from one to another, paid or unpaid shelter. I had been leading the Gypsy life, which continued in the future for an unknown period of my life. Personally for me, the therapeutic effect of those drugs on me still remains doubtful.

There is a very good chance that my first suicidal attempt was the end result of those psychotropic drugs initially forced on me on my 68th birthday! Of course, there is no proof, but if one reads the label, each and everyone of those medications says in very small letters that there's an increased risk of suicidal tendencies.

In the time period that followed, who knew if their effects on this patient (myself) would be tested again?

Chapter 36: Beggars Can't Be Choosers

The first stop as a gypsy was at Columbia S.C. sometime in 1st week of August 2016. There was very little time for my children to give instructions as to how to use the iPhone. On the plane, I requested one gentleman next to me to show me how to keep my phone in Airplane mode? This was after the loud announcement that the plane was about to take off.

Chimi was at the airport to receive me. She had expressed her intention of taking care of her younger sister as long as it was needed. Apparently, she had told her daughters and maybe other relatives that she had considered this as her duty. Within 2-3 days, she drove me to my appointments with the psychologist and psychiatrist. If I remember correctly, the oldest of the two psychiatrists I saw was the one who understood my situation correctly. First he stopped the Depakote. Unfortunately I don't remember the details as to which drug was prescribed instead. But the situation didn't change much. The only thing I had always preferred nowadays was lying down on the bed for as many hours as possible. The Curtains were always drawn and very little entry of bright sunlight and very little interaction with other people could be considered some contributing factors. Sujata, her older daughter lived nearby. Passing the time with her, her children, her husband and the two big dogs could be considered one of the best therapy for my mind. Luckily I was able to meet with them much more frequently than expected.

My retired senior brother, we call him Nana, is a US Citizen and lives with his younger son in California. Somehow he came to know my situation. And totally out of real concern, he, his wife whom I call Vahini and their older son flew from California. The next morning there was a detailed discussion of the exact events that took place. The very fact that I could explain everything without a single tear in my eyes, in detail with all the boldness and courage was totally surprising for my nephew. The plan was I should visit California on a trial basis in the month of October for the Festival of Lights. If I feel more comfortable, the plan was to spend an unknown period of time there in the company of them and their two granddaughters.

By the end of 1&1/2 to 2 months, I could sense that my sister's physical, emotional as well as mental capacity to be my caretaker was obviously diminishing. And I could totally understand that. She clearly told me that the fact that I do nothing except lying in bed etc is making her feel depressed. It was equally true that she couldn't contribute much on her own to make me feel better! She started making appointments for herself with some of her friends for breakfast or lunch. Another most disappointing statement of hers repeated often was, "There must be some valid reason why Shrikant behaved the way he did!!!" She was another one so far, other than my children and their wives who had a hard time believing in me. In fact, these all were the ones who had spent the least amount of time with Shrikant and myself. Anand and Atul had left the house at the age of 18 when they entered college. At that time I was working full-time. There was very little interaction between Shrikant and myself especially in front of them. Their presence in the house, later on, was almost like being the guests. Each and every friend of ours who had spent much more time with us over the years believed in me 100%. "I don't have to take you each and every place I go!" was Chimi's sentence that alerted me and realized it was time for the gypsy to find another shelter!

During the Festival of Lights period, I did stay with my brother and his wife in their younger son's apartment in California. The environment was 100 times much more favorable for any person in depression.

The Middle of November 2016, was the last time I was in Columbia, S.C. I packed everything, first flew to Chicago, stayed with Chimi's younger daughter in Milwaukee for a week. She drove me to Atul's in-laws in Indiana for Thanksgiving. Here, even under the influence of those psychotropic drugs which had failed so far to improve my mind positively, I did try my best to behave like a good girl! Without any doubt, I was making EVERY CONSCIOUS EFFORT to mix with all the wonderful people I was surrounded with. For my two beautiful grandchildren, Khelan and Lila, who all had come there for the holidays, I always was their happy Aaji. But in my own bedroom there, each and every night and the next morning without failure, it was Atul's mother-in-law, Atul and Rina, they were all witnessing my despair, I was always crying uncontrollably. From Chicago airport, I flew to San Francisco. Nana's older son Samir was there to pick me up. The next 3 months, I spent in the company of my brother and his family. Each and everyone had welcomed me totally open heartedly without any doubt. They all did their best in helping me to behave like a normal person at least when I was surrounded with all these loving people. But left to myself, the ONLY THING I was doing was CRYING, alternating with solving Sudoku and Free sell game on my iPad! My Vahini, did her best to be my friend rather than a sister-in-law.

I will always be in everyone's debt for providing me with shelter, comfort and unconditional support, and I will always be in everyone's debt forever. My brother's family did it all keeping me as their No.1 priority. Someone's presence with that unavoidable negative energy could have been potentially harmful to the innocent minds of their children. None of the elders expressed that as their primary concern.

Unfortunately nothing was really changing my own personal situation. My life remained in TOTAL LIMBO. Besides, my own brother Nana had two very obvious and distinct sides of his own coin! A couple of visitors from Shrikant's family had come a few times to see me. Nana, another control freak, always had a very clear warning for me. I was not allowed to talk anything about my own story! He is always an expert in showing off his own colorful achievements! Vijay, Shrikant's very close cousin, had stayed with us in NJ many times over the years before he moved to California. I distinctly remember him bringing up the subject of knives being used by me! He never asked me directly or clearly, exactly what was in his mind? Some very shocking information got revealed later on in the middle of 2017. I was not even allowed to cry! Nana and his wife, my Vahini, had a clear warning for me! As long as I was under their shelter, I was to behave by their family's rules. This side of their coin was never complained about or revealed by me to both of their sons during that time period.

If I was given a choice, if I was in a sound state of mind, then staying with my sister in S.C. or in the vicinity of my brother in California for an extended period of time would have been my last option! I knew better than that! Occasional short pleasure trips would be a different story.

This unexpected detour in my life taught me one of the major Life Lessons, BEGGARS CAN'T BE CHOOSERS! It so happened, my life was being managed by others including my own two sons.

My best friend Prema and her husband Anil had moved to California. I wanted to talk with their lawyer daughter Sheila, if possible. Anil and Prema picked me up. During my stay there, Sheila came to see me. Obviously, she was sorry to hear my story. In fact, she, her brother and my other best friend Alaka's both children, had known us for a much longer period and we had met each other many more times than my own relatives. They all 4 had eventually told me about their observations. Very clearly Shrikant would never miss an opportunity to put me down, or make me feel inferior in front of the spectators!

Sheila suggested me to write down my story in detail as it had happened. Just in case I needed a lawyer in the near future, it would come in handy. I followed her recommendation. I spent hours typing my story on the iPad. Getting the copies printed was no problem at all! Anil didn't have much input but Prema did try to point out the reality. She presented her own clear understanding about the facts of life. "Pratibha, Shrikant's behavior was always like that. Why did you expect anything different after so long? Also Pratibha, you know, always one of the partners is left behind and eventually will have to lead the life as a single person!" Unfortunately it was not comforting enough for my tortured mind!

I was back in Cupertino, California. Here my brother and Vahini were living with Salil, their younger son. He had won the limited custody of his two beautiful daughters. On every alternate day, they were there. I used to play cards with them almost every evening they were there.

February 26, 2017 was Lila's 3rd birthday. Atul wanted my presence during the celebration. I had clearly mentioned that I would prefer not to return to California. New York was where I belonged once I was made to believe 58 Greenwoods in NJ was not for me. Just prior to my return, Shaila called me in California. She had fractured her left wrist. She was going to be home for at least a month and a half. She had welcomed me again to stay with her in New Milford, NJ. After attending Lila's birthday, Atul dropped me at Shaila's house on March 2nd, 2017.

My mother had taught me well. For every unpaid shelter I was accepted, I made sure to compensate them monetarily or otherwise for their hospitality. For me, it was the MUST, but whenever I had been of any financial help to anyone, the only thing I used to say was, I did it because I could do it. I NEVER expected anything in return except the fact that I always wanted everyone to be happy!

Chapter 37: Nothing Seemed Like Working Though—

Without any doubt, the next door kept on opening right from the time when the front doors to my Home Sweet Home were shut off for me for good on Christmas Eve 2015. Even the locks were changed right away. If Shaila had not called after she fractured her left wrist, my one-time student Dr. Koti Nara had plans for me to work hard and sweat in her 100 acres land of winery! After retiring, that had become her passion.

She is the one who had diagnosed my situation right away to be situational depression. I was never a Bipolar. I am positive that this depression was definitely not there when I was forced to get admitted in the Heaven Facility on my birthday. It was that first night when I had lied down for the first time on the brand-new bed in my rented apartment. That time the reality had finally struck me. That was the origin of my Situational Depression.

Again absolutely no words can express how I continued to feel. I always was one of the luckiest in millions to have so many of these outside of the family members and friends there for me. Shaila's extended family had accepted me as one of them. In return, I tried as much as I could to show them my thankfulness. Once in NJ, several of my O.T. Women's Club friends came to visit me. I even tried venturing looking for a place to stay in the Villages of Old Tappan. It was actually one of my future dreams to live there after downsizing 2 years from 2015! I was going to have everything there till my remote future of very old age. I actually felt sorry for myself for being in the situation I was in. When Donna, one of the members of WCOT, also a Realtor, showed me a place there, I actually started having palpitations again! It was impossible for me to think about the end result of feeling all ALONE again! I gave up on that idea for good.

Shaila could have easily accommodated me for a very long time even after she had started working again. Unfortunately, with all the so-called therapeutic medications, my mental situation remained status co! She couldn't take the chance of leaving me alone the whole day while she was eventually at work.

While in California, on Valentine's Day, February 14, 2017, I had written a note for Shrikant. Because of the restraining orders, I had included that note in the email for my two sons. "please let your father know that I want to go back to him more as a true friend than anything else. Upon my return from the trip to Egypt, I had spontaneously hugged him telling him that I had truly missed him. He was the No.1 member of the DREAM of my intact family of 10. I have only one life to live which is extremely lonely and I have a strong desire to hold on to someone and that someone is nobody except him. My only request to him is to give it a sincere thought to make this Journey of Life happier mainly for the sake of our four beautiful grandchildren, two wonderful sons and the love of their lives with their own families including. Thank you!"

Not sure if my children showed that note to their father. Later on, in fact a point came when I had finally decided to defy the law. None of the lawyers his or mine were lawful in many ways. I started sending him messages through WhatsApp and emails. Absolutely nothing had helped. I finally gave up.

When I returned back to Brookdale Battery Park in April of 2017, after an absence of about 9 months, I was offered the same room at Apt 606. It was considered the Respite Facility. I started seeing a psychologist in my building named Dr. Krohn and a psychiatrist named Dr. Yemins in Mid Manhattan. During the summer, I went to Alaska with Shaila. She had arranged such trips before through the travel agency. Definitely, it was supposed to be a very good change. But still the wounded mind of mine won't give up being sad. In the sightseeing bus, I preferred sitting at the back seat so that no one saw me sobbing!

During the summer of 2017, my cousin had come from India to visit her daughter in NJ. She apparently was trying to contact me. Finally, Rajesh, her son-in-law contacted my husband. Shrikant did not know my whereabouts but did go to see him in his office. There during lunch hour, Rajesh heard something totally unexpected. Shrikant told him that Pratibha had stabbed him in the abdomen on Christmas Eve, 2015! Somehow my cousin got my contact information from my brother in California. Their family of 4 came to visit me at Brookdale in August 2017. That was the first time and then several times afterwards from different sources, I became aware of the pathological lies my dear husband was spreading towards as many people or friends as he could. This included his multiple phone calls and hours of conversation with multiple of my friends from Florida, Delaware, England, California, and Texas all over.

Being a perfect and seasoned pathological manipulator, he knew though very well whom not to tell. He never told such things to my children and their wives or anyone whom I may be in touch with. This was too obvious because there was no such thing as even a remote occurrence. And because Anand, our older son had never heard it from his father himself, he didn't want to confront him. It took me a long to understand his rationale! As it turned out, Shrikant was not even consistent in spreading those rumors. Apparently, he was allegedly stabbed at different locations of his body! In one instance, he was bleeding so profusely that he ended up in ER and didn't even know what happened to his wife!

This was the first time I decided to notify one of his very close relatives, his youngest aunt in India. Over the years, we had met her several times including at our place in the USA. I just needed someone to understand the whole situation, including in Shrikant's own words. I hit the dead end again.

I really wanted to end my life. I wanted to die with dignity. I googled and wrote to the appropriate person in charge. They denied saying just by suggesting to me, they would be potentially responsible if I finally succeeded in ending my life. I pleaded with my children and their wives to take me to Switzerland, where Death with Dignity is practiced. No one was ready.

More the dose of the antidepressant increased by Dr. Yemins, the more I was getting desperate to die. The only one thing I dreaded was, if I don't succeed, then again possibly, I would go back to the Heaven Facility. I imagined a few options. If I just carried a fake gun and kept running on the West Side Highway, either the police will shoot me or will get killed in the traffic. Another convenient place I thought of several times was going to a relatively remote place on the Hudson River in the dark hours. I would walk there, imagining the perfect spot to jump from. Nothing became a reality. I had failed one time. While receiving those ECTs in that Heaven Facility, at least there was one favorable outcome. On May Friday the 13, 2016, my (The Defendant's) motion to be terminated from ADV was granted by the Hon. Judge! Friday the 13th was not so bad after all! This time I really wanted to be successful in ending my life.

Finally, I came up with one more plan. Somewhat similar to before but definitely I had to swallow many more of those pills than last time. I had only 1 Tylenol # 3 left. As per plan, at night I sat in the tub after swallowing the pills. I had a kitchen knife. I tried several times but for whatever reason, I just couldn't get to the radial artery of the right wrist! With all the pills on board, I guess I fell asleep.

Next thing, I woke up to throw up all the stomach contents. So that they don't have to clean the blood all over the carpet, that was the reason I sat in the tub even though it was not comfortable. No luck again! I had no choice but to clean up after myself and go to bed and continue sleeping. This being in a Senior living facility, they have some kind of monitoring. Some time the next day, there was a knock on the door. Because I was not in a position to get up from the bed, it was Alison who came into the room using the master key. I am just a bit tired, that is the only thing I said.

Obviously, I had no intention of telling this to my children. One of the best thing ending up in this facility was I had the most beautiful company of my two little grandchildren, Khelan and Lila. Almost every evening, Farah, their nanny will make sure that they both spend time with Aaji. Anisha, and Kira had the opportunity to spend time with me several times at 58 Greenwoods. They both did crafts with me to their heart's content. Both the little ones did do crafts with their Aaji as much as possible. At night I would go to the little ones' apartment, many times had dinner and then will be reading them the books. The most favorite books for both of them were from "Ramayana."

When I had arrived in NY back in February, I wanted to take some actions with the help of my children so that I could go back to my home. I always believed that it would have taken care of all that "Situational Depression." Unfortunately, the general consensus of my 4 loved ones was, I needed to get SETTLED before taking any actions. Any legal action was rightly to be too lengthy and unpredictable. Little did I know!

My mental depression got obviously too worse, every evening in front of my Atul and Rina, after the kids went to bed, I would start crying. I just couldn't help it. Keeping a 24/7 Aide was absolutely No for me. Finally, Atul called Dr. Yemins. For the meeting, for the first time, Anand was able to make it.

"Sue, I think you should file for divorce!" To this, Anand said, "Dr. Yemins, are you sure?" His answer was that in any case, I was going to be miserable. At least Shrikant will know that his wife can make her own decisions.

With the help of Atul, we arranged a conference call between Silvana, Atul and myself. I retained her as my Divorce Lawyer and filed for divorce, I think on November 19, 2017. Papers were served to Shrikant when he ignored Silvana's letter to think about reconciliation. Silvana was recommended by the president of WCOT. Pamela's lawyer husband had known her.

I think I spent one more Thanksgiving in Indiana with Atul's in-laws and went back to California by December of 2017.

Chapter 38: Scene IV, Act II

This time in California, Salil arranged a trip for Christmas vacation, my brother Vahini, Salil's 2 daughters and myself. I think I was in much better shape with the same amount of medications. Nana was planning his trip to India during the month of February and March 2018. We had to be back before my court date. I was really not keen on joining him and his wife during their trip to India. But didn't want to be in NY during winter either. In retrospect, it turned out to be a good decision to join them. I was able to meet my cousin/ real brother, Sharad Dada. He did talk some sense that I think was most needed verbal spanking! Also I needed to be in touch with my lawyer, Silvana through emails. Otherwise, I mostly remained in my Cocoon.

In preparation for the first meeting with Silvana, I wrote a very lengthy email to her from India in February 2018. It explained why my case may not be anything but normal. If she doesn't inform Shrikant's lawyer in advance that his client is suffering from a complex personality disorder and doesn't take necessary actions, this case will NEVER END. I provided her the proof of June 1, 2010 incident when police had arrested my husband. I thought Silvana will use her proper judgment.

On the contrary, the case got dragged on and on and on...which the reader will come to know later.

Overall, I was much more upbeat than last more than 2 years. Vahini was undergoing some major dental work in Pune, India. So, my brother and myself flew back to California as planned. Just before we departed, one totally upsetting incident had taken place which I was made aware of.

Another totally shocking incident took place at the San Francisco Airport. At the customs area, the machine denied me reentry in my country of citizenship when I scanned the passport! There was actually a Cross mark!

I was denied reentry in my country of citizenship.

The customs officer, looked at his screen and was reading something for a very long time! Obviously I was not able to see it. My brain, not so bad in imagination, got it right away! The officer asked me if there was any incident at home etc. I didn't miss a single moment and started crying uncontrollably and loudly. My brother was in another line and had already finished the reentry requirements. He watched me being escorted to the Customs Office. I continued crying while sitting on the bench till my term came. The officer checked everything, marked OK and I finally joined my brother. His older son, Samir had come to pick us up. While in the car, I finally started crying again, talking in between. While in Pune, during one discussion, Nana debated with someone in his own defense, "Anyway, Pratibha had tried to murder her husband, Shrikant!!!"

Can anyone imagine witnessing two very harsh blows both at the same time? I actually had no desire to go back to his Son's apartment. I wanted out. I called a couple of friends including Prema, my best friend. I was hoping for her to pick me up ASAP. Of course it was not practical. I had no choice but to take a deep breath and think of another alternative.

While lying in bed at night, I did some serious thinking! Vahini had not come back. I still had about 10 days before I went back to NY. I told myself it was going to be my duty to feed everyone including Nana, Salil and his two daughters when they stayed with him on alternate days. I made peace with my rebellious self and indirectly with my brother. The next morning, I took charge of the kitchen. It was not difficult at all to find the whereabouts of all the Indian ingredients for cooking.

Everyone was happy. Both the girls loved tasty food. I got a chance to show off my culinary skills. Finally I had found some purpose in my life.

Sometime by the end of March 2018, I was back in NY. Again the same Apt 606 was waiting for me! How strange. Someone had used this respite facility in my absence. It was again made available to me. Am I not the lucky one!?

Chapter 39: There Is a Myth About All Lawmakers Being Lawful!

There was an old retired lawyer named Dorothy in my building. I had known her since 2016. We used to have dinner together for a very long time. "Judiciary department is one of the most corrupt departments!" she had said. "Sue, yes, you can represent yourself in the court for the restraining orders to be removed. But make sure that the Judge is the right one! Only 1 out of 7 are the good ones!" Now can anyone tell me how I was supposed to know whom and how to choose one as my judge!? I assure the reader that this statement is not applicable to each and everyone.

I had retained Silvana as my divorce lawyer on September 18, 2017. Divorce papers were served to Shrikant in November 2017.

Total Email Paperwork after Filing for Divorce in November 2017

Her contract clearly said that "The law firm will represent your interests in the matrimonial dispute. The client must provide full and accurate information." Not only this lawyer but each and everyone I dealt with, especially the Forensic Accountant, paragraph after paragraph were the details regarding the payment for the services. This was in their printed application forms.

Before the first court date on April 12 of 2018, one of my very good friends, Olivia came with me to see Silvana. Olivia was willing to submit 200 signatures from our town of Old Tappan regarding my character. Apparently, it was not going to be useful. I provided in person, a copy of the June 1, 2010, Shrikant's arrest material. I gave her a copy of what I had written according to Sheila's instructions in California. I repeatedly told her that my case was not a normal case and that my husband had a major personality disorder which includes pathological lies. And if she doesn't warn Mr. Galler, Shrikant's divorce lawyer, this case will never end. Silvana told me that she would read it and won't charge me for that!

The first court date was on April 12, 2018, Jyoti, my daughter-in-law was there with me for support. The first thing Silvana told me was about Mr. Galler mentioning to her regarding his client's repeated remarks. Shrikant was surprised that Suhasini had filed for divorce!

As I entered the courtroom, Shrikant was already seated as per the restraining orders. When I looked at the back of his partly bald head, I heard a soft whisper in my right ear. "Pratibha, why are you wasting your life for this man? He is devoid of any feelings for an intact family. Your children's definition of family may be different. Wake up, take control of yourself and your destiny!" It was my mother, my Angel had whispered in my ear. Once more maybe for the 101st time, she had come to my rescue.

The next date in the court was scheduled for July 19, 2018. We were to provide ALL the financial and any other assets information. The independent appraisal of the 5 rentals and our home was ordered and completed. Shrikant not only didn't provide complete information but adopted delaying tactics. Before our next appearance in the court for supposedly "FINAL SETTLEMENT" I wrote to Silvana, "I am hoping and pray for peaceful and complete closure on October 17, 2018." It got postponed till the next date December 6, 2018 because of Shrikant's request based upon pathological lies, but it was accepted by Silvana.

On November 5, 2018, Silvana wrote to me, "We are moving to the conclusion soon, as the court will not allow the case to go on for much longer after January."

On November 6, 2018, I wrote to Silvana, "I do have the sincere desire to get rid of the Restraining Orders only for emotional purposes. I have the constant feeling of being imprisoned even being outside of the prison."

On November 19, 2018, Silvana wrote, "The goal is to maximize what you can obtain without spending money on legal fees unnecessarily(?)!

Mediation was arranged, got postponed till January 29, 2019. This was because of Shrikant's alleged sickness. I think by now the lawyers from both parties had realized whom they were dealing with. So the two attempts at mediation before the final judgment NEVER took place. Finally, the Intensive Settlement Conference took place on February 7, 2019. Outside the courtroom, both lawyers had a lengthy and heated conversation with Shrikant. I was not allowed to hear due to restraining orders. No one had accompanied me in the court that day.

Totally unexpected, on February 7, 2019, in the courtroom, we were actually declared "Divorced!" Verbally. The Hon. Judge made that announcement! I had absolutely no other feelings except being shocked! But still was definitely in complete control over my mind. In the end, the Judge asked if anyone wanted to say anything. I did raise my hand halfway. The Judge noticed it. All 4 of us stood up. With the permission of my Divorce Lawyer, Silvana, I turned myself in the direction of Shrikant, and I said to him, "Shrikant, I want to thank you for everything you've done for me!" I really didn't care what anyone else in that courtroom thought. I felt good about myself and my presence of mind, and I had meant it all from the bottom of my heart. There was ZERO PRETENSE.

The terms of the divorce settlement were such that it was very obvious to me that my lawyer Silvana had not acted in my interests at all. She had not given special consideration to my request. She had indirectly catered to the opposing party, my now EX! Right from the beginning, Shrikant himself had prepared a spreadsheet and had very clearly divided the bank accounts and the appraisal values of all 6 houses (rentals and our home) 50% each. Except, he had not revealed all of his own bank accounts and more importantly, he didn't correct the appraisal values to the independent assessment. When he realized the newly assessed values were more, he immediately came up with the pathological lie of tax implications! Given the full account of his behavior well in advance and requesting Mr. Galler to kind of forcing him to stick to his own proposal with some changes would have saved so much time, money, and emotional meltdown and it would have been eventually much better for him to move on! Shrikant's behavior was so obvious, they both together could have easily convinced the Judge. Anyway nothing like that happened.

This is how I learned my major LIFE LESSON. The lawyers of opposite parties are NOT enemies of each other. They both engage in communication and CHOOSE THE LEAST RESISTANT PATH! They obviously knew that Shrikant was wrong but it was extremely difficult to deal with. Just like my chairman, Dr. Bizzari and multiple others over the years including my husband, my so-called some family members and friends, they knew it all. They all knew that it was not difficult to handle Mrs. Suhasini (Pratibha, Sue) Joshi.

According to the settlement that day, I was to own 2 of the rentals, 2 would be by Shrikant, the remaining one rental and our house would be sold ASAP and money would be divided equally along with the other assets especially the bank accounts.

This is the time for the first time even Anand got involved. Atul had been in the loop from the beginning. On March, 2, 2019, Atul wrote to Silvana, "My mother is not in a position to take over the ownership of those 2 rentals and to manage them." There were multiple back-and-forth email exchanges going on between Anand, Atul, and Silvana on just this real estate deal. On March 26, 2019, in the court, outside the courtroom, for the first time, I met Silvana's assistant, Danielle Cardone. I was excluded. Not too far from me, there was a heated conversation going on between Shrikant, Mr. Galler, Danielle and Atul. Mainly it was my husband. Now he, who himself had proposed the deal, refused to cooperate in owning all the rentals in exchange for 1/2 of the appraised values. Shrikant was shouting at Atul, telling him to get out of the court! It actually brought Atul to tears. I could hear everything but just couldn't do anything again because of the restraining orders. I did say something loudly enough that they could hear from 4 screens and tables away. I was given a warning by Danielle against repeating it again. I knew at that time my husband was severely mentally disturbed. While driving me back, Atul reminded me again at least for the 2nd time, that he had to take time off for me!

The most important issue of concern for me as I had repeatedly said before was that of the rental properties. I was really petrified by the thought of owning and managing them. I proposed to both my children they could own those two just by providing $1 for each property to change the title on the Deed. They both declined. I suggested through my lawyer to let Shrikant have both of them on top of the 50% of the rest of the division of the assets. Both the lawyers thought that I was crazy! Finally after multiple back and forths, I wrote to my lawyer, yes, I will accept that term of the deal. This was not for money but mainly to show my children and my husband that I was accepting the challenge. My lawyer provided me with a wonderful manager named Fred, who happened to be from Old Tappan.

On March 29, 2019, we both voluntarily entered the agreement, signed the PSA and were officially divorced just like that! Even on the morning of March 29, I had very lengthy discussions and disagreements with Danielle and finally, I had literally given up and then signed the PSA. (Property settlement agreement). There was the signature of both of us, both the attorneys, the Hon. Judge, with the gold seal!

March 29 happens to be Atul and Rina's wedding anniversary too! Without ever entering both of those rentals in almost 30 years of being the co-owner, both the properties were sold with the help of Fred and Pinna, whom I had known before. I had met her then against the wishes of Shrikant. Before December 31, 2019, one major headache and also a major factor accountable for sleepless nights in the past was taken care of. There was no urgency in informing my children.

Follow-up of the very PSA that we had both willingly signed was another issue! I was not allowed to enter the house to remove my belongings. It was Atul who had volunteered. I gave him a very simple list, not too much at all. I even alerted my whole group of friends from WCOT, to go with Atul and remove as many beautifully created and repurposed pieces of art of mine as they could. The major hurdle for both my sons again was the total noncompliance of Shrikant. My belongings needed to be removed before the house could be put on the market! We had only 1 month to sort it out! It is sickening to keep telling about the ordeal and real resistance by the control freak Mr. Shrikant Joshi.

The first thing Shrikant did after we got divorced was that he fired his divorce lawyer, Mr. Galler. He started representing himself. The story is literally ENDLESS! His letters to Danielle with regular and certified mail, clearly showed that he is totally mentally sick and totally out of reality. But no one could do anything! He was literally possessed by his Type 2 personality!

On May 7, 2019, Atul wrote to Silvana and Danielle, "It would be accurate to say that his dad has been found to have many ways to throw sand in the gears but I can't think of a way to make that a productive comment! It has become very difficult for me and my brother to get through to him. What next do you want my mother to do?"

By May 2019 beginning, I had repeatedly told Danielle that we must bring him to court ASAP. Finally on February 21, 2020, we entered the court for the second time. One obvious delay tactic was he hired another divorce lawyer named Marilyn. In court, we both signed another consent order. He obviously looked both mentally and physically sick in the courtroom that day. Everyone including the Judge had obviously noticed that my ex was lying. They did nothing significant except the Judge added one major hurdle! He appointed Ms. Carleen Gaskin as a forensic accountant to look over and solve the problem. Shrikant was told to pay her retainer fees. He also appointed a Lawyer In Fact, Mr. Landel to take over if there is resistance from Shrikant in signing the papers.

The Hon. Judge actually lied to me that day. He said ours was the first couple to come back to the Judge for the second time after signing the PSA in the last 13 years since he has been on the bench! Later I confirmed it was a big fat Lie!

As any human being can do, I did thank Shrikant's new lawyer Marilyn for representing him! The whole atmosphere was pathetic!

I was finally allowed to enter my house on March 6th and 13th, 2020. Many friends came along with me besides Drew Craft, the police officer I was supposed to pay while he was monitoring my every move and the movers that he arranged for me. The scene inside the house was SHOCKING beyond anyone can imagine! Only the pictures can be the witness!

Atul and Anand came each on one of the two days. They came mainly to remove their own belongings. I had mentioned to them that I had enough help. They didn't have to waste time for me.

Love, Laugh, Dream & Inspire frame was displaced from the foyer and was laying in the pile of garbage!

By the weekend of March 14&15, 2020, my apartment #606 at Brookdale, Battery Park got decorated with as many belongings as I was able to salvage from my beautiful home sweet home at 58 Greenwoods. My umbilical cord attached to that house of mine over 31 years was finally cut off for good. The worst thing that happened was I had to leave all of my stained glass supplies there to be thrown in the garbage along with so many more beautiful things scattered all over the house.

Right after that the COVID PANDEMIC hit! In the senior building where I live, we were quarantined! I believe that I definitely had Covid related abdominal symptoms. Later that year, during my doctor's visit, antibody testing came positive. During that quarantine period, my creativity got a boost! I created 104 different gifts and made a card for each individual. They all were working 24/7 to keep us healthy and happy. Each individual from top to bottom got Thank You note and a gift.

Payments to my divorce lawyers continued. The monthly bills started increasing up to now $10,000.00 or more. Finally, the Google Search I was forced to do had exposed the TRUTH!

On August 23, 2020, I read in Google Search that my lawyer's Firm is known as "billing machines." The advice given was not to sign their retainer agreement, instead take it back with you! It also said the following— There is a site where Judges are "Judged!" My lawyer's firm is a cornerstone of this racket where abusive judges extract money from families to enrich their lawyer friends like her. Their basic playbook is to milk you over 12 months. You are hiring this firm to sell you out in the judge's chambers to let the judge know how best to cause the break up of your family! This review was the revised one in June,13,2020. It did have some more to shed light on.

Finally I had it!!! The amount of total bills paid was about $195,468.00. The only thing that got resolved for me was the two rentals forced on me to own got sold with the help of the Firm's real estate attorney. Silvana herself did nothing significant except promising me and submitting the total hours spent on her client! I think I was charged $475/ hour.

From here on, again I ended up handling everything by myself. I could totally understand. The children had absolutely no more time to waste. By now I think they had given up on both of us, their parents. It was going to be a really very long road ahead, the duration unknown to me. I am writing this chapter now on January 22, 2023, Sunday night. The assets division is still not complete. It is almost 4 years since we have been divorced. But unfortunately the reality has set in, and I am afraid for good. Just two months ago, Shrikant's very close cousin and his wife came to visit him from Chicago for the first time after 7 years. From the pictures and the video they shared, the mental and physical condition is just shocking! The Alter Personality has taken over for good. I sincerely hope I am wrong. I did contact the Old Tappan Police, the social services chief and the adult protective services. They assured me that Anand was aware of the situation. Not that I can do anything anyway. My restraining orders are still in effect.

Chapter 40: Hoping To Finish Act II and Move On To…

It is simply unimaginable for anyone to comprehend the ordeal involved in completing even a minor aspect of the PSA agreement. Eventually, in accordance with my ex-partner's unreasonable demands, I had to remove my belongings from the property at 58 Greenwoods. This was supposed to be done within a month of signing the PSA on April 30, 2019, and exclusively through Atul. However, it took almost a year to complete.

In addition to this, there were several other matters that required attention. Anticipating a lack of cooperation, I prioritized the significant task of dividing our bank accounts. My previous divorce attorney, Steve, whom I had hired for restraining orders, had advised me to separate our funds as early as 2016 due to his distrust of my husband. By mid-August 2019, I had successfully handled most of the accounts, with the exception of one major joint account. Unfortunately, dealing with Carleen, the forensic accountant, proved to be another hassle! She was appointed by the Judge, and it was not possible to refuse her services! Interestingly with all the loopholes in the law system, the circle of MUST communicate with widened. This meant the number of internal communications between them and my divorce lawyer, Silvana increased, reflecting that the amount of money billed to me per month also increased. My lawyers- Carleen- myself- Shrikant's lawyer- Shrikant, and the two secretaries of the two lawyers. Shrikant had already fired his Attorney #2, and Rick # 3 was in the picture. I doubt very much if Mr. Rick got to see his client at all! Also, it is hard to believe that Rick made an attempt to get familiar with the case by getting input from Marilyn, Shrikant's previous counsel. I did get to see Rick, though, in one of the zoom meetings with the Judge! To this, they then joined two realtors, Mr. Cortez and Paula. One was for the remaining rental to be sold and money divided, which was thankfully sold eventually. Paula's ordeal with Shrikant was such that finally, she emailed all the parties involved that because she was being harassed by my ex, and if he didn't stop, she was to have restraining orders against him! Apparently this is because Shrikant had gone to the police with the complaint against Paula.

One more thing of the recent past was on February 7, 2020, Shrikant filed a complaint with the Old Tappan Police that his house was burglarized! I am 99.99% sure it was not true at all. His brilliant psychopath mind had come up with multiple ideas for the plot because he wanted to renovate the house to 'Stage it up' before it goes on the market! Nothing materialized for him. The police did their usual search but were unsuccessful in finding any evidence that he was hoping to claim with the insurance. That house belonged to me also, so naturally I ended up being in touch with the OT Police through back-and-forth emails.

In the meantime, this Carleen, the forensic accountant, came up with her brilliant idea. With communication between her and two lawyers, they decided to send about 28 to 30 subpoenas to all our banks, his, mine and ours! Her complaint was both Shrikant and myself were not cooperative! As far as I knew, whatever was required of me, including detailed and accurate calculations of ALL THE ASSETS, I had provided multiple times. Apparently it was not enough. My lawyers, Silvana and her associate Danielle NEVER supported me. Instead, they all agreed it was the quickest way to solve the matrimonial dispute! A minimum of 700-800 or maybe over 1,000 papers got printed and were sent to me to go through! I did come across 3 accounts that Shrikant had not previously reported!

On July 16, 2020, a total of 27 subpoenas were sent to the banks. The two lawyers on both sides divided the required task! To me it was nonsense, delaying tactics and money rip-off! The Judge said on February 21, 2020, that he was against wasting time and money. He had even criticized Shrikant in the court for hiding behind the curtain, giving the excuse of those Restraining Orders. In fact this was actually the No.1 defense mechanism for my own lawyer, Silvana! And many other parties involved in our case used the same excuse of myself bound by restraining orders!

Just to let the reader know, finally with multiple email correspondences and with my new set of lawyers retained as my counsel, by the end of 2022, Carleen's discovery process was completed almost 3 years after she was appointed on February 21, 2020. Because the report was acceptable to what I was expecting by August 2019, I decided to go with the flow! It was just recently presented by my divorce lawyer Brian to the current Hon. Judge at Hackensack Court. The motion was OKAYed by the Judge. And hopefully sometime this year, 2023, the division of assets will be complete!

With the help of the original real estate lawyer Andrew Naideck, the 5th joint rental was sold and money got divided. Mr. Cortez was the realtor, and Mr. Mills was Shrikant's real estate attorney. For the final division of assets and for the home at 58, Greenwoods, my then-newly retained Divorce attorney, Brian Shea, and Andrew Bolson, the real estate attorney, were involved. For my EX, Rick remained the divorce lawyer and Mr. Mills the real estate lawyer. Then once the contract was signed, Justin, the buyer's attorney came into the picture!

The reason I include all these names is that, FINALLY, I had decided to defy the law. Very good chance that I may forget someone's name but eventually, I started including each of my eX's and my lawyers including my ex himself in the email correspondence. My behavior was totally against the law in normal terms but I had NOTHING TO DO WITH THE LAWLESS LAW! At one point, I included all the past lawyers of Shrikant also. I had only one question for all of them, this was fully knowing that no one was going to reply. My question to all of them was, if the unique and complex nature of my case was made known to them, would their conscience have agreed that the outcome may have been different and better? The direct or indirect feet-dragging tactics continued even when I was warning all of them that maybe my ex was on the verge of a mental breakdown. I believe this lawless law system was responsible for the present irreversible alter-personality transformation of my ex.

Rob Landel, the attorney in fact appointed by the Judge, did nothing. He was actually afraid of my EX'S threats.

After the divorce was completed, on May 24, 2019, I requested Silvana to bring my ex back to court. Didn't happen. On April 17, 2019, she told me that including Shrikant's attorney, no one believed in my EX'S nonsense excuses. I asked her 3 questions very clearly, 1) if I had no money, what would she have done? 2) did her knowledge regarding our assets influence her decisions? & 3) if she was in my shoes, what action would she have taken? Her answer was, "I realize that this is unfair but this is the way the system is set up! It is not very good at getting compliance quickly. Other than simply walking away from what you are required to get, there is no other way to compel compliance from a recalcitrant litigant who ignores the law! But we are almost there!" She also said that they are all equally frustrated but not because of me, "You are a lovely client!" This is actually her writing!

Finally, by August 31, 2020, I wrote an email to Silvana and included each and everyone I could think of in CC, telling her that her advice was well received and that I do not need her services anymore. Her firm was literally sucking thousands of dollars with ZERO outcome!

I have mentioned about my Google search in the last chapter. "Their company is known as Billing Machines!" There was criticism about some of the abusive Judges from Hackensack who aid their lawyer friends by extorting money from the families to enrich them! This is what my old lawyer friend Dorothy had meant. She had told me to find the correct judge! I requested Andrew Naideck to finish his real estate deal regarding 58 Greenwoods. Eventually Silvana withdrew his name also from not serving me as a real estate attorney. Between all those involved in the deal regarding the sale of 58 Greenwoods, all came to a decision, and there was no sense in bleeding my money anymore. The house was under actual contract. We both had signed it. But Shrikant kept convincing the whistleblower that he had no intention of selling the house.

He wanted this defiant Suhasini to suffer! He had many more tricks up his sleeves to achieve that goal of his pathological mind. Strangely, no one dared to bring him to court. Shrikant had even harassed the Old Tappan librarian. She had contacted me. I was actually willing to back all of them up. This is not because I wanted my ex to be punished for his actions. I really wanted him to get treated for the genetic complex personality disorder he was suffering from. One of the best clinical psychiatrist friends of mine named Padma had known him and had diagnosed him accurately. There is treatment available but he needed to be kind of forced to get the treatment using proper psychotropic medications. Nothing like that happened.

I knew for sure that if my children really wanted to avert the situation, it was possible. My best friend from first grade had a very similar mental illness. It was her Dr. son, Dr. Husband and lawyer daughter, they all had discussed the alternative. They actually brought her to court, proved her to be invalid to make any decisions, and forced her to take the proper medications. Just last year, I visited her in Chicago. Her Dr. husband is back with her. They actually remarried!

Being one of my best childhood friends, I stayed with her in 2003 for a week. I had firsthand witnessed her dissociative behavior at that time and was actually scared of the way she was behaving at that time. It was her Dr. son from Boston who had told me on the phone that theirs was the most dysfunctional family known to him! I had heard that word for the first time that day. Again, the reason why I am going into details is that the same Dr. son of my friend had diagnosed my EX'S condition right away. This was last year when Shrikant called him out of the blue after almost 22 years! Within 5 minutes of conversation with my EX, he knew that something was drastically wrong and had actually called the police on his own to visit my EX!

Anyway, such is the story of me and my simple dream of an INTACT FAMILY OF 10! The beautiful home now belongs to Shrikant. By the end of 2020, he had declared victory over me. He had mentioned to my whistleblower that he hopes that Suhasini has finally learned the lesson!? I still don't know what lesson he was trying to teach me. The only thing I can think of, I guess, I should have never crossed him or defied his SUPEREGO, I should have just obeyed and accepted his superiority!?

This is my Knitting and Chrochet Group for last about 7 years. We meet every Thursday afternoon. These friends have first hand witnessed my Uplifting Progress since 2017.

Now I commute from Manhattan to meet my friends from Woman's Club Of Old Tappan (WCOT). I had joined this club in 2003 right after my retirement.

Closing Chapter

"Act II is finally over!" I may have said that. But it is so only as far as the ongoing legal issues are concerned past Christmas Eve of 2015. In every other sense, I had already moved on in a very positive way. The way the description of my book goes is my story has turned out to be the most compelling, seemingly never-ending one! Given the opportunity, volumes can get written! The huge Treasure of Life Experiences that have been gathered so far during my life journey still remain sealed.

Some totally unexpected, beautiful but at the same time emotionally devastating circumstances had taken place in the year 2022. Being creative, I was able to complete my own picture of being in that La La Land of dreams since the second year of medical school. Finally, I had come to realize now after so many years that there always must have been the presence of a Divine figure of beautiful Lord Krishna tucked somewhere deep in my mind in a tiny cute box. The presence was unknown to me for so long! Now that I am convinced about its existence, I can converse with that figure, my own conscience, my own friend, my own God, any time and at my own will. Interestingly the repercussions of this new discovery continue to amaze me and the radiant smile on my face continues to be the witness!

Finally, by October end of 2017, Dr. Yemins, my psychiatrist, had suggested that I should file for divorce. I had done that. On February

7, 2018, I entered the courtroom crying but had exited it smiling. Some miracle had taken place in that courtroom. My Angel, my mother had given me the "संदेश"! She had told me to move on. She had explained to me why so.

Now I could feel the difference in my own thought process. Dr. Yemins had continued prescribing the psychotropic medications but had decided on his own to slowly decrease the dosage. In May 2018, I had gone to Costa Rica with Shaila. This time I thoroughly enjoyed it. In the summer of 2018, I went to Ireland with Anand and his family. After spending 2-3 days in their company, I took one of a kind tour of Ireland by myself. Anand had arranged it with Tauck Tours. What I had realized over the years was there was absolutely no need, no desire for me to be exposed to the luxurious lifestyle on a daily basis. But at the same time, I had no problem indulging the same for a week or so when I got to join the sightseeing tours. They were all arranged by someone for me as per my request, as per my strong desire (OCD).

We even celebrated "Diwali" the Festival of Lights at the beginning of November 2018 and then the early Thanksgiving in the same month of that year. There was a gap of at least 4 years that I recall. My loved ones tried convincing me to accept this as our new "Whole Family!" It was impossible for me to accept that concept as It was always going to be 10 minus one! Shrikant was the one who had helped me to create this family. My children, born in America may never understand what it meant to me. In early December of 2018, I went to Iceland with a group of friends.

And another memorable trip to North India took place in late December 2018. It was most wonderfully arranged by Jyoti, our older daughter-in-law. I was with my two granddaughters as well as Anand, Jyoti and her parents. On Christmas Eve, 2018, in the company of all these loved ones, in a five-star hotel in Jaipur, I enjoyed not only one but two glasses of "Cosmopolitan!" Didn't even know what the heck I was drinking! But the fact was, I didn't want anyone to notice that I was actually missing Shrikant, who was soon going to be my ex! The memory of Christmas Eve, 2015 for me will exit only when my soul enters another world.

On March 29, 2019, we had both signed the PSA agreement and were declared divorced. The legal process had continued as I said till after I came back from India on February 23rd of this year 2023. Obviously, by now, my derailed life train from June 1st 2010, was brought back on the right tracks. Especially after my homelessness on Christmas Eve 2015, I was alive only because of the Virtual Life Support. Without any doubt, all my loved ones had kept me alive by their tireless efforts. Now I was ready to be weaned off gradually from that support. By middle of 2019, Dr. Yemins decided that I didn't need the support of those psychotropic drugs anymore. In my final visit to him, I did ask him a straightforward question. "Dr. Yemins, do you really believe that the medications worked?" He understood what I meant. "At least the medications brought the positive thoughts to your mind!" Looks like he had forgotten, just a year an half ago, I had attempted suicide for the second time as he was increasing the dose of those antidepressants. I thanked him, paid the last bill and left his office near Bryant Park.

By then I had already started attending the social gatherings, both Indian as well as those with my friends at the Woman's Club of Old Tappan. Again I joined Shaila for the Australia- New Zealand trip in November of 2019. On the way there, I made sure to celebrate the return of my usual positive energy with my nephews and their families including my brother and Vahini in California. Eventually, by the end of October 2022, I confirmed and decided to close one of the major chapters with my own brother and his control freak behavior. I had it by then. His behavior had made me loose the peace of mind several times before. The time had come to act on it for good, forever.

In January of 2020, I had made one more trip to India. This medical reunion after 54 years of joining the medical school was the second one and that also after being divorced. I thoroughly enjoyed this one. During our 25th reunion, I became very ill and was not able to enjoy it at all. The best thing that happened during the second reunion was I got connected to the BJMC WhatsApp group. Then during Covid for the next almost 1&1/2 years, my legal work was only via emails or Zoom. My precious gift of creativity was the key factor in the continuation of a positive attitude for myself as well as for those seniors in my building. Due to Covid, I was unable to see my children and their families. For me, it was necessary to make sure and they all four did assure me. It was good to hear that my ongoing saga of last almost 10 years had not created major turmoil in their own families. My desire always will be that they continue to remain as intact families. It was never intended to, but when I had first approached all 4 of them after June 1, 2010, I had ended up taking too much of their time for me in those 10 years.

Till the end of February 2022, I was busy sorting out the best way to simplify my life further. After all, this had been my desire from as early as the age of 40! If I get a call from Heaven or Hell, I should be ready with just a change of clothes and all of my mother's letters to me! The move from a 6 bedroom house on a one-acre property to a small, fully furnished one-bedroom apartment at Brookdale Battery Park had already simplified my life significantly.

Now I was freed from all the responsibilities towards my ex. Besides, for the last 49 years, there was ZERO presence or entrance to my mind of any "Man" other than my now ex. From the Honeymoon night of December 31st, 1972, my life, my destiny had already taken the path of no return. My job was just to follow whatever was expected of me by my now ex as assigned by that same Destiny. The lust, having children, loving them and the families they both created, this was the job assigned to me. My job as a doctor was to work hard and make money. My art of creating something out of nothing and making wonderful friendships was also part of that same destiny but not inclusive. Basically, my outlook towards the world was very much limited, from within the walls created by these same duties towards my now ex, my job and our children.

For the first time by the end of February of 2022, in a certain way, my mind was exposed to the whole world! This Ken, a widower of my age, speaking my native language, was part of that unknown world. Just those hours and hours of phone conversations had changed my world! Part of his email on March 30, 2022, just 5 days after we first met, had said, "Dear Dreamer, This is also new to me. Let us take one step at a time. I need to tell you something. I did not want the phone call to end!" And then within a week after we first met, he decided to visit me again in my apartment. This time, while leaving, he hugged me and kissed me! "At least accept the fact that you are much better looking than the average!" Truly, this was all new to me! My father had told me that they had bought me by selling the hay! What really did my father mean? "we should meet earlier than later!" This was Ken's text right after he had reached his home that Sunday.

The effect of this newly found feeling on me was too obvious. The glow on my face, the bubbly happiness, and the change in my behavior were witnessed not only by my usual friends in the building but even by those observing me while walking on the streets! One lady actually asked me about my age! Somehow she had noticed that the salt and pepper color of my hair didn't match with my smooth and radiant skin! This new experience had caught me by total surprise, totally unexpected. Ken himself had admitted on the phone that he felt like a 20-year-old boy! I had felt the same way! He had called me a magnet! He promised me to be there for me forever!

For the first time at the age of 74&1/2 years, I had experienced this 3-way attraction towards Ken. 5-10% romantic (that is also age-related like being able to hold hands while walking!), 70-75% emotional and 20% divine, I still refuse to use the word " Love" to describe it. At the same time, I understood what my own children must have felt like at their appropriate age. I had always honored their feelings without experiencing them myself.

And then merely after 17 days, the WhatsApp message came, "Our wavelengths are different!" This had followed by Zero explanation. In the meantime, most of our conversations had changed too. He was mostly complaining about his health constantly and I was encouraging him to consider health as his No.1 priority. His family, his daughter, and his cute little grandson always had to be his first priority. This is what I had suggested to him. Same way, my responsibility was always going to be to my vast family here at Brookdale Battery Park. For me, after the first wave of that crazy "Love" feeling had mostly vanished within less than a week, I was thinking way ahead for my future age beyond 80+. This was when I noticed people started feeling lonely. And maybe just the companionship with this Ken in the future is what I was hoping for.

Anyway, there were a few very important outcomes of this short-lived affair! My bubbly nature has refused to abandon me even now. Ken became the vehicle through which I met my classmate after 55 years and his wife for the first time. Actually, a few more really beautiful friendships got created. This only one incident, the devastation I witnessed, left me being much more strong. Because I was convinced that all of my thoughts and behavior were genuine, I had no problem in discussing this experience with a few of my close friends. They clearly told me falling in love is a dangerous game. Looks like I was not the only one who had experienced this devastation. No wonder so many of these songs in Hindi, Marathi or

English or maybe any other languages unknown to me have this deep, powerful meaning. Now I know why my very good friend's most beautiful daughter had finally given up the dating game. It was too torturous for her vulnerable mind.

Recently my astrologer had noticed this change in me after 8 years of first seeing him. I had to confess that yes, for whatever reason, a few more pieces of evidence of this "Pheromones" phenomenon have been experienced! His recent advice to me was something that I have decided to follow. " Remain Neutral" is what he had suggested.

Because I have found my own friendship within myself in as pure form as it could be, I am able to share this friendship with those who come or may continue to come in my picture on their own. Being able to put myself in their shoes is something that helps me to understand them and then again, I end up feeling this strong desire to be there for them. This is only if they approach me on their own. There is absolutely no compulsion. This feeling is the same for both sexes, with maybe a slight + with the opposite one!! And again, there is something else! Again my own OCD tries to take over. I have this strong urge to try to peep into that person's personality!

I have reluctantly accepted my defeat of losing my ONLY DREAM of an intact family of 10. Finally, I have made peace with my rebellious mind regarding it. The Destiny has offered me this BIG family at Brookdale Battery Park in lower Manhattan. I have every intention of holding on to it as long as I can.

I was under the impression that the position of the North Star is constant in northern skies. And then I was forced to leave my constant at 58 Greenwoods. Then again after being promised to be cared for forever, it became an instant history, something of the past. The situation is such, I may continue to bump into one or more of such seniors who will desire my company either to talk with or to walk in the company of or just to dine with or to do small chores for them because they are unable to because of physical ailments. I want to be happy. But my happiness depends on those surrounding me to be happy! So this is exactly what I desire to practice. I think I have finally Almost settled down as far as my feelings are concerned.

My obsession with that ring with 3 stones is over by now. About 4 years ago, one ruby had fallen off. A new ring was needed to replace the old one. I was in India that time. I just decided to sell the damaged ring. Now I satisfy my obsession about the rings by wearing a variety of rings, multiple of them at a time, 99 cents + tax on each!

I am aware of being bound by the restraining orders against me. My OCD is such, and I am still thinking of some creative ways to approach my ex. It is my strong belief that his mental illness can be tackled. I believe that he has been stuck in his type 2 personality for the longest period by now. He had come out of similar situations before. I know it for sure because I was the only one who had witnessed it all firsthand. I am still hoping for some miracle. It is solely for the sake of himself and his four most precious grandchildren. On CBS Morning News, I watch a show called

Kindness 101. The kids have admitted that the distinction between perseverance and OCD is very minimal.

As for myself, I am trying to be only in the Present moment. I am still the same Dreamer, a big-time Dreamer, except that now I am an Experienced Dreamer.

At night, I do my quick prayer and exercise for a minute or so, and start listening to one of the songs forwarded on WhatsApp by music lovers of my medical group. Then I turn onto my left side, on the left side of my Queen size bed. Before the 3-minute song is over, I have invariably entered my La La Land World, full of Dreams!

These are some of the photos of the seniors from my Large Family at Brookdale Battery Park for last about 7 years.

After being able to abandon the Gypsy life, this is part of the one bedroom apartment I moved in. Ours is the Huge Family Building. The apartment was furnished before I moved in. I was able to decorate it by using any thing that I was able to kind of salvage from whatever was the all over the house. The police was there to supervise and my friends and the movers were there to help me.

Current pictures of my one bedroom apartment at Brookdale Battery Park.

Made in United States
North Haven, CT
13 December 2024